Gentleman Soldier

Joseph G. Dawson III, General Editor

TEXAS A&M UNIVERSITY PRESS COLLEGE STATION

Gentleman Soldier

John Clifford Brown & the Philippine-American War

EDITED, WITH AN INTRODUCTION BY

Joseph P. McCallus

Library of Congress Cataloging-in-Publication Data

Brown, John Clifford, 1872–1901
    Gentleman soldier: John Clifford Brown and the Philippine-Ameri-
can War / edited, with an introduction by Joseph P. McCallus.—1st ed.
        p. cm. — (Texas A&M University military history series ; no. 89)
    Includes bibliographical references and index.
    ISBN 1-58544-274-7 (alk. paper)
    1. Philippines—History—Philippine American War, 1899–1902—
Personal narratives, American.   2. Phillipines—Description travel.
3. Brown, John Clifford, 1872–1901.   I. McCallus, Joseph P.
II. Title.   III. Series.
    DS570.K37B76   2003
    959.9′031—dc21   2003005684

To Joseph & Margaret McCallus

Contents

Illustrations

Preface

*S*EVERAL YEARS AGO, while working on a project concerning American expatriates in the Philippines, I inadvertently found a rare ceremonial book published in 1901. The book, titled *Diary of a Soldier in the Philippines*, was a first-person narrative of the Philippine-American War by a soldier named John Clifford Brown. I remember reading it quickly at first, and then, as events unraveled and his character emerged, more slowly and with considerable delight. Finally, as the story ran to its penetrating conclusion, I read quite deliberately and with substantial contemplation. I thought then, as I do now, that this is certainly one of the most important and compelling primary accounts of America's first war in Asia.

At first glance the above claim might seem a bit dubious. John Clifford Brown's military career lasted but a year and a half, and though he was formally cited for his industry and energy, he won no decorations for valor. Moreover, as an enlisted man, he had nothing to do with the strategic conduct or outcome of the war. With the exception of drafting a number of maps for his commanding officer, his service was undistinguished. Yet there are a number of factors that set Brown's diary apart from other primary accounts: because he witnessed a very broad sweep of the war, his journal paints a panorama not seen anywhere else; he was a sophisticated person within a historic moment, whose words, especially when seen against his personal background, provide pathos on a significant scale; and his prose, particularly its rich detail, is the most developed and polished to come out of the war.

To fully appreciate Brown's life and his tenure in the Philippines, the reader should approach his work from several standpoints. One of these is military history. The importance of Brown's diary is that it sheds valuable light on a variety of military operations during the war. Unfortunately, the 1901 edition offers no explanatory information whatsoever regarding his soldierly activities. This new publication attempts to illuminate Brown's travels and assignments during the war through the use of ancillary material, most notably his commanding officers' war reports. I try to give as encompassing a view of Brown's military life as possible through the use of other primary sources, media accounts, and existing scholarship.

This is also the story of one person and his family. Aside from this diary and a few records, little is known of John Clifford Brown. To better present Brown as an individual, I make extensive use of his sister Helen Clifford Brown Holt's unpublished 1951 memoir, "Recollections of an Old Lady," which her descendants so graciously allowed me to read. I interviewed two of Helen Clifford Brown Holt's daughters—Helen Holt Emerson and Julia Holt Bradford—and include their memories of the Brown family as well. The reader might find it odd that descriptions of Brown's home, childhood, and adolescence are incorporated here, especially given the fact that this is essentially a military journal. However, the central theme of the story is that Brown disguised his background— or, perhaps better put, his real self—while he was in the army. To understand Brown in the Philippines it thus is imperative to see Brown in Maine.

Another feature of this collection is a discussion of Brown the writer. With the exception of his senior thesis in electrical engineering at the Massachusetts Institute of Technology, there are no other extant examples of his prose. This lack of comparative material makes a rhetorical analysis of Brown's diary entries extremely difficult. In an effort to understand the writer, I have examined the author-audience relationship and the context from which this relationship was addressed. Perhaps the most intriguing contextual aspect is his health and how his deteriorating condition may have impacted his thoughts. I believe that Brown contracted typhoid fever (not dysentery, as the introduction to the 1901 edition claims) and suffered from its symptoms until his death in January, 1901. Whether Brown was really aware of his condition is a major point of conjecture and thus crucial to the reading of his diary. Consequently, I discuss typhoid fever at length in an attempt to illustrate how his worsening condition may have affected his writing.

In 2000 I retraced Brown's route in the Philippines. Despite my sixteen years of travel and academic research in the Philippines, I was consistently surprised at how much of John Clifford Brown's world is still accessible. In an effort to provide readers a contemporary association with Brown's words, I have included a description of present-day places. Furthermore, I believe many readers, especially those not familiar with the Philippines or the Philippine-American War, would be interested in knowing the effects of Brown and his comrades. To this end, I briefly illustrate some of the changes the United States rendered in the islands.

Diary of a Soldier in the Philippines's complete text is reproduced here; nothing has been abridged from the text of the 1901 publication. The short introduction to the 1901 edition is succeeded by a continuous chronological sequence of the original letters and diary entries without structural breaks of any kind. The only change I made in this new collection was to divide the narrative into chapters, being careful to keep the chronology intact, beginning with his journey to the Philippines and followed by chapters on his fighting in Pampanga, the "north hike" to Bangui, his stay in Manila, and the building of the Paranaque bridge. I conclude the story by adding Helen Clifford Brown Holt's account of Brown's hospitalization in San Francisco and death in Los Angeles. Each chapter is introduced by a short discussion of the major events, placing them within the larger military, personal, and Philippine context. In the case of misspellings, the correct form accompanies the misspelled word in brackets after the first occurrence only. I have similarly kept Brown's version of place names, putting the present-day spelling in brackets immediately afterward. The 1901 edition identifies several places where Brown made drawings in his diary; I have also retained these notations in the text.

I am indebted to John Clifford Brown's descendants for their constant willingness to share family stories and photographs: Helen Holt Emerson and Julia Holt Bradford in Portland, Maine, and Frances Holt Smithwick of Beverly Farms, Massachusetts, the three daughters of Helen Clifford Brown Holt; Howard H. Dana Jr., Portland, Maine; and George Clifford, Los Altos Hills, California. Simply put, the project would not have reached fruition without their enthusiasm. This book stands as a testament to their kindness.

I would also like to thank my colleagues at Columbus State University. The help of the staff at the university's Simon Schwob Memorial Library has been crucial, especially that of director Callie McGinnis, who allowed me to periodically present my findings in the library's scholarship series, and Cheryl Hewitt of the Interlibrary Loan Section, whose efforts permitted this project to be completed. The Instructional Technology Department under the direction of Sandra Stratford provided invaluable technical assistance, especially Jon Haney, who gave much time and expertise with the maps and photographs.

Numerous persons at research facilities and within other organizations have also been of immense help. I am particularly indebted to Cindy Murphy of the Maine Historical Society; Michelle Crowley of J. B. Brown and Sons; William C. Baldwin of the Corps of Engineers History Department; and Serafin D. Quiason at the Lopez Museum Library, Manila. I was also fortunate to have the aid of persons at the Portland Public Library; the Massachusetts Institute of Technology alumni office; the U.S. Military History Institute at Carlisle Barracks, Pennsylvania; the University of Georgia Library; the Ayala Museum Library, Manila; and the American Historical Collection at the Rizal Library of the Ateneo De Manila University. The Columban Fathers at the Malate Church in Malate were very helpful. The nourishing manna continually provided to me by the American Association of the Philippines and the American Chamber of Commerce of the Philippines is, as always, much appreciated

A number of individuals lent me their experience, critical eye, and goodwill. Jim Halsema and Craig Lloyd read the manuscript and offered valuable advice. In the Philippines, Orlino Ochosa and Antonio Lahoz Sr. gave me their time and kindness. For sixteen years my parents have never faltered in their support of my research in the Philippines. Finally, this book simply could not have been completed without Juliet.

Gentleman Soldier

Introduction

Joseph P. McCallus

THE FOLLOWING IS THE STORY of a young man who died a century ago. Today he is unknown, save for the few who have read his letters and journal. His name was John Clifford Brown, and he lived the last years of his life as a gentleman soldier in the Philippines.

John Clifford Brown was born in Portland, Maine, on March 28, 1872. His family was the wealthiest in Portland and was comfortable within East Coast social circles. A Massachusetts Institute of Technology (MIT) graduate, Brown worked for five years as an electrical engineer with the New York Telegraph and Telephone Company. When war broke out with Spain in 1898, he resigned his position and joined the volunteer army. He served as a lieutenant and a captain in New York regiments, but was mustered out without seeing an overseas post. In 1899 he reenlisted as a private in the regular army's Corps of Engineers and was immediately sent to the Philippines, where he served as a cartographer for Brig. Gen. Samuel B. M. Young, making maps of previously uncharted areas of northern Luzon. During this time he kept a detailed journal of his experiences, which he sent home piecemeal as correspondence. Later that year he contracted typhoid fever while still on active service. Unable to continue his duties, he was ordered home. He died in Los Angeles on January 16, 1901.

In his will, Brown left a sum of money to erect a "suitable memorial" to his life. A few months after his death, his brother Philip collected the letters and journal entries Brown had sent to the family and had them privately published as a book titled *Diary of a Soldier in the Philippines*. Only fifty copies were printed, all of which the family distributed. This small, nearly forgotten paper memorial is essentially all the world knows of John Clifford Brown.

There are a fair number of primary accounts of the Philippine-American War, but Brown's journal stands apart for several reasons. One is that few of these narratives address the cultural conditions of the era.

Brown's story of life in the "old Army" is complemented by a fine description of life in late-nineteenth-century America, a period often misunderstood by later generations. The 1890s are commonly envisaged as a golden time of enlightenment and invention. It was nothing of the sort. The turn of the century was marked by confusion and change—and with it, anxiety and mistrust. There was a wide disparity in wealth, and with the rise of the trusts came a feeling of financial helplessness for many individuals. Labor unions, as well as the migration of African Americans to northern cities, were changing the economic landscape. Indeed, the 1890s saw perhaps the worst labor violence in American history. Racial discrimination was rife, with lynching being widespread in the South and race riots occurring in the North. The cities were awash in immigrants—mostly Catholics and eastern European Jews, nearly all non-English speakers—creating teeming urban ghettos and marked unease in the minds of the largely Anglo society. The American West had been conquered, the Ghost Dancers crushed, and the cultural psyche was walled in by the Pacific Ocean. Outside the United States it was the age of empire, with European colonies marked by severe racial chauvinism and segregation in Asia and India and unspeakable horrors in Africa. In short, the 1890s may have been a gilded age for a few, but most Americans lived in anxious circumstances with a very dark undercurrent.

Perhaps nothing reflects this dark anxiety better than the Philippine-American War, known for decades as the "Philippine Insurrection." It was a conflict in which Americans, having been swept away by a powerful and little understood sense of nationalism, were forced to confront their self-image through the political and social dynamics of imperialism. Americans, bred on the notion of independence from European powers, became the possessors of millions of Asians inhabiting islands with impossible to spell names an ocean away. American troops, who had been reared on stories of defending the Alamo and defeating the Sioux, found themselves across the Pacific confronting a brown-skinned enemy who spoke a multitude of languages. The army was strictly segregated. White officers commanded African-American regiments and racial tension prevailed within the military. Back home, the guilt associated with subduing a foreign people split American public opinion. Yet many soldiers, much like their counterparts decades later in Vietnam, would sacrifice their lives knowing their countrymen only half-heartedly supported their efforts.

Brown's work reveals both the complex state of American society and the conduct of the war. His story contains a storm of national and cultural issues: imperialism, racial prejudice, and social class. The description of military life is one of the finest to come from that era. In particular, his chronicling of the grueling march from central Luzon to the northern tip of Bangui Bay is a fascinating daily log of the most decisive campaign of the war. Afterward, he was tasked to supervise the construction of a bridge outside of Manila. The one-time destroyer became a builder, and his prose reflects the awkward transition from conqueror to colonizer.

Brown's journal stands apart for another reason: he is a compelling character. In reading the collection of his letters and journal from June, 1899 to August, 1900, augmented by excerpts from his sister's 1951 memoir, the reader will consistently find that Brown's actions raise a number of irresistible questions. Why did a wealthy, twenty-seven-year-old man, trained at MIT and appreciative of the arts, leave a comfortable life of privilege for the military? Why did he trade a promising career in New York for the rice paddies of the Philippines? Why did such a person eagerly move downward in rank from captain to private? His words show this remarkable transformation of character during the last two years of his life. Brown's metamorphosis includes the daily cloaking of his social background from other soldiers, the personal sacrifices made over a harsh terrain, and his enjoyment of war and the military lifestyle. He often juxtaposes his former professional career with the sights and sounds that confronted him as a soldier in the Philippines, and the reader will quickly grasp that here is a person undergoing an immense change of perspective and temperament. This transformation, full of realism and pathos, is amplified by his ongoing illness and eventual death. It is a moving experience.

The Brown Family of Portland

The coastal city of Portland, Maine, owes much of its development—and probably its survival—to the Brown family. John Clifford Brown's grandfather, the artificer of the family wealth, was John Bundy Brown.[1] He was born in 1805 in Lancaster, New Hampshire, one of ten children to a man some say was a tavern keeper and others say was a farmer. John

Bundy Brown came to Portland as a dollar-per-week grocery clerk, but at the age of twenty-three joined a fellow clerk in a start-up grocery business. Soon they were importing large quantities of sugar, molasses, and rum from the West Indies. Observing the popularity of molasses and the public's unrelenting appetite for anything sweet, Brown took advantage of the new technology that transformed brown sugar into the fancy white and yellow varieties. Its success was immediate, and he soon had Portland's first and America's third sugar factory. Built in 1845, within a decade Brown's eight-story factory employed more than two hundred persons who processed thirty thousand hogsheads of molasses and produced 250 barrels of sugar a day. The product was transported to customers on Brown's own ships.

His initial success was magnified by tragedy. On July 4, 1866, a fire broke out on the Portland wharf. It quickly jumped into Brown's supposedly fireproof factory and burned it and much of the surrounding area to the ground. Brown, however, was reportedly insured in gold by English and Scottish holding firms, and he soon poured large sums of money into rebuilding Portland. He also began investing in banks, railroads, and glassmaking. By 1880, he was the city's largest landowner. The fire thus not only increased his wealth, it also created an image of him as a paternal benefactor.

The resurrection of the city and the resurgence of its patron were synchronous. With his amplified wealth Brown built "Bramhall," the city's largest and most elegant mansion. In it he housed an important private art collection, including commissioned paintings by Winslow Homer and sculpture by Franklin Simmons. Unlike the caricatures of nineteenth century American industrialists, Brown was typically regarded as being community minded and very progressive, funding a number of philanthropic endeavors, including scholarships for Portland High School and nearby Bowdoin College. He died in 1881 after suffering a simple fall on a patch of ice.[2] His company, J. B. Brown and Sons, is still one of Portland's major investment firms.

It is with the sons that this story develops. John Bundy Brown married Anne Matilda Greely, and the couple had three children, Philip Henry, John Marshall, and Ellen Greely Brown. Philip Henry, the eldest son, was born in Portland in 1831.[3] After graduating at the head of his class at Bowdoin College in 1851, he returned home to help his father manage the sugar factory. He later went into banking and subsequently expanded

J. B. Brown and Sons into areas such as railroads and real estate. In 1854 he married Fanny Clifford (18??–1900), daughter of Justice Nathan Clifford of the U.S. Supreme Court. Theirs was a large family, with twenty years separating the oldest, Philip Greely Brown (1855–1934), and the youngest, Helen Clifford Brown Holt (1875–1965). Between them there were four children: Nathan Clifford Brown (1856–1941), Frances Clifford Brown Prescott (1859–1940), Anne Ellen Brown True (1860–1946), and John Clifford Brown (1872–1901). Philip Henry Brown died suddenly of heart failure in 1893, but as Helen Clifford Brown Holt remarked in an unpublished 1951 memoir titled "Recollections of an Old Lady," all of his children "lived all to a good age except one."[4]

Helen Clifford Brown Holt's "Recollections" reveal that it was the family that anchored John Clifford Brown. Her observations are invaluable because she builds a psychological foundation for our understanding of her brother, and her lucid and detailed prose allows us to see into a turn-of-the-century household. The characters portrayed here, like those in her brother's letters and journal, emerge as complex human beings, replete with weaknesses and humorous foibles:

> My parents were very different in character and disposition. My
> father was a man of extraordinary cultured tastes. He loved beauty to
> excess, which, I suppose, was the reason he loved to travel. Beautiful
> scenery, pictures, music, flowers, and plants moved him sometimes
> to almost tears. He loved the theatre, but filled me with embarrass-
> ment when I went with him, because he wept so easily. But books
> were his obsession. When he was not at the office at the bank, he
> read constantly, and I mean that literally. . . . He often went to the
> greenhouse or in the garden, as soon as it was light, but most often
> he read in his room. He read late at night too, had a shelf that fitted
> over his tub for his book, and a metal stand for his dressing table.
> He always had a book in his hand when he was driving home to the
> Cape with his old horse, from his office, and sometimes entirely
> forget to pay attention to his horse. But she always turned into the
> gate at Glen Cove, and stopped at the door of the house. Often
> there they would remain, the horse drowsing, my father deep in his
> book, unconscious of the time or place. As he usually brought out
> the order from the market, the servants turned to watch for him, in
> order to get the dinner started on time, and my mother too, waiting

with the rest of us for our daily sea bath, which we had every day when he came home, never allowed him to stay there for long.[5]

Brown's father and grandfather both blended industry and the arts, business acumen and literary sensitivity. It would be a compound he would share with them in his adult life. His father's love of travel and his mother's social awareness also earmarked Brown. His mother is described below once again by his sister Helen. The counterpoints between husband and wife are striking:

> My mother had the sweetest disposition I ever knew, but she did not share his passion for books. Flowers, yes, scenery, but I never felt she cared very much for the pictures which meant so much to my father and to his father before him. But she loved the theatre as much as he did, and travel, although she was always deadly ill on a boat.
>
> She was intensely interested in the problem of unmarried mothers. In those days they were, in reality, turned out of their homes, in the most horrible disgrace, and had no where to go. Even at the time of birth, they were accepted only at the Poor-house, where they were treated as criminals and, after they left the hospital, there was nothing left for them but a life of misery and disgrace. Mrs. Longfellow, whose husband was brother of the poet . . . was equally interested and the two of them with Miss Cornelia Dow, sister of Neal Dow, the well known fighter for temperance and prohibition, founded the Temporary Home. At first it was an entirely private enterprise, and it was many years before they could get a state appropriation for it. . . . Here they had a cook as well as the matron and began to train the girls to help with the work and to care for their babies. Then they placed the girls with their babies in accredited country homes where they worked for nothing, if you please, and almost always became worth while women, often married to respectable farmers and so on. . . . When I was considered old enough, I joined the Board of Managers. I used to visit them at the Home.[6]

Her practicality, outgoing manner, and progressive attitude seemed to be a perfect complement to her husband's mercantile and artistic energy.

*Brown family, circa 1890. John Clifford Brown is in the front center,
wearing the striped jacket. Courtesy Helen Holt Emerson.*

Mrs. Brown's social concern, a trademark of the family, surely affected
John Clifford's view of the world, at least before he saw war. Her son was
devoted to her, and as her daughter notes, he was the apple of her eye.

It seems clear that Brown grew up in a stable, close-knit family. John
Clifford's brother, Philip Greely Brown, who like his father and brother
Nathan Clifford graduated from Bowdoin College, was well known within
the city of Portland as the president of the First National Bank and general manager of J. B. Brown and Sons.[7] Like his father, he was a great
lover of books and the arts. In fact, he was a major benefactor of the
Portland public library. He must have had a strong sense of history because he belonged to the Society of Mayflower Descendants, the Society
of Colonial Wars, and the Sons of the American Revolution. Mrs. Helen
Holt Emerson, the daughter of Helen Clifford Brown Holt, recalls the

following about the man who is most directly responsible for keeping the memory of John Clifford Brown alive:

> Every Sunday night we three little girls [the three Holt sisters circa 1920] or however many of us were there used to go down and call on Uncle Phip. Mother used to live there alone with him and a housekeeper for years before she was married. They were very close. We would walk down Bowdoin Street one block and go and call on Uncle Phip. He was seated on a little chair, and it had a built-in footrest, and his feet were on that. He had a big cigar and a big silver cigar cutter. He would affect a Maine accent, which was no more true than the man on the moon. He talked in this really outlandish way. He used to startle people, I guess. My youngest sister, Frances, she was, evidently, a disappointment to him because she wasn't a boy. He said, "I'm going to call you Frank." So he called her Frank.
>
> Uncle Phip did very smart in business and was president of the First National Bank. When the Depression happened and everything shut down for a long while all of the bank directors were liable for the contents. They were supposed to pay you your deposit if demanded. Evidently the directors did not care what the banks were supposed to give to these depositors. Uncle Phip paid the whole difference out of his private money, which, I was told, made him really a kind of a hero because of that.
>
> Then they wondered if there would be anything left in his estate to take care of Vaughan Street [his residence] and the greenhouse and the garden and all the land. The actual fortune that was supposed to come to the rest of the family wasn't there anymore because of the debts to the bank.[8]

His kindness was apparently legendary. One newspaper account shortly after his death said the following:

> For many years the people of Portland have been used to the sight of a small, unassuming man going about the streets, sitting in his office on Middle Street or in the First National Bank, or wandering about the rooms of the Public Library. . . . Now that he will be seen no more there are many persons who will wonder why the

anonymous gifts that came to them have ceased; why a subscription marked "a friend" is not forthcoming; why a strange name assumed by him for charitable gifts, sometime, appears no more. . . . Many a woman in need of advice and help, many a man in financial difficulties, many a member of his family looking for cheer and encouragement will be at a loss where to turn to now that death has claimed Philip Greely Brown.[9]

Philip Greely Brown seems to have been a larger than life populist banker, and it is through his concern for the memory of his brother that we are able to access the journal. As the copyright holder, and as executor of John Clifford's will, we can reasonably assume it was he who championed the publication of *Diary of a Soldier in the Philippines.*

Another family member whose kindness plays an important part in the John Clifford Brown story is his first cousin, William Henry Clifford Jr.[10] Referred to as "Billy," he was three years younger than John Clifford, and they were close childhood companions. After an unsuccessful attempt at MIT, Billy Clifford began his illustrious military career at the Shadman School in Annapolis, getting his commission in 1899. He arrived in the Philippines in December of that year as a first lieutenant with the 3d Marine Battalion. As Brown's journal tells us, Clifford left the Philippines for China in June, 1900, and participated in the famed Boxer Rebellion. It does not tell us that he returned to Manila in October of that year to find his cousin in a pitiful state. Clifford was responsible for arranging Brown's care and transportation home in November. He left the Philippines in 1902 and returned in 1906 as a marine captain. Several months later he was again sent to China. After leaving the marines, he became a successful Virginia farmer. He later served in the army during World War I. Mrs. Helen Holt Emerson later said of Clifford: "We were very fond of him. He was very handsome. He was called 'Chudleigh Bill' because he had an estate called 'Chudleigh.' Chudleigh Bill had a cane and he swaggered. He was fun, lively, and he had a great estate [in Virginia], and he had tales of working down there and what went on. He was not really interested in Portland at all, I don't think."[11]

Brown was thus seemingly surrounded by a family full of love, success, stability, and a healthy dose of comic relief: a millionaire father who read so deeply the horse took him home, a socially concerned mother, a kind older brother who affected strange accents, and a close cousin who was a dashing marine officer. The Brown house in Portland seemed both formal and warm, extravagant and relaxed. Below, John Clifford's sister Helen remembers growing up in Portland:

By the time I was born the family was living in a house built and given to his son by my Grandfather Brown. It was on the corner of Vaughan and Bowdoin Street, and it was built there in order to be near the very large estate of Grandfather Brown, who undoubtedly had grand ideas. There were no houses then in this western part of the city, and most people felt it was practically out of town.

The Clifford family was closely affiliated with ours, for my mother's brother, William Henry Clifford, married my father's sister, Ellen Greely Brown. There was, as we used to say, a "matching" Clifford child for every Brown one.

Our house was, for those days, very luxurious and elegant, and the household ran like oiled silk, owing, I suppose, to the fact that my mother had in her youth done every branch of household work herself. . . . The staff usually consisted of a butler and his wife, who was the cook. A chambermaid, laundress, and three men—a coachman, head gardener, and assistant.

All the rooms in the main house were very large, and all were rather dark, owing to the heavy draperies and the color used in the decorations. There were on the top two floors, twelve rooms, one on the top floor, however, was not a bedroom, but my father's study or book room. It was lined with book shelves, and we were not allowed to go in there without permission when we were children.

The drawing room was done over by a New York decorator when I was a grown child, in pale blue, with a dado of dark cherry wood, pale yellow ceiling, and rich oriental rugs. But the rest of the house was in its original dress. My father had a beautiful stained glass window, a half circle, put in at the end of the room. It was of dark red poppies against the most beautiful blue background. . . . It was designed by Sargent, whom my father admired tremendously.

The big library, because there were two, was painted dark red, and the small library was entirely glass enclosed bookcases, no walls showing at all.

The kitchen was enormous. It had a regular hotel range, and many pantries adjourning. In one was a built-in ice box, and shelves for the uncovered milk pans. There were no screens in the house in those days, but I do not remember flies in the milk room.

We lived with a good deal of formality. Everyone dressed for dinner, the women in evening dress, the men in more formal clothes than the daytime, but I do not think they wore real evening clothes. I was always arrayed in white, or pale blue, with sashes. At first I came down only for dessert, but I was very young when I allowed to come to the table, for I remember being teased by my brothers on account of my huge appetite. Also I remember a dreadful experience when I tried to outdo my brother Jack. There was a set of plates, decorated with different varieties of fruits, one of which Jack and I thought particularly fine. It had a cluster of strawberries on it. (These plates are in the pantry here now.) We used to hate the person who got it at the table, and Jack was always trying by sly means to be the one. One evening I went boldly into the pantry, and asked Oscar, our butler at the time, to please give me the plate. He said he would if I would give him a kiss. This was a perfectly harmless suggestion on his part, but, to my mind, it was beyond words horrible. However, so anxious was I that I said yes. Feeling no less than a fallen woman, when at dessert the plate was put in front of me, Jack's rage was no consolation. Bursting into tears, I fled to my room.

There were eight of us at the table when the family was at home. My two sisters, Annie, always called Nan, and Frances, always called Tot because she was so tiny. Three brothers, Philip Greely, Nathan Clifford, and John Clifford, called respectively Phip, Cliff, and Jack. It is terrifying to the modern housewife to remember those meals. The man or maid never left the room, but stood at attention near the pantry door, ready to pounce if anyone finished their vegetables, or plates needed replenishing in any way. . . . Claret was always on the table, usually Pontet Canet, and all took it except Jack and I, who, being twenty years younger than the other members of the family were too young to have it.[12]

The house at 85 Vaughan Street no longer exists, torn down shortly after Philip Greely Brown's death in 1934. Yet through its memory, we see that the Browns seem to have been a solid, even idyllic, representation of late-nineteenth-century American family life. They worked hard and had

85 Vaughan Street, where Brown grew up.
Courtesy Helen Holt Emerson.

wealth. They believed in education. They were artistically sensitive. They were socially concerned, even progressive. The parents were loving, the children obedient, and all were supported by a close network of family members. And the youngest son, John Clifford, was the finest America had to offer: a public school graduate, he had gone on to excel at MIT. He acquired an outstanding job as an electrical engineer in New York City and served his country by joining volunteer military regiments. In 1898, at the onset of the Spanish-American War, he was a handsome man, popular in the elite social circles of New York and New England. He was in every sense a fine young American gentleman. A year later he would be immersed in a conflict that would challenge his moral fiber and alter his perceptions of life. Like thousands of other American men in 1899, he would play a part in the country's first dirty little war: the Philippine Insurrection.

The Life and Character of John Clifford Brown

Despite lacunae in the historical record, there is enough public documentation to establish a thumbnail of Brown's life. Not surprisingly, such documents reveal little of the man's character. We know that Brown was born on March 28, 1872, in Portland. He graduated from Portland High School in 1890. At MIT, from which he graduated in 1893, his coursework included a variety of engineering and technical classes such as dynamo testing, hydraulics, electrical instruments, and electrical engineering, plus several courses that would serve him overseas, mechanical and freehand drawing being among them. His senior thesis at MIT was titled, "An Investigation of the Causes of Variation in Stray Power." Liberal arts classes were also part of his curriculum: French, German, English literature, and political history. He also had several courses in military drill. Legal documents show he performed his family fiscal responsibilities after the death of his father. He died, single and childless, on January 16, 1901, in Los Angeles. He was interned in the family mausoleum at Evergreen Cemetery in Portland. The Reverend Fenn of the High Street Church (Congregational) officiated. Military honors for a soldier holding the rank of corporal were executed by troops from the Portland barracks.[13]

Brown's military records also reveal the basics, but with some interesting contradictions.[14] His papers from the New York Volunteers reveal very little, save that he enlisted in May, 1898, as a captain in the 8th New York Infantry; was mustered out in November, 1898; reenlisted as a first lieutenant in the 203d Regiment of the New York Volunteers; and was discharged on March 25, 1899. Brown, according to these sources, was single, fair complected, had blue eyes and blond hair, and stood five foot seven. His next of kin, listed only as "P. J. Brown," was surely his brother Philip.

Little else is known of Brown's volunteer experience, save that he was stationed at Camp Chickamauga, Georgia. After mustering out in 1899, he presented himself at the Washington, D.C., barracks and reenlisted in the regular army for a three-year term on June 21, 1899. The records state that he was twenty-seven years and two months old, his previous occupation was that of electrical engineer, and his residence was New York City. The soldier had "Blue [number] 10 eyes, L[ight] Bro[wn] hair, W[?] Fair complexion, is 5 feet 7¾ inches high." He had a permanent mark described by the initials "R.L.S. [measuring] 1 3/4" palm of R[ight] Hand from center to wrist." The next day, June 22, Brown was assigned to Company B, Battalion of Engineering, at Willets Point, New York.

His "Descriptive and Assignment Card of Recruit," dated June 22, 1899, provides the same information as above, but with a few deviations. His eyes are here listed as "Blue 12," his complexion as "Ruddy," and his height as "5 8¼." While one person might judge a shade of blue differently, and while "fair" and "ruddy" might be seen as the same by two different evaluators, the half-inch discrepancy in height seems odd. His weight is not given, but in a letter home Brown tells his mother that he was over the weight limit (he seems mildly concerned about this), which was probably in the area of 130 pounds. This description should be seen against the one of him in the introduction to the 1901 publication, where Brown is said to be "a tall, lithe, very handsome man, of the pronounced blonde type." It is doubtful that even at the turn of the century five foot eight would have been considered tall, and one can only wonder just what "pronounced blonde type" entails. In any event, it is certain that Brown was of average height, of sleight to medium build, and had light hair and complexion.

His death records reveal contradictions that are somewhat more troubling. The Adjutant General's record of January 26, 1901, states that Brown "died 12:05 A.M., January 16, 1901 . . . at Van Nuys Hotel, Los Angeles, Cal. while on furlough from this [U.S. Army Hospital, Presidio] Hospital. Remains shipped to Portland, Maine, at private expense." The cause of death was "Enteritus." An inventory of his personal effects dated two days later noted that there were "no effects," and that the remains were taken to Portland "by his relatives." The Final Statement record of the Adjutant's Office, dated January 30, 1901, gives the following details: the army owed Brown $6.33 for clothing not drawn, while he owed the army $0.15 for a tin cup, $1.27 for a shelter tent, and $0.35 for a mosquito head net. In the remarks section, the report says Brown's "[s]ervice honest and faithful. Soldier sailed from Manila, Nov. 2. 1900. on Transport 'Thomas.' Serving in the Third year of continuous service since Sept. 28. 1900. Previous service: Capt. 8th N.Y. U.S. Vols. May 2d. to Nov. 3d. 1898. 1st Lieut. 203d N.Y. Vols. from Jan 2d. 1899. to March 25. 1899." Importantly, the report states that Brown "died while on furlough, at Los Angeles, Cal. January 16th, 1901, of Enteritus. Contracted in line of duty."

There is some question as to how Brown died. His obituary says only that he was "seriously ill." The introduction to the 1901 collection of his letters and journal states that Brown died of "dysentery," as does an MIT alumni memoir written thirty years later. As just seen, all of his army records show that the cause of death was enteritis. Helen Clifford Brown Holt, who was with him in the last month of his life, declares on a number of occasions in her "Recollections" that her brother "succumbed to enteric fever." She said that a relapse of enteric fever resulted from over-eating on board the U.S.-bound transport ship, and that more relapses—including the final one—occurred in San Francisco and Los Angeles. Her daughter, Helen Holt Emerson, said that the family had always been told that Jack Brown died of typhoid fever, the more common name for enteric fever. Clouding the issue even further are Brown's own statements. On January 30, 1900, feeling recovered from his three-week sickness, he states—presumably based on what the doctor told him—that he had "acute gastritous. Must have eaten too much." Yet on February 14, after a relapse of the illness, he writes, "Doctor told me this morning I was pretty well saturated with malaria." He has yet another relapse on June 4, when he says he has a low fever. The diary stops abruptly and with no explanation on August 23, 1900. The last sentence reads, "A large portion of the company is sick."

While Brown may indeed have caught malaria, the three illnesses officially attributed to his death are dysentery, enteritis, and typhoid fever. The type of sickness is important in attempting to understand his mental state during the last few months of his life, so a short discussion of the different illnesses should prove beneficial. It is clear that from January through August, 1900, Brown was, at several points, seriously ill. It is unclear, however, whether Brown suffered from one illness throughout the last year of his life or a combination of several. It is also unclear whether Brown believed he was well or if he was disguising his condition in his correspondence home.

It is doubtful that Brown died of dysentery. Dysentery is a term applied to a number of conditions causing ulceration and inflammation of the large intestine. It is characterized by blood and mucus in the stool. The two most common types, bacillary and amebic, are both contracted by consuming contaminated food or water. Amebic, the more chronic and insidious of the two, causes severe pain through ulceration of the intestines, with death caused by intestinal hemorrhaging and gangrene of the bowel. All evidence shows that Brown died of an intestinal condition, but nowhere in the journal or family accounts is dysentery discussed. It is possible his army doctors lumped dysentery under the general title of enteritis, but dysentery, which was rife among U.S. soldiers in the Philippines, was usually identified as a distinct item. Furthermore, while dysentery, enteritis, and typhoid fever all have some common symptoms, Brown complains of high fever, stupor, and loss of appetite, all of which apparently came on quite suddenly. At no time does he mention the abdominal pain and bloody flux characteristic of dysentery, although one might speculate that he simply chose not to include such a description in his journal.

Enteritis is a general term for a variety of problems associated with inflammation of the intestines, but it is not a term commonly used for dysentery. The army doctors who signed Brown's death certificate were undoubtedly correct that Brown succumbed to an ailment associated with the intestines, but what specific problem is not given (if it was even known). One textual link is that enteritis has often been associated with acute gastritis, and Brown reported having acute gastritis, although, as will be discussed in a moment, there are some questions regarding his statement. Acute gastritis—the symptoms of which are loss of appetite, nausea, headaches, and vomiting—can be a secondary symptom of typhoid fever.

Helen Clifford Brown Holt says that her brother suffered from enteric fever, an alternative term for typhoid fever. Ingesting contaminated food or water causes typhoid fever, which also results in inflammation of the intestines. Before antibiotics, typhoid was the scourge of armies. The disease has a ten- to fourteen-day incubation period, followed by early symptoms of head and body aches, fever, loss of appetite, and diarrhea. A high fever follows, sometimes accompanied by delirium or a stupor and red patches on the body. This condition may last from seven to ten days, followed by a lowering of the fever for another ten days. The person then returns to normal, with relapses of a low-grade fever being common. Importantly for our purpose here, typhoid is a disease of complications. Intestinal ulcers caused by the bacteria can eventually lead to massive hemorrhaging. Another complication, perforation of the bowel, often results in peritonitis, which at the turn of the century was usually fatal.

Problems with the gall bladder, heart failure, and pneumonia can also occur in the latter stages. Death is usually the result of toxemia and general debilitation. In Brown's time, it might be twelve to eighteen months from infection to death.

Without an autopsy performed within a few days after death it is impossible to say with certainty what caused Brown to die; however, I ask the reader to entertain a probable scenario. Brown became infected with typhoid fever in the late fall of 1899 during the "hike" through northern Luzon, or perhaps as late as Christmas while he was in Bangui. His early symptoms arose in Laoag, and on January 12, in Vigan, the severe symptoms left him prostrate. He says, "I don't how many days I laid around headquarters," which suggests a stupor. The fact that he was discharged from the hospital on January 29 leaves a three-week period from the beginning of the symptoms to his supposed recovery. This is roughly the time frame of a person's first bout with typhoid. He goes back to work happy and with an air of confidence; at least that is what is presented in his writing. Brown, of course, was neither recovered nor cured. The bacteria in his intestine caused relapses and complications throughout his service in the islands. Moreover, without antibiotics, such a salmonella bacteria would certainly have resulted in irreversible damage. In the last week of August, 1900, a relapse brought an end both to his active service and his journal keeping. From then until January, 1901, his body deteriorated from one of the complications of typhoid.

This scenario, of course, raises several questions. One obvious question is, if Brown was diagnosed as having typhoid, why was he not treated for it? The answer is that army doctors of the time often misdiagnosed typhoid as malaria, which Brown was told he had contracted.[15] Was Brown misdiagnosed? It seems likely: typhoid does have symptoms similar to malaria, as well as a variety of intestinal ailments. Was Brown really treated for typhoid but chose not to tell us?

The last two questions conceivably carry heavy implications for the reading of the text. It thus is important to speculate as to just how much Brown knew of his condition. If Brown was cognizant of its severity, how might this have affected what he recorded in his journal? Unfortunately, Brown does not give us much help. After the first bout of sickness he says, "I knew any way it was nothing serious," and that it was "acute gastritis. Must have eaten too much." Acute gastritis may have indeed been a problem; recall that it can be a symptom of typhoid. Yet surely Brown would have known that overeating does not incapacitate a young man for three weeks, and anything that does prostrate someone for that long is most likely quite serious. Was the overeating statement a glib remark uttered after months of hiking through north Luzon? Possibly. Or, knowing that his mother would read the entry, was he trying to mask the real state of his health? Probably.

Whatever the case, his entry for June 5, 1900, is interesting. Brown, then in Paranaque, states laconically: "I am, so the Doctor tells me, going through that agreeable state call [sic] convalescing. . . . I have not much confidence in him even if he did cure me. His theory seems to me to give medicine by shovelfuls, which is not, I believe, in accordance with the latest practice."

The passage points to a number of telling signs. One is that Brown assumed he had an illness and that he had been cured. Another is that Brown seems to have known something about medicine at the time. Nonetheless, no actual identification of the malady is presented. This is a puzzle. Brown is a detailed diarist, getting down the sometimes smallest of particulars. Why would he not record in more detail an ailment that is threatening his life?

There are two possibilities here. The first and more probable is that Brown simply did not want to alarm his family. Given the care that he demonstrated when writing to his mother, it seems consistent that he would mask his condition. Less likely is that the family or publisher edited the comments concerning his sickness. This speculation arises from the fact that none of his obituaries reveal the exact cause of death, save the mention of "sickness," even though the family was there at his bedside. Furthermore, the erroneous report of dysentery in the 1901 introduction suggests that someone either mistook or disguised the real nature of his illness. At that time typhoid was thought contagious; rather than casting the likelihood that the family was infected with typhoid, they may have thought it prudent to edit the manuscript and publish he died of dysentery. This idea is made more plausible when one remembers that Brown's mother and grandmother both died within weeks of Brown. Considering that three members of the same family passed away nearly at once, it is certainly imaginable that the Browns did not want the people of Portland whispering that typhoid had infected the family.

The fact that he does not reveal the name of his condition frustrates our understanding of his life and shrouds his character with mystery. It thus is beneficial to turn to the personal memoirs and private memories of those who knew him to learn more about the man. At a distance of over fifty years, Brown's sister Helen portrays him as an intelligent, social being, patriotic, with no discernible idiosyncrasies other than enjoying practical jokes at the expense of his sisters' suitors. Her "Recollections" show that he was devoted to his mother, a relationship with strong implications to the journal. Brown's writing never reveals that he was something of a ladies man; indeed, he never mentions the concept of sex. However, Holt tantalizingly mentions "Jack's love affairs" and "Small dances at home and suppers after theatre parties." She also mentions "Jack and Polly," but does not further identify the girl and offers no details of their relationship.[16] Helen Holt Emerson recalls that her mother Helen "Loved Jack. Of course, he was closest to her in age. The others [siblings] were of another generation." She adds that as a child she had heard that "All the girls wanted to dance with him but he wasn't a very good dancer. They thought they would be able to sit out with him," meaning that they would get to know him while sitting on a sofa or garden bench.[17] He apparently was seriously involved—within the late-nineteenth-century context—with a Portland woman named Florence McMullen. However, it is difficult to ascertain how much influence McMullen had on Brown because he never mentions her in his writing.[18]

An extended observation presumably comes from one of his classmates. In MIT's *Report of the Thirtieth Anniversary of the Class of Eighteen Ninety-Three,* the anonymous writer, from a three-decade distance, says the following about Brown:

> As to his life and work at the Institute, the following lines, from one who knew him at that time, give a very vivid impression:
> "John Clifford Brown was one of the youngest and brightest men in '93. He was, perhaps, slightly too boyish in appearance to impress those who did not know him well with the full maturity of his mind, and too uncompromising to be what is called popular. These things, no doubt, kept him from holding many class offices, without lessening, however, his interest in class affairs, regarding which he was not only always willing, but also able to give valuable advice.
> "As a student, his work was well above average. He was intellectually very capable, indeed, though the formal record of his work may not show this; for he was full of the animal spirits of youth, and

could not always resist the proffered frolic. Indeed, these same animal boyish spirits and the sincere love of companionship were his worst enemies, and forced him unconsciously to undertake, in addition to his studies, more than his physique was intended to stand. As a student outside of Tech, he devoted considerable time to history and military affairs, and was able to talk very interestingly on such matters relating to his country, although he was not often willing to do so. Ornithology also seemed particularly to attract his attention.

"During his Freshman year he roomed on Charles street and for the remaining three years on or near St. James avenue. His room was always open to friends or strangers, and his hospitality never failed. As intimated previously, he never held an office of prominence in the student body, though he was class auditor for three years, and a member of many committees.

"Socially, 'Jack' Brown was kind-hearted, sympathetic, and true, though independent. He had the natural ability to command respect and devotion wherever he chose. He was quick to discover and admire real ability in others, wherever he found; and the friends he made during his four years at the Institute were from all walks of life. He was a member of the Theta Xi fraternity, K2S Sophomore Society, Hammer and Tongs Club, and the Electrical Engineering Society. He was American to the core, and martial in spirit; and it was not a surprise to those who knew him best that his death occurred while serving his country in the army in time of need."

Upon leaving the Institute, Brown entered employ of the Metropolitan Telephone Company of New York, serving in various capacities until he was promoted to the position of assistant engineer. He was always interested in military affairs, and soon after reaching New York, joined the Seventh Regiment, and was advanced to grade of captain.

On the breaking out of the Spanish War, he was made captain of Company C, Eighth Regiment, of the New York Volunteer Infantry. With his regiment he went to Chickamauga, and remained there until his regiment was mustered out in November, 1898. On January 22, 1899, he was commissioned first lieutenant of Company F, Two Hundred and Third New York Volunteer Infantry, and was mustered out March 25, 1899.

On June 22, 1899, he enlisted as a private in Company B, United States Engineer Corps, and at once was ordered to Manila, where he arrived August 13, 1899, having sailed there on the transport *City of Vaza* [*sic*]. He was at once ordered to the north of Luzon, where he saw a great deal of active fighting. His work was highly commended by his superior officers, especially that of plotting and mapping in the northern part of the island of Luzon. While in active service, he was promoted to the rank of corporal.

He returned to Manila somewhat weakened from the exposures and rigors of his active campaign, and was taken sick with dysentery, and ordered to the hospital at Manila, where he remained until ordered home, November, 1900. On his homeward voyage, although very weak, he would not give up; and by the exercise of great will-power he went through the voyage without allowing himself to be taken to the hospital. He repeatedly stated that, as soon as he reached this country, and could once more see his mother and the other members of his family, he would get well. One of his brothers was spending the winter with his wife in California, and they met him upon his arrival in San Francisco, and, seeing at once his weak condition, telegraphed immediate[ly] for his mother. When Mrs. Brown reached California, she would have never recognized her son. He weighed less than ninety pounds, and was so wasted as to remind his mother of the Indian famine sufferers. About a week after her arrival in San Francisco, Mrs. Brown was taken ill with pneumonia, and died after a few days' sickness; and after her death his grandmother also died in Portland. Jack had begun to improve somewhat, but his mother's death had a very bad effect on him. As soon as he was able, his brother went with him to Southern California. The first reports after his arrival there were quite encouraging, but the fatal disease had so weakened him that it was soon seen that there was no hope for him, and upon January 16 he died in Los Angeles.

His funeral took place in Portland upon January 26. He was buried with military honors, with pall-bearers selected from among the soldiers from the regular army at Fort Preble; and a corporal's guard escorted the remains to the family lot. At the grave a corporal's salute was fired.

He was a member of the Racquet and Tennis Club and University Club of New York and the Cumberland Club of Portland, in all of which he was a popular and prominent member.

While in the Philippines, he kept a voluminous diary, and this, together with many letters which he wrote home, has been printed for private circulation among the immediate friends, and is said to be most interesting.[19]

There are, of course, some obvious errors in this account. For one, Brown sailed to the Philippines on the *City of Para*. As the previous discussion adduced, Brown was ill for nearly a year before his death, which was probably the result of typhoid, not dysentery. According to his sister Helen, he stood the death of his mother rather well. These errors aside, the MIT alumni report provides invaluable evidence for an analysis of Brown's character. The writer, who obviously knew Brown at least fairly well, suggests several attributes that are clearly seen in his letters and journal, and may be crucial in understanding his mental makeup. One is his independent, perhaps stubborn, streak: he was too "uncompromising to be what is called popular." A second is his inability to resist adventure: "he was full of the animal spirits of youth, and could not always resist the proffered frolic." The prophetic observation that "[his] animal boyish spirits and the sincere love of companionship were his worst enemies . . . [which] forced him unconsciously to undertake . . . more than his physique was intended to stand" stands as a testament to what would befall him in the Philippines.

These traits—independence, a romantic call to adventure, fellowship, and physical challenge—all come alive in his words, helping to construct a psycho-social composite. It is important to remember that letter and diary writing, arguably the most intimate types of composition, employ common rhetorical principles. As in an essay or speech, the writer creates a particular ethos, usually with reference to events and a perceived audience (in a diary this would be the person who might actually read the work). In Brown's case, the character that emerges is a combination of the one he created for his mother in his letters and the one he kept secret in his journal. All of the letters are addressed to his mother, and nearly all reflect a conscientious son attempting to placate her worries. For example, the letters he wrote in June and July, 1899, while traveling across the United States and over the Pacific, speak of plenty of food, good health, excellent, even luxurious, accommodations, and that "The men are quiet and well behaved. There is not half the bad language or horse play that there was among the officers I went South with when I was in the Volunteers" and "Most of the men in the room, there are ten of us, were writing. One was reading his Bible. I am sure if it had not been for the rifles and the equipments I should have thought myself in a dormitory at school." Later, after he had been in the Philippines for more than a month, he wrote: "the life out here is much pleasanter than we had any idea of. You notice I have not had any of the hard, dirty work you anticipated. On the contrary the various duties, the constant change of scene and duty, the excitement and the knowledge that you are doing your duty makes it the pleasantest life I have had."

Brown and his mother obviously had a discussion on the merits of enlisting. In fact, according to his sister Helen, Brown "was advised not" to enlist by "his older friends in New York," and when he did, "it nearly broke my mother's heart. But nothing would move him."[20] Brown seems to have realized his enlistment raised personal questions and was a professional gamble: at a number of points in the journal he seems to reassure himself that joining the ranks was the right choice. Although Brown enjoys the life of a soldier, he knows his mother is surely reading the dispatches about the fighting in the Philippines, so he continually tries to soothe her worries. In January, 1900, at the beginning of his illness, Brown wrote to his mother: "Don't worry about me as I am all right now. I would have written you when I was sick but felt too miserable. I knew any way it was nothing serious. You can hardly imagine what good care they took of me in the hospital or how comfortable I was there."

Brown's concern for his mother's state of mind is understandable. His solicitude should also be seen against the backdrop of the family's history. Philip Henry Brown died suddenly six years prior, and the family was still sensitive to the mother's condition. Brown himself had caused some serious anxiety within the house. Helen Clifford Brown Holt recalls this about her brother a few days before her sister's wedding and shortly before her father's death:

> Jack, then in his senior year at Tech, where he was majoring in electrical engineering, had his vacation then [January 1893]. . . . Nan was wonderfully happy, now that her mind was made up to marry a boy, as she said. And Frank was exuberant, dashing about, giving us

all presents, and helping in any way he could. He had a beautiful young spirited horse, and he would come to the house every afternoon with him in a stylish single sleigh, to see if he could take Nan out for a drive, or do any errands for my mother or father. Three days before the wedding, as I came up Pine Street from the Bellows School, where I was in my senior year, I saw a crowd gathered about the small house on the corner of Pine and Emery Street. The front door of the house was open and more people were inside. When I asked what the trouble was, I was told that young Mr. Brown had been badly injured, having been thrown from the sleigh. I went in and saw Jack lying on the floor, blood coming from his mouth and ear, and Frank holding his hands. A doctor had been sent for. It had just happened. A snow slide came off the Pine Street block in front of the horse. He shied and bolted, and Jack was thrown from the sleigh with the side of his head against a tree. Some one who had a carriage there, took me home to tell the family and get ready, but Frank said not to tell them what he and others firmly believed—that Jack was fatally hurt. My mother was wonderful in an emergency. Jack was the apple of her eye, but she went right to work. With my help, Nan's and the maids', the guest-room was made ready, and before Jack was brought home, everything was done. We were told that it was impossible to tell before two or three days if Jack would recover. But the chance was slim. Frank went home, got some clothes, and spent the rest of the time with Jack, helping out the nurses and being wonderful. He would dash off to his office in the morning for an hour or two, that was all. You can imagine how he felt about the accident, which was, however, quite unavoidable. As we were told that if Jack recovered consciousness it might mean either the end of the beginning of recovery, he was never left alone a moment, and Frank took many night hours. My mother had to be re[s]trained from being in the room every moment. If she ever slept I did not know it. At times Jack would utter queer guttural sounds, as if in pain, but we were assured he was not suffering. But when my mother heard those sounds, she would fly into the room, thinking consciousness might be on the way.

Meanwhile the whole household was suffering from a double dose of confusion. That of the imminent wedding and a severe illness. One of these is quite enough! Jack was ordered extreme quiet, so heels were muffled, servants crept about, telephone the only lively thing, and orders were given to all not to use it. A notice was put in the paper that the wedding would take place quietly at the house, with no guests outside the household and Mrs. True. Word had been sent to Tot to come just for the day. Cliff went to a hotel when he came, and not even the Clifford family was to be present. Jack might die at any moment.

My father, I learned afterward, had to pay for the elaborate wedding feast as ordered, but of course it was cut down for us to feed about twenty persons. Dr. Gordon said he would stay in Jack's room all the time the ceremony was going on. I have a clear picture of my father, standing at the end of the drawing room from which the piano and all the furniture had been removed, directing Samuel and the two gardeners who were bringing in the plants, to make a solid bank of flowering plants as a background for the wedding party. The tears were streaming down his face, and it seemed as if we were getting ready for a funeral. The beautiful colors of the stained glass window, under which the flowers were banked, made a beautiful picture. (That window is in the attic. It was designed by Sargent). Presents came thick and fast, but no callers came near us. It was the most extraordinary combination of events.

However, the actual ceremony was happier than we had dared to hope. While we were waiting for Nan to come down, and Tot and I were standing in the hall to follow her in, Dr. Gordon came down stairs hastily. Holding up his hand, he said, "Jack is going to recover." And he remained for the ceremony instead of going back. So the wedding feast was really quite pleasant; the reaction, though, was hard on us all. I thought my mother, who did faint occasionally, might do so, but she held on bravely. Although Jack was on the road to recovery, Nan and Frank postponed their trip for a few days, going to their new house on Danforth Street to start their new life together. It took Jack a long time to get well. At first he could not talk, and then he would get his words mixed up. I would enrage [engage?] him, but he would say, "Please give me some toast," and he might want a book, and could not under-stand why we would not give it to him. But he was back at Tech in time to graduate fourth in a large class, with no bad after effects from his terrible blow.[21]

Holt's poignant picture of the mother being restrained from seeing her son makes Brown's apprehension all the more understandable. The journal entries show another Brown. First, it is interesting to note that Brown had some type of literary intention for his journal; just what kind of plan will probably never be known. On June 25, 1899, Brown wrote to his mother: "I am going to send home from time to time letters addressed to me. I wish you would put them in my desk unopened. They will be nothing but rough notes which I may some time expand into something. Everything important I will put into my letters."

What Brown did was place his journal entries into envelopes, address them to himself, and mail them to his home. His reason for doing this seems to be the result of pragmatic planning: carrying a journal though a military campaign would be hazardous, and mailing it home in segments would undoubtedly the more prudent course. The secretive nature of his request, including the red herring that everything important would be in the letters, seems intended to ensure his privacy was not violated. Clearly, Brown saw his journal as a conduit for private thoughts and observations, as well as for military matters that he did not want to reveal to his mother. The journal, at least at the onset of his Philippine experience, was an introspective exercise, confiding to the reader Brown's appreciation of his surroundings and experiences.

The reader is thus confronted with a bipartite voice: simultaneously there is the epistolary character predicated on the grace and responsibility of a good, caring son, with a second character living within a sealed envelope kept inside a desk drawer. However, as the campaign on Luzon progresses, these two forms of communication, and so the two characters, interfuse. In an undated letter—but one that must have been written on either July 31 or August 1, 1899—Brown tells his mother: "I send you these few pages from my journal instead of a letter. . . . Please save these pages after you have read them and put them with the letters I have sent home addressed to myself." A curious parenthetical element in his journal entry for September 10 reads: "(It is the same moon, dear mamma, but we see it some hours later.)" This clearly shows that he was at least thinking of his mother as he wrote in the journal. More directly, Brown ended his April 19, 1900, letter with the question, "Do you still like the journal?" This serves as yet another indication that his mother was the intended audience for at least some of the journal entries.

Brown family, 1892, including the husbands of several sisters.
In the front row are John Clifford Brown (center) and his sister Helen (right).
Courtesy Helen Holt Emerson.

There are a number of possible reasons for this melting of two voices into one. The most probable is the lack of paper. Brown complained on several occasions about not having enough of it and on January 9, 1900, wrote, "I would like to write many letters but have no paper nor can any be obtained." Indeed, he confessed that some of the paper he did use was captured from the insurgents or looted from civilians. Another reason could be that his initial plan to "expand [the journal] into something" may have disintegrated along the hard road chasing Aguinaldo through northern Luzon. Or perhaps he did not have the time or energy to continue the dual correspondence and decided to condense them. In any event, a number of journal entries sent home, especially after Christmas, 1899, often have direct and implied references to his mother, which calls into question the extent he was tailoring his account to his audience.

Although vague, there is evidence of another audience for his journal entries besides his mother. The entries for May 16 and July 13, 1900, seem markedly different in that they use the second person singular, yet are not signified anywhere with the term "mamma," which Brown always used with "you." Furthermore, the content of these two entries is unusually personal for Brown, perhaps even passionate—subject matter that does not seem to fit a mother-son relationship. One involves Brown, sounding exceptionally forlorn, recalling songs he and his intended audience heard in the past. The other involves Brown sounding uncharacteristically confused, hesitating to discuss something "purely metaphysical," about which he hurriedly added, "you need not show it to any one if you think it unsuitable." The tone of both entries is a notable departure from the rest of the journal, and one wonders if he sent them as correspondence to someone other than his mother. But whom? His sister Helen or his brother Philip? Or perhaps Florence McMullen, his supposed sweetheart? Brown's secret audience—if it is secrecy and not the result of an editorial decision—will surely remain secure.

The conflicting characters within his communication reflect Brown's identity in the military, creating a thematic tension that runs deeply throughout the work. Without question, the idea of disguise is central to this story. Openly, Brown is an enlisted man in the U.S. Army. He eats, sleeps, and works with men of the same rank. Unlike them, however, Brown is wealthy, highly educated, and a world traveler—a man brought up to appreciate literature, art, and ornithology. He is a gentleman. Moreover, he served as an officer in the volunteer army. The conflict between outer and inner identities manifests itself at all points of the work. Attempting to come to grips with the paradox, Brown tries to conceal his identity throughout his Philippine experience, often without much success. For example, while still aboard the transport ship, Private Brown found himself being asked to cross social and military boundaries: "The doctor who enlisted me at Washington barracks asked me into his stateroom a few evenings ago and we had a long talk, with drinks and cigars. He told me to come in whenever I had time, but I hesitate to accept favors which I cannot repay until so long. . . . I have an idea the men are beginning to find me out. They all know I was an officer in the

Volunteers. There are two men from the 8th and one from the 203d in the company. Several have asked me why I did not try for a commission."

The men did indeed know that Brown had been an officer. The *New York Sun,* reporting how Company B marched out of the Willets Point post, observed that the outfit "contains a number of men whose services were thought indispensable here . . . Lieut. John C. Brown of the volunteers, who served throughout the Santiago campaign, went along as a private."[22] That he never went to Santiago might have caused Brown a great deal of discomfort, and his letters reveal that he asked specifically for the article, so he must have heard of its contents. The feeling of unease resulting from being in the ranks must also have been acute, at least at first. On August 5, 1899, while still aboard the *City of Para,* Brown, seemingly paranoid, wrote: "I find I am getting to be known among the officers, whom I avoid as much as possible. When I am on duty it is quite usual to hear, "Is that him?" Lieut. o. of 'ours' made some advances to-day, asking me if it was true I had graduated from M.I.T., saying also they would give me a chance when we get ashore."

A rather dramatic instance that again promotes the theme of a cloaked identity occurred on May 8, 1900, when a civilian foreman approached Brown, the military inspector overseeing work on a bridge, and offered him a bribe to look the other way with regard to construction specifications: "I looked at him and felt myself flushing as I did so. I felt my fist close, then, well then I laughed. What did it matter. How could he know that I was anything but a Corporal of Engineers. I am no fool. I know how often it is done. . . . It is not his fault he is detailed with a gentleman in disguise."

Brown is clearly cognizant of his prince-in-pauper's garb pretext, and a remarkable revelation on August 6, 1900, gives the reader more clues as to Brown's hazy identity within the ranks: "We were fighting the war over again in the canteen this evening, and one of the Sergeants in speaking of my trip and the occasional reports they heard of me from other organizations reminded me of a fact I have always considered curious and yet do not remember to have ever mentioned. I never was with an organization long that it did not turn out that they were guessing about my nationality. It is a curious fact that I was never suspected of being an American. I have been called German, Swedish and English, but have always had great difficulty in persuading any one that I was a pureblooded Yankee. I don't understand it either."

He was never thought to be an American: a fascinating problem of appearance. Obviously, language had to be at the center of the uncertainty. Perhaps his upper class New England accent confused his comrades. Or, remembering Helen Holt Emerson's disclosure that Brown's brother Phip would "affect a Maine accent, which was no more true than the man on the moon," perhaps Brown concocted a speech he thought would camouflage his background. Whatever the reason, this passage and the ones before it all underscore the importance of outward exhibition and concealed identity and highlight the remarkable situation that Brown faced. He obviously wanted to do his job well, and he mentions numerous times that he hoped to get a commission. Indeed, by the end of the narrative it is clear that Brown intended to make the military his life's vocation. He knew his success depended on his ability to get along with his fellow enlisted men while demonstrating his value to his officers. To accomplish the latter, he had to bring to bear his training as an engineer, the professional discipline he developed as an as an officer in the volunteers, and, one assumes, the social graces valued by commissioned personnel. Yet these hard-won qualities could weaken his ability to work with his peers, thus undermining his chances for promotion and commissioning. He ran the risk of being labeled by both the enlisted men and the officers as a "dude," or "upper class," or a "gentleman." The former might see him as a rich man "slumming it" with the lower class, whereas the latter might see him as a professional threat. For both he must balance tact and ability, the present and the past, the open and the closed.

The idea of duality within Brown's character is also seen in the balance between the practical and the poetic. Brown was a trained engineer: mathematical, scientific, exact. His ability to draft was immediately put to use upon his arrival in the Philippines. Afterward he was detailed to build one of the many bridges the Corps of Engineers constructed in the Manila area. For recreation, he read books on geometry, one of them written in Spanish. He also knew French and Latin. To help pass the time he would write out problems in geometry from memory, which he called, "Good mental gymnastics, splendid practice." His fascination with Filipino technology and architecture led him to sketch stone mills, bird traps, furniture, houses, towns, and, of course, geographic areas. His powers of description were disciplined and formidable. In his journal and letters he employs strong detail and precise language to depict his daily activities, his comrades, his quarters, his surroundings, and the minutiae of his life.

What makes Brown's character so stimulating is that his MIT training was tempered by his artistic and philosophical sensibilities. As his sister related, he grew up in a home surrounded by a superb private art collection. His father was a passionate reader and devotee of the theater. Brown took, in a fashion, the European "grand tour," seeing Versailles, Venice, Naples, Capri, Dover, and assuredly other cities and places not mentioned. In the Philippines he read newspapers, Dickens, Kipling, *Century*, and the *North American Review*. He pondered philosophical questions. He enjoyed watching sunsets alone, which made him feel "capable of writing volumes of descriptive poetry." There is other evidence, such as the odd inclusion of the sailor's story, that Brown had ambitions to write creatively. The brutality of war is seen within an artistic context. The following passage is indicative of Brown's complex character, and, it might be added, his rather developed prose style. Note the remarkable interplay between the physical labor of battle, the comedic chase of the pony carrying his clean underwear, and the horror of the execution of the Filipino prisoners, all punctuated by a deep appreciation for art as seen by his description of the painting.

Started at daylight and went up the creek bed, a steep and difficult trail, until the guides said the insurgents were right ahead. . . . Finally rested. Pretty well blown, on the top of a little hill, firing still continued, and commenced to write up my notes, regarding the whole affair as a joke, when word came that a man in A Troop was killed. Poor fellow, he was buried where he fell with five insurgents, not buried, to keep him company. It were easy to wax sentimental was there time. A considerable wait while the horses were brought up (I came near losing my pony who broke away, as it was I chased him much nearer the insurgents than I cared to go and much further than I would had he not had all my rations, the blanket I had been so long without and clean underclothes strapped to his saddle), then forward again for another mile, when we were fired on again from ambush and lost another man killed and one wounded. Finally the ambush was discovered and the men run out. The rest is not pretty reading, but it seemed natural enough at the time, when men had been toiling and fighting (it was now 3 P.M.) in the broiling sun all day. When the men in ambush, they were in a cave, were located they were rushed and ran, threw away guns, etc., and turned weeping saying, "Much amigo, you amigo,"—bang, the last from a revolver. When it was over there were three "good" insurrectos, and incidentally a man had a carbine broken off short at the stock. Another hasty burial, and then a climb as straight up as it is possible to go for a thousand feet and then three miles along the ridge top, commanding two as beautiful valleys as it is possible to see. The trail was frightful, horses falling and rolling, and hot and tired men swearing, and officers hurrying the little column ahead. It was sunset when we began to descend into the little town of Banne, some 1000 feet below us and three or four miles away. The artist that painted the sunset in the mountains that grandma has in her gallery was a genius. I thought of that picture a thousand times and will own it, if money can buy it and I get out of this alive, to commemorate this day.

The combination of struggle, atrocity, and conquest seemingly arouse his artistic pathos. It also shows Brown's ability to compartmentalize conflicting values, a necessary component of soldiering. As his story develops it becomes apparent that this is one of Brown's strongest faculties.

Brown, as the MIT memoir notes, was "martial in spirit" and enjoyed the military lifestyle. Testimonies to this are found continuously in both the letters and the journal, helping tie the narrative together. As also noted, he had decided to push for a commission and thus make the military his career. This decision in itself raises a number of questions about his character. Brown was twenty-six years old at the outbreak of the Spanish-American War. He was an electrical engineer with the New York Telegraph and Telephone Company, and he surely would have been considered at the cutting edge of his profession. Like thousands of other American men, Brown felt the patriotic call to arms, so his commission in the volunteers should not be considered unusual. Yet a year later, after serving but not seeing duty in Cuba, he enlisted as a private in the Corps of Engineers. At first, this may seem odd, but Brown was not the only man of means or college graduate to enlist in the ranks; in fact, there seems to have been some type of movement among wealthy East Coast university men to join the service. The prospect of adventure also enticed many professionals to travel to Santiago or Manila. Finally, the lure of heroic enterprise is a strong probable cause for Brown's enlistment. But why, after having served in the Philippines, does Brown decide to try for a commission? By 1900 he had served in the military and seen combat. Surely he must have considered the fact that he was a nearly thirty-year-old man giving up his civilian profession. Was Brown running to or away from something?

His journal provides clues that suggest Brown was dissatisfied with his chosen vocation, as lucrative and promising as it may have been. It may have been this dissatisfaction that, at least in part, drove him to the service. His description of the private broken in rank seems to suggest that Brown's career with New York Telegraph and Telephone contained some troubling moments: "He [the private] sat at the side of my bunk . . . and told me his troubles with a pathetic little catch in his voice. . . . I woke up some hours later and he was still turning and muttering. His mental state reminded me of some of my New York experiences."

This intriguing line offers a glimpse into Brown's mind-set as a young professional. Moreover, there is conspicuous evidence throughout the journal that he was dissatisfied, or at least bored, with his career as an engineer. Concurrently, he was intoxicated with the excitement of soldiering. In New York he maintained the "martial spirit" first noticed by classmates at MIT. Early in his stay in the Philippines he wrote about taking point on reconnaissance patrols, "My curiosity that leads me to volunteer on such work will get me in trouble some day." As he began his duty as a freelance cartographer he wrote: "I cannot imagine any work more to my taste. . . . This is a delightful detail. I am my own boss and going when and where I please." While working on his map at General MacArthur's headquarters, he recorded: "It seems strange that after joining the army to be rid of desk work I should have so much of it to do. I shall ask to be relieved if it threatens to be permanent. I think, and it is this that keeps me cheerful at it, that I will be sent out on the reconnaissance and get my chance again the next time there is anything risky on. I do not like the rear when there is a chance for adventure."

Later, at Christmas time, lying on the beach at Bangui, his self-examination revealed perhaps one of the more telling clues of his character: "[I] wonder how it was possible for me to endure the life I led in New York for five weeks, let alone for years. There is no use disguising the fact, I have found what suits me, and that even though I realize that I have been exceptionally lucky in having a detail that allows me to wander without restraint where my own sweet fancy dictates."

It is the unconstrained, adventurous lifestyle that seduces him, and this need for independence and excitement should be seen as the engine of his character. Such an appetite is hardly uncommon in young men, but the dichotomy of Brown's career—that of the professional and the soldier—reflects almost perfectly the clash between two conditions that was beginning in the late nineteenth century: the economic man versus the martial man. During the 1890s, Theodore Roosevelt, one of the chief proponents of American expansionism, saw the future of American culture in terms of the conflict between the material man—embodying industry, wealth, and inflexibility—and the martial man—who personified struggle, creativity, and virility. Roosevelt, who romanticized modern warfare, saw the economic man as a huckster, subordinating the country to the ease of life, while the military or martial man was necessary for continued growth and development. He deemed that robust patriots, men of fighting qualities, should determine our national policies.

The now nearly forgotten concept of the "dude" helps explain how Roosevelt may have influenced Brown's character. The term, which came into vogue in the 1880s, referred to a well-dressed and pretentious city man. A decade later it denoted a wealthy, well-educated young professional from the Northeast. The middle and working classes, as well as members of their own class, considered dudes—the privileged descendants of the men who built nineteenth-century America—to be snobbish and inconsequential, or even worse, soft-handed and effeminate. During the years before the Spanish-American War the concept was drawn into the ideological struggle between the corporate and the military man. Calls went out from different parts of the political arena, including, of course, from Roosevelt and another politician Brown read, Albert J. Beveridge, for elite young men living in the East to develop "manly" virtues. The military was seen as the natural vehicle for such development, and when the Spanish-American War broke out, a number of Harvard men enlisted as privates. Yale men followed suit. Dudes from other schools, apparently eager to show their true sprit, enlisted with them. Soon, volunteer outfits such as Roosevelt's famed "Rough Riders" featured a hodge-podge of western cowboys and eastern college boys.[23]

While there is no evidence that he read about or knew of Roosevelt's sociopolitical views, there can be no doubt that Brown was a dude. Given his MIT background, he would have been aware that the men of Harvard and Yale were enlisting as privates to prove themselves. Although the alumni memoir states that Brown was interested in the military as far back as 1893, it is entirely conceivable that other men of his social class who joined up as privates directly influenced him. In fact, Brown mentioned while in Hawaii that he had heard Mrs. Sewall's brother, who certainly would have been a member of the upper class, "did the same thing I am doing, going out as a private." It thus is fascinating to consider that Brown's preference for life as a soldier in the Philippines over life as a corporate man in New York or young scion in Portland may have been a reaction to his perception of society and how it related to his personal identity, particularly in terms of his masculinity. He refers to the idea of class and position several times within the journal, and, as discussed, Brown was keenly aware of his awkward place within his own outfit. It thus is easy to imagine that his embrace of the military was a successful test of his social class and probably a form of reaffirmation of self and family. It was certainly an expression of reaching for Roosevelt's concept of the ideal man.

Brown's father was a Republican, Roosevelt's party, and Brown, like Roosevelt, was an ardent nationalist. As remembered by his MIT colleague, he was "American to the core," so it should not be surprising to find Brown's perspective on U.S. involvement in the Philippines corresponded closely to Roosevelt's ideas on expansion. Indeed, Brown lauds the writings of Sen. Albert J. Beveridge, an arch expansionist in the Roosevelt mold. Proponents such as Roosevelt and Beveridge were driven by a fierce national pride. This pride was in no small way the result of the conviction that America was a morally just country and thus could not act wrongly. For example, Roosevelt and others saw the war with Spain as a righteous war because America only fought just wars. Moreover, Roosevelt believed that Anglo-Saxons had the special ability to govern "backward" people; indeed, such an ideology put America at the apogee of historical development. This attitude should not be confused with that of the Nazis or the Ku Klux Klan, in which racial hatred was both the essential principle and the modus operandi. Roosevelt's beliefs were the product of a type of social Darwinism that viewed Filipinos and other non-Europeans as inferior, but not inherently so. In fact, he expected African Americans, Asians, and others to develop through the service of the superior white man. It was, as Kipling called it, the "white man's burden," a moral responsibility to govern, to extend Anglo-Saxon thought in an effort to uplift the entire human race.

Given this tri-part concept of expansionism, it is easy to understand how U.S. forces saw themselves as liberators who must subdue the folly of native self-rule.[24] This monumental paradox is evident in Brown's thoughts. On September 17, 1899, he wrote: "The sentiment of the company is strongly against cheating the natives. When we first landed the men, judging entirely from what they had heard in the States, were loud in their denunciations of the country. Now almost all admit it is a fine country. Personally I, and I think all thinking people here agree, cannot help seeing that the country will amply repay the States for their trouble in subjugating it."

The Philippines and its people should be happy to "repay" the United States for its troubles—a common expansionist sentiment and a hallmark of manifest destiny. Brown again expresses such cultural dogmatism in this observation: "This native civilization is a curious thing. It does not seem able to stand alone. With the Spanish it rose to a certain height, just high enough to want to go further, but it can't do it alone. With America back of the government it will reach a high standard, but I am convinced that at no time will they ever be capable of really governing themselves. Even the educated Filipinos are childish. It seems to be their nature. I do not think time will ever change it any more than it has the nature of British India. I do not think any one will say they are capable of self-government. Am pleased that the sentiment in the States seems so overwhelmingly in favor of keeping the islands."

While American sentiment was not as overwhelming as he seems to have thought, Brown's perspective on the Philippines reflected much of the attitude in America and certainly echoed the thoughts of those in the military. Brown was clearly influenced by the people around him, and the prevailing military thought of the time was formed in a large measure by recent American events. The United States had just finished conquering its own West, a conquest morally sanctified from podiums and pulpits across the land. For American military planners at home and officers in the field the Indian Wars had an enormous impact on U.S. strategy and tactics in the Philippines, as well as the character of American troops. Virtually all of the higher-ranking U.S. officers began their professions fighting in the West. Many of the enlisted men had also fought in those conflicts, and those who were too young grew up reading about or listening to romanticized accounts of the U.S. Cavalry chasing the Apaches and the Plains Indians. Such a history formed the distinctive contemptuous temperament of the American soldier, a disposition reflected by Roosevelt, who when not referring to Filipinos as "Malay bandits" or "Chinese halfbreeds," compared them to the Sioux and Commanches.[25]

Old Indian fighters commanded Brown and he interacted with enlisted men who were also frontier veterans. The American military commander in the Philippines, Maj. Gen. Elwell S. Otis, spent fourteen years fighting the Plains Indians. Brigadier General Arthur MacArthur, Douglas's father, served twenty years on the western frontier. Major General Henry W. Lawton, a hero to the U.S. troops, including Brown, captured Geronimo. Brown's commanding officer during part of his march through the Ilocos was Col. Luther R. Hare, a captain in the famed 7th Cavalry and a veteran of the Little Bighorn. It should not be surprising to discover that Brown idolized the troopers of the plains. Relaxing in Laoag, Brown says that he "sat there and alternately listened to the band and to the Corporal with me, who told me stories of Wounded Knee and the Fight at the Mission." In describing one of the older soldiers, Brown, clearly obsequious, evokes images from Frederick Remington, the romantic chronicler of the white man in the American West:

> I don't think I have mentioned the old Sergeant (Lanney, twenty-two years in the service) who has made my lot such a comfortable one since I have been with K Troop. He is Remington's beau ideal of a cavalry sergeant. To see him at the head of the column, he always had the advance guard and I always ride with it, is a delight to the eye. Thin and wiry, he seems a part of the horse, the best in the troop, by the way, he rides. Long service on the Indian frontier has made him cautious, and the advance guard is run as an advance guard should be run, to the discomfort, openly expressed, of the men who are apt, unless the enemy is seen, to look at the advance as an opportunity to "rustle" and a freedom from the restraint of the column. He took a fancy to me and so I share all his privileges, of having my meals cooked, dishes washed and the pony fed. Also I always get good quarters, sleeping next to him, and listen for hours to tales of the frontier and the army in the old days.

Brown's struggle with his prejudices is a theme that runs the length of the document. Like his position on American expansion, it is important to place his attitudes on race within the perspective of the period. His view of the African-American soldiers he fights alongside is consistent with the prevailing attitudes of the late-nineteenth-century American military, and it could be easily argued that his racial feelings mirrored the civilian sentiment of the era as well.[26] While his opinion on race relations before the war is not known, something apparently happened on the transport ship that later caused Brown to say, "we hated the colored men on the ship." He refused to salute black officers (white enlisted men were not required to do so). While at Paranaque, when the doctor of the 49th (Colored) Infantry offered to have him over to his quarters for drinks and cigars Brown remarked that he would not be "patronized by any one, least of all a nigger." He said that African Americans "do not seem to think like white men," and, more onerously, "I am rapidly acquiring a very poor opinion of the race and should heartily support any attempt to disfranchise them, or to limit their suffrage."

John Clifford Brown is a character built on a series of dualities—hardly an uncommon condition, although seldom are readers allowed such an intimate exploration of the conflict. Progressing through his letters and journal, the reader is faced with a number of perplexing, sometimes troubling, questions about Brown's persona. Here is a man trained in the practical sciences and consumed by romantic adventure; one who rebels against the mundane regularity of a daily job and yet is comfortable in the autocratic military; one who enjoys the arts and admires, or is at least at ease with, the vulgarities of war; one given to profound intellectual activity and base racial chauvinism (the latter not necessarily a contradiction at that time). Amplifying these dualities is the theme of disguise that prevails throughout the narrative. Brown, through his own admission, is a man who has assumed a life at odds with his upbringing and experience; a man who, because he must mask his background, has created another identity. As he was consumed by the sickness that ravaged his body, he camouflaged his anxiety with work, thought, and perhaps, bitterness. It is through his costumed self and the tensions inherent in such a drama that the reader should appreciate the character.

The Importance of Brown's Observations

Until the publication of several works during the last fifteen years, the study of the Philippine-American War has been split neatly by chronology and ideology. For the first fifty-odd years after the war the common interpretation was by the Americans, whose writers usually claimed some type of justification for the violent annexation of the country. With the postwar rise of Filipino nationalists such as Renato Constantino—and later with a slew of postmodern, poststructural, post-Constantino scholars—came a very narrow understanding of the war, constructed chiefly through instances of American racism and brutality. While both views have credibility, they are usually laden with polemics and often championed by ideologues. Neither perspective makes substantial and/or objective use of the primary accounts of the war.

The Philippine-American War is fairly rich in firsthand material. Collectively, these testimonies offer an encompassing view of the conflict, from Commodore George Dewey's victory at Manila Bay in 1898 through the conflicts with the *pulahanes* in 1905. Published works include Bradley Fiske's *War Time in Manila* (1913), which gives one of the few navy accounts of the conflict, showing the remarkable change in American temperament between Dewey's defeat of the Spanish navy (which Fiske documents superbly) and the arrival of the first troops assigned to fight the insurgents. Clarence Lininger's *The Best War at the Time* (1964) recalls being a volunteer in the Visayas; although told at a temporal distance, the work is interesting in that it shows how counterinsurgent warfare operated. *Manila Envelopes: Oregon Volunteer Lt. George F. Telfer's Spanish-American War Letters* (1987) is a collection of letters that document another volunteer's experience. Telfer's profound religious beliefs give the work a somewhat moralistic bent, which inadvertently provides for a dour commentary on American imperialism. Still another volunteer account is Needom N. Freeman's *A Soldier in the Philippines,* published in 1901, which gives impressions of the army and Filipino culture. James Parker's *The Old Army: Memories, 1872–1918* (1929) is an excellent work that spans his Indian-fighting days through his experiences in northern and southern Luzon, highlighting his command at the battle of Vigan in November, 1899.

One account that is particularly appropriate to this study is *We Thought We Could Whip Them in Two Weeks* (1990), by William Oliver Trafton (edited by William Henry Scott), a memoir of life with the 33d Infantry in northern Luzon. As a soldier in this Texas volunteer outfit, Trafton was often in the same area at the same time as Brown, including San Fabian, Vigan, and the Benguet region. Although not as detailed or precise as Brown, his observations of the conduct of U.S. troops and the reaction of Filipino civilians are especially revealing. The work serves as a solid cross-reference to some of Brown's activities, from both a personal and military perspective.

The works just mentioned are hardly an exhaustive list of the primary sources available. The military history collection at the U.S. Army Military History Institute at Carlisle Barracks, Pennsylvania, contains many pieces of official and personal correspondence of Philippine-American War veterans. These works and those mentioned above formed the foundation for a new perspective in Philippine-American War scholarship. Studies by Brian Linn, Richard Welch, Stuart Creighton Miller, William Henry Scott, and Glenn May have used primary accounts and official correspondence as the basis for their explorations into the causes and methods of America's venture in the Philippines. The result (especially in Linn's case) has often been a thorough, objective approach to the war. Earlier studies such as those by John Gates, Russell Roth, and Leon Wolff also use the soldier's words to illustrate their critical inquiry. This is true for only a few of the pre–World War II studies, like those of William Sexton and the official history of the war by John Taylor.[27]

It is somewhat surprising that Brown's journal is so little used by scholars. He is cited as a source in Gates, Linn, Miller, and Welch, but the references are minor or auxiliary, and there is no discussion of Brown or his observations. For example, Gates uses Brown's one-sentence account of anti-Chinese insurgent sentiment on September 5 to discuss the Chinese community. Linn cites Brown in *The U.S. Army and Counterinsurgency in the Philippine War, 1899–1902* as one of a number of sources to describe military rule in northern Luzon. Likewise, Miller and Welch simply use Brown as a source to substantiate the activities of U.S. troops.

Yet Brown's work provides a vivid chronicle of the American soldier in a number of different situations. Most noteworthy is his account of the effort to smash the Army of Liberation in Pampanga and northern Luzon during the fall and winter of 1899. His writing provides some of the best historical documentation of the campaign. The drive on president and military leader Emilio Aguinaldo, now largely forgotten, was one of the most arduous marches in American military history. After suffering catastrophic defeats around Manila, Aguinaldo was forced to the Pampanga region, where his troops were soundly defeated in more or less set-piece battles during the summer. With his family he fled to Tarlac. General

Otis, his adversary, fearful of a guerrilla war, devised a plan to capture Aguinaldo using a complicated three-pronged entrapment before the renegade leader could reach the mountains and continue his insurgency. Two forces, under Lawton and Brig. Gen. Lloyd Wheaton, would encircle the insurgent forces and in doing so block mountain and coastal escape routes; a third force under MacArthur was to drive the fugitive government up through Pampanga and into the guns of Lawton or Wheaton or both. By taking its leader, the United States could thus eradicate the fledgling government by crushing its military. The rebellion would be over. Another objective was the freeing of American and Spanish prisoners who had been captured during the past year. These were held by Gen. Manuel Tinio and were dragged from Malolos up into Ilocos Norte.

There were a number of elements that Otis and other U.S. officers inadequately considered prior to initiating the largest operation of the war. First and foremost was the terrain. By November, 1899, no American force had gone farther north than Pampanga, the flat, wet plain of Luzon. Otis began sending men past Pampanga and into essentially unknown areas such as Nueva Ecija and Pangasinan. Later, U.S. troops would be ordered into the mountains of Ilocos and Abra, the latter being particularly rugged and, as the Japanese found out forty-odd years later, absolutely perfect for local guerrilla activities. Roads were barely passable even in dry weather. There were few bridges in areas prone to flooding. Maps were poor or nonexistent. Supply lines were tenuous at the start and would become nearly impossible the more the army advanced into insurgent territory. Worst of all, no one really knew just how hostile the local population would be or how much support they would give the insurgents.

The operation began in the fall of 1899. After securing the important railway junctions at San Fernando and Angeles in October, American forces began to push north after the fleeing president. Supply lines, an obsession with Otis, immediately became a problem; indeed, Lawton's advance stopped completely at Cabanatuan because of swollen rivers. In early November the bogged-down Lawton received word that Aguinaldo was moving his capital from Tarlac in central Luzon to Bayombong in Nueva Viscaya. Nueva Viscaya is mountainous, so it was imperative that Aguinaldo be cut off before he could reach the safety of the province. It soon became clear, however, that given the state of the roads and rivers, American forces would not be able to accomplish this.

Brigadier General Samuel S. B. Young, former Civil War hero and commander of all cavalry units in the Philippines, offered a remedy to the situation. Young proposed the creation of a mobile column that would rendezvous with Wheaton and block the mountain passes before Aguinaldo reached them. Reminiscent of Sherman's earlier march in Georgia, nothing but the absolute minimum in the way of supplies would be taken. All heavy equipment would be left behind. This included stoves, ovens, and nearly all vehicles save for the lightest of supply wagons. Young's men would live off the land.

After hesitating, Lawton (who knew the cautious Otis would never approve such a plan), gave Young the okay. On November 8 the make-shift column—which included cavalry, Macabebe Scouts, and a young engineer named Brown to make maps—moved out. For more than a month the column suffered true hardships. The few light supply wagons were quickly abandoned to the impassable roads; likewise the only am-bulance. Daily rations were cut in half. Clothing, especially shoes, rotted away. Malaria, dysentery, and stomach problems set in. Morale plum-meted. Men had to be threatened to get them to continue.

Ultimately, Otis's operation was successful, despite the hardships and poor communications. Wheaton failed to rendezvous with Young, and Aguinaldo escaped. Young chased him unsuccessfully up Luzon's west coast, but he was eventually captured in 1901. By then, however, all sem-blance of a Filipino national government was shattered. Tinio and his brigade, first mauled at Vigan and Tangadan Mountain, were soon deci-mated at Dingras by Col. Robert L. Howze, bringing an end to major hostilities by insurgent army troops in northern Luzon (but not guerrilla activity, which would go on until April, 1901). All of the Spanish and American prisoners were freed. Tinio and others would come in from the mountains to surrender. American-backed or sympathetic politicians were installed in cities, towns, and barrios throughout most of Luzon.

Brown's narrative is at the center of all this and is historically valuable for several reasons. First, Brown was involved in the major stages of the northern Luzon campaign. His journal describes the drive to secure the railroad in Pampanga in late September and October, 1899. Brown and his Company B took part in the battle at Porac, where American forces drove off entrenched Filipinos and thus helped secure the area around San Fernando and Angeles. His observations of the battle are striking in their detail and clarity, making his one of the best accounts in the corpus of Philippine-American War material. Brown was also there at San Fabian, where Young's and Wheaton's columns finally met. Traveling north along the coast, he eventually took part in the battle at Tangadan Mountain, a crucial event in the offensive. Finally, he reached the campaign's terminal point, Bangui Bay. For any student of the war, especially the northern offensive, Brown's work is an indispensable reference document.

Brown's narrative of the northern "hike" also makes an important contribution to the history of the engineers in the Philippines. The story of military engineers is but slightly recorded in most conflicts, and in the case of the Philippines conflict, virtually nothing exists. While in Pampanga, Brown took part in the backbreaking work of building bridges and ferries in towns such as Santa Ana and Arayat. He relates the difficulties of fording rivers and building roads, often at the expense of the local populations, whose trees and sometimes houses were used as material. Luckily for Brown, he was taken off the heavy labor of road and ferry building and pressed into service as a draftsman. Again, his work provides an insight into a rarely seen, or even considered, aspect of warfare: that of the cartographer. In Smith S. Leach's short history (1903) of the three engineer companies sent to the Philippines, a passage reads "one private left with General Young's Flying Brigade from Cabanatuan and made maps of all the roads traveled until Vigan was reached."[28] That man was Brown, and his orders were simply to go north with any available troop and map all that he saw. This essentially means that Brown acted as a sort of lone wolf mapmaker, able to jump from outfit to outfit.

Brown's unique detail allowed him to travel with a number of different companies. No other account by an enlisted man offers such broad look at commanders and troops, all of which he describes in great detail. In short, Brown became an accidental historian of the northern offensive, providing for readers intimate glimpses into the U.S. military hierarchy and the order of battle. As noted, Brown served under Lieutenant Oakes as an engineer. In San Fernando he acted as a guard at MacArthur's headquarters, where he also came in contact with Lawton and Maj. Gen. Joseph Wheeler. He joined Lawton's 1st Division in October, when he served closely under Young, commander of the Cavalry Brigade. He also spent time under Capt. John G. Ballance of the 22d Infantry, one of the finest U.S. officers of the war, and served briefly with Lt. Matthew A. Batson and his Macabebe scouts. Lieutenant Colonel Edward M. Hayes of the 4th Cavalry was interested in Brown's drawings and spoke to him about them. Brown rode into the Ilocos with Colonel Hare of the renowned 33d Infantry, and later, with Maj. Samuel M. Swigert of the 3d Cavalry, took part in the smart skirmish near Banna. He finally arrived in Bangui with Capt. George C. Hunter, also of the 3d Cavalry, and served briefly there with a contingent of marines from the USS *Wheeling*. Even after his northern experiences, his assignments included interaction with a variety of persons and companies: he worked in the Intramuros, the headquarters of all U.S. operations in the islands, and he was sent to Paranaque to work with the 49th Infantry.

While Rudyard Kipling and George Orwell immortalized England's colonial forces, few Americans today have a grasp of what it was like to be a U.S. imperial soldier. Brown's journal gives some understanding of the experience. With the northern offensive over, his narrative changes to a description of the occupation. The last third of the story involves his stay in Manila, where he finishes his maps, and the building of the Paranaque bridge, which furnished him a good deal of frustration. His focus changes first from the calamity of war to the pleasant rhythms of city life: his work at the palace, the restaurants, the promenades around Manila's Luneta Park, and the warm daily interaction with his fellow soldiers. It is nearly an impressionist painting of a city and a soldier at peace. Things change when he is given the bridge assignment at Paranaque. There he had to deal with American contractors and workers, the first wave of what would be an ocean of colonizers, as well as with Filipino laborers. The experience was not a positive one for Brown, and the reader is treated to the difficulties of empire building.

Perhaps the most striking aspect of the journal is its strength as a travelogue. It has all the elements of a superb journey piece, one that describes the military conflict, the land and people of the Philippines, and the development of a man's character through conflict. The reader is allowed to follow Brown throughout his journey, from Talavera in central Luzon all the way to Bangui Bay at the very north of the island. His diary gives a superbly detailed step-by-step account of the trip, allowing the reader to witness the incredible hardships endured by U.S. troops: the sickness, the lack of shelter and shoes, and the poor food. It also demonstrates what living off the land actually entailed, including the copious looting, the destruction of private property, and, as demonstrated earlier, the humiliation and even summary execution of military prisoners. He gives his impressions of Filipinos, at this point mostly positive. Not only are events, places, and people described, we also see Brown's character metamorphose from soft-handed recruit to callused veteran. The John Clifford Brown who stretches out on the beach at Bangui has seen much and changed considerably since his innocent romance with the New York State Volunteers and his wide-eyed arrival in Manila. His thoughts reflect a marked maturity. Brown at Bangui is a young man with a realization of life that came about through the mud of Pampanga and the slopes of Tangadan; it is a mind that can now appreciate the beauty of nature moments after a brutal murder. But at Bangui, at the very top of Luzon at the turn of the century, Brown does not realize he is about to or has already contracted the disease that will shortly take his life. Brown's journey does not end at Bangui, nor does his character remain static. He must travel south to build a bridge over a foul river at Paranaque. That is where his story really ends.

Brown's narrative thus spans the American military experience at the turn of the twentieth century. Beginning with conquest on the battlefield, the story moves to the heavy work of colonization. In spanning this experience, his descriptions bring a sense of historical intimacy not found in most of the other primary accounts of the war. This, coupled with his extraordinary personal situation, make Brown's story surely one of the most important and entertaining of the conflict.

The 1901 Text

Just how Brown's narrative has reached its present form needs some explication. This collection uses as its source the book titled *Diary of a Soldier in the Philippines*. It was published in 1901 by Lakeside Press of Portland in a run of fifty copies, all numbered save one. It is the only edition and Philip Greeley Brown copyrighted it. The book contains 248 pages, including a short introduction and frontispiece photograph of Brown as an officer with the New York Volunteers. The document is structured chronologically beginning with a letter dated June 22, 1899, and ending with a journal entry dated August 23, 1900. There are no explanatory notes or ancillary information of any kind. However, there are parenthetical statements marked "Illustration" where Brown's journal entries included drawings that were not reproduced.

Although there is no documentation revealing exactly how the letters and journal came to be published in 1901, it seems fairly clear what happened. When Brown died, preceded shortly by his mother and followed soon after by his grandmother, Philip Greeley Brown collected the letters and journal entries and had them bound and published as *Diary of a Soldier in the Philippines*. Evidence points to this because of a will notice that said John Clifford Brown "leaves to his brother Philip G. Brown of Portland $2000 for the erection of a suitable memorial to his brother." It is probable that the money left to his brother was used to publish the book. Because Philip Greely Brown held the 1901 copyright it seems certain that it was he who carried out his brother's instructions regarding a memorial. Furthermore, other than the giant family crypt that was there when he died, there are no stone memorials left to John Clifford Brown. There are no grants or scholarships in his name. There are no buildings or rooms in tribute. Based on this evidence, it is safe to assume that the fifty copies of his overseas narrative were intended to serve as Brown's memorial. As far as this writer knows, sixteen copies are still in existence.[29]

What happened to the original letters and journal? An extensive search has not revealed any of the material. There is no mention of them in Philip Greely Brown's will. The direct descendants of the Brown family do not know of their whereabouts. The author has contacted other relations through a stockholder's list of J. B. Brown and Company but has not found the documents. Portland institutions like the public library, of which Philip Greely Brown was a major benefactor, do not have them. Neither does the Maine Historical Society, to which descendants of the Brown family have contributed memorabilia. The Lakeside Press has been out of business for decades and the author has been unable to locate their records. The original papers were not bequeathed to MIT, Brown's alma mater, or Bowdoin College, Philip Henry Brown's and Philip Greely Brown's alma mater. West Point does not have them, nor does the collection at Carlisle Barracks.

The apparently missing original letters and journal, as well as the complete set of maps Brown copied and sent home, are troublesome, and a few words should be devoted to their possible whereabouts and the consequences of reading this text without them. It is quite conceivable that the papers have long since disappeared. Perhaps, with Brown and his mother dead, they were simply thrown away after *Diary of a Soldier* was published. They could have been destroyed or lost through the inevitable housecleaning that comes after a family member's death, such as Philip Greely Brown's in 1934, or the destruction of the Vaughan Street residence shortly thereafter. It is also imaginable that the originals vanished with the Lakeside Press. Of course, it is entirely possible that the documents still exist, perhaps buried deep in a box in some relative's attic, held in a private collection, or unrecorded in a library somewhere. At this point, however, no person or institution has claimed them. Thus, given that many of Brown's descendants did not know of the book's existence, and given that no institution close to the Brown family has them, it seems most likely that the papers Brown sent home to Portland passed out of existence shortly after the printing was done.

There are, however, reproductions drawn from Brown's roadmaps. In volume one, part four, of the *Annual Reports for the War Department for the Fiscal Year Ending June 30, 1900* (1901), there are ten maps directly attributed to him, as well as a highly probable eleventh. The maps are identified as "sheets," numbered one through ten, and further identified as "road maps" between two places. For example, the first map that he drew, which corresponds to the events of August–November, 1899, is noted as "Sheet No. 1, Road Map from Mexico to Cabanatuan, plotted during advance of Gen. Young's Brigade, prepared under direction of J. Oakes." The "road maps" (all wonderfully descriptive) accompany a lengthy report by Lt. John Oakes on the activities of Company B, Engineers. While the maps are described as being prepared under the lieutenant's direction, Oakes gives Brown credit for drawing the maps, as well as high praise for his service. The eleventh map, which is included in the same set as the ten road maps, is of the battlefield at Tangadan Mountain, and it is marked as being drawn under the direction of General Young. It is known from the journal that Brown was responsible for drawing the battlefield and that he reported directly to Young at the time. Consequently, it is a safe guess that Brown drew this map as well.

Does the lack of the original papers hinder a reading of the work? Yes and no. It is extremely disheartening not to be able to see the illustrations Brown made during his travels, including those of houses, bird traps, and even benches, which he sent home and which the editor at Lakeside Press chose not to include, probably due to reproduction methods and costs. In a few places Brown refers to attachments such as the notes describing the fight near Santa Rosa, the Manila housekeeping list, and the pass to cross the American lines outside of Manila, that he sent home but

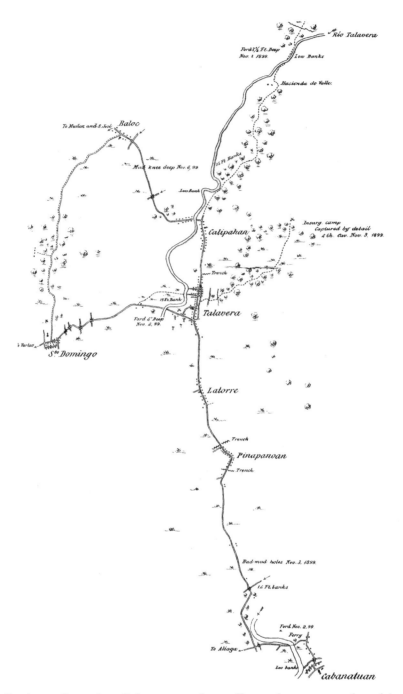

Road map of route from Cabanatuan to Lupao. From volume one, part four of the Annual Reports for the War Department for the Fiscal Year Ended June 30, 1900.

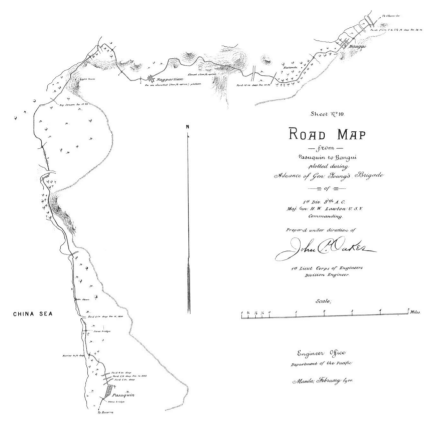

CHINA SEA

Sheet N° 10.

ROAD MAP
— from —
Pasuquin to Bangui
plotted during
Advance of Gen. Young's Brigade
= of =

1st Div. 8th A.C.
Maj. Gen. H. W. Lawton U.S.V.
Commanding

Prepared under direction of

John C. Oakes

1st Lieut. Corps of Engineers
Division Engineer.

Scale,

Engineer Office
Department of the Pacific

Manila, February 1900.

Road map of route from Pasuquin to Bangui. From volume one, part four of the Annual Reports for the War Department for the Fiscal Year Ended June 30, 1900.

which are also not included in the published text. There is no way of telling why these were not recorded, but a number of assumptions can be made. It could have been that either Philip Greely Brown, who would have been the first to consider editing the documents, and/or the Lakeside editor, deemed such auxiliary information unimportant. Or, like the illustrations, they may have been too problematic or too costly to reproduce. On balance, however, the narrative reads superbly without the illustrations or the few attachments, and their absence does not seem in any way to diminish the work.

There are more questions to be asked about the editing of the 1901 text, but before addressing them one point needs to be considered: Did Brown have an editorial role in the book's publication? The possibility exists that Brown and his brother Philip, and perhaps even his brother Nathan, discussed the matter of publication while in San Francisco together. Brown, although very sick, was communicating with his family, and it is conceivable that the brothers talked about what should and should not be included in the published journal. Such editorial planning, however, seems doubtful. While Brown may have certainly requested that his journal be published as a memorial, given his condition and that of the family it seems unlikely they would have been able to do much in the way of editorial decision making. First, Philip Greely Brown was with his brother for but a few days, perhaps five or six, and during that time the family was in the process of grieving for the mother who died the day before the eldest brother's arrival. In addition, Philip and Nathan must surely have been preoccupied with making arrangements for transporting their mother's body back to Portland. Brown would live for only three more weeks, during which time he was moved to Los Angeles. He surely was affected by his mother's passing, and he was emaciated and not completely ambulatory as a result of his illness. Thus, his mental and physical condition make it unlikely that he would have been able to contemplate what should or should not be included in the published diary—if in fact he requested that it be published, which is not certain.

It seems then that if there were any editorial decisions they were made by the family, and probably by Philip, who lived in Portland where Lakeside Press was located, and who was, as noted, the copyright holder. Having said that, one might ask why only letters to the mother (and perhaps only chosen pieces sent to her) were included when Brown mentions that he engaged in correspondence with others. Again, there is no real way of knowing but there are some ideas. The Brown family in 1901 was undoubtedly devastated: Brown, his mother, and Anne Matilda Greely Brown, the paternal grandmother, all died within a four-week period. It is certainly plausible that the book was intended to be at least in part a tribute to the obviously close mother-son relationship, and thus only the letters to her were recorded. It is also possible that other family members, such as Philip and sister Helen, simply did not want their letters published. It should be noted that no correspondence between Brown and anyone else is extant.

Two further questions might be asked about the editing of *Diary of a Soldier:* were certain journal entries omitted and why does the journal end so abruptly in August when Brown was in the Philippines until November? Perhaps the best approach to both questions is to consider Brown as a writer. As a diarist, Brown was dedicated and fastidious. Although his journal keeping was a bit spotty while he was aboard the transport ship, once he landed in Manila on August 13, 1899, his entries were quite regular. From that day until August 23, 1900, he failed to record daily entries only thirty-eight times. However, seventeen of those days occurred during his hospitalization in Vigan in January, 1900, eight during his first relapse a month later, and eight more during his second relapse in May-June. Thirty-three of the missing entries thus are directly attributable to his illness. Of the five remaining days, there is little explanation. One, December 4, might have been the result of marching into the mountains near Tangadan, but the others simply are not there. The military did not censor mail at the time, and there is no indication of any mail being lost. The days bracketing the missing dates show no great activity. It just seems Brown did not record what happened on those days.

Brown's illness and its effect on his writing probably explain why the journal ends so suddenly. The last journal entry is dated August 23, 1900, and there is no record of any other journal entries being sent afterward. What seems likely is that he had another relapse of his illness and suspended his journal keeping, as he did in Vigan and Paranaque. This time, however, he never felt well enough to continue. Unfortunately, the introduction to *Diary of a Soldier* clouds the issue with uncertain information: "Brown was put in charge of building a bridge at Paranaque. It is characteristic of him that he worked upon this bridge for weeks while so ill that he should have been in the hospital. He stuck to the work until it was finished, and thus made his death certain. Had he lived he would soon have received the commission in the Regular Army which he coveted."

That he oversaw the bridge being completed, while possible, is hard to imagine. Government records show that it was "probably" finished in 1900, but work was stopped entirely on the date of his last entry owing to a lack of piles.[30] Brown mentions that there might be an official inquiry into the contractor's procedures; in fact, there were major problems with building materials. Perhaps the introduction means he stuck to it until work was suspended in August. That, however, infers he was extremely ill in July or August, and there is no indication such was the case in the journal. Moreover, the reference to his obtaining a commission is equally baffling because we know he was not accepted for the commissioning examinations that year—unless for some inexplicable reason the army reversed its decision after August 23, and there is no record of that happening. Even if he was allowed to take the examinations, we know that his illness caused him to be hospitalized after the August date, and that he was shipped home on November 2. It thus seems doubtful that he could have studied for and passed the exams.

A more intriguing textual question concerns the willful omission or alteration of specific information within the letters and entries. Did the soldier's older brother Philip, surely an early reader of the material, change or drop portions of accounts within Brown's story? It is the contention here that few if any of Brown's original documents were altered for content. The voice of the writer offers evidence to substantiate this. As discussed earlier, because the letters and at least some of the journal entries were written for Mrs. Brown, he surely adopted a particular voice for his mother, and certain elements of a soldier's life overseas would undoubtedly not be chronicled. And, as also noted, it is obvious that Brown was trying to placate his mother's anxiety when he reported his good health, the good food, and excitement of military life. It thus is predictable that the voice and its content promote the image of a "good son" in a safe moral environment. How would Brown have deviated from this voice? Why should anything be modified in these almost bucolic letters? Paradoxically, however, elements of *Diary of a Soldier* are quite candid in revealing his racial prejudices, his vivid descriptions of battle and war atrocities, his accusations of corruption at the Paranaque bridge, and his dislike for certain persons he encountered. If an idealized memorial for their lost soldier was the family's intent, why did it allow these to be printed? Philip Greely Brown could have trimmed references that might somehow have compromised the memory of his brother, but given the frankness of what is included, what would have been offensive enough to be dropped or altered? A sexual reference? Vulgar language? Disparaging remarks made about persons in Portland? Considering the writer's voice and existing content, this seems doubtful.

Perhaps the most perplexing question is the total lack of reference to Florence McMullen, the young Portland woman Brown was apparently "sweet" on. According to the family it was assumed that the two of them would eventually marry, so it is quite strange that she is invisible within the narrative. It is possible—in fact, probable—that Brown carried on a separate correspondence with McMullen, and given Brown's penchant for separating identity, audience, and medium, it is conceivable that he willingly kept all thoughts of her to letters. We most likely will never know: she married after his death and passed away decades ago. It is doubtful she kept any letters from Brown, and if she did it is equally doubtful any would exist today. Even with this scenario, it is still troubling to think that her name does not appear once. Perhaps brother Philip, knowing that McMullen was still a family friend and member of Portland society, decided to cut any mention of her from the original documents in consideration of her social future. There may have been legal concerns if the references were deeply personal. But is Florence McMullen really there? As noted earlier, there is the astonishing change of voice on May 16, 1900, highlighted by the melancholy statement about songs, "I suppose you have forgotten them by this time," which certainly could have been a lonely man's sigh to a woman at home. A similar change in voice occurs on July 13. Again, are these passages the result of rather dubious editorial modifications to the original correspondence? If so, it weakens the narrative because an example of Brown's romantic voice would certainly have broadened his character.

Copy wise, *Diary of a Soldier* is remarkably clean. With the exception of place and personal names there are few spelling errors. It seems certain that any miscues in the letters or journal were corrected before printing, a custom of the time. Even so, Brown was a solid student at MIT; spelling and grammar were probably not among his weaknesses. The discovery of the original documents might reveal that his brother or the publisher stylistically distilled Brown's prose, but it is unlikely that this would significantly have changed the effect of the work.

It is, of course, a shame that the original correspondence cannot be found. All in all, however, the 1901 edition provides a more than adequate text for contemplating Brown and his service in the Philippines. Hopefully, with the added information contained in this new edition, readers will be able to see Brown within the larger and more dynamic contexts of U.S. military history and American-Philippine relations.

John Clifford Brown as a captain in the New York Volunteers, 1899.

Introduction to
Diary of a Soldier in the Philippines
(1901)

CAPTAIN JOHN CLIFFORD BROWN, United States Volunteers, died January 16, 1901, at Los Angeles, Cal., of dysentery, contracted in the Philippines. Captain Brown was born at Portland, Maine, March 28, 1872. He early showed a strong taste for electrical science, and made a special study of this at the Massachusetts Institute of Technology, of Boston, where be graduated with very high rank in 1893. Almost immediately he was employed by the New York Telegraph and Telephone Company in its engineer department. His advancement was rapid, and at the breaking out of the war with Spain he occupied a position of responsibility not often given to so young a man. He had, however, been a member of the Seventh Regiment for several years, and he believed it his duty to go to the war. He went as a captain of the Eighth New York. It should be said that he went eagerly, for he was a born soldier—a tall, lithe, very handsome man, of the pronounced blonde type, quiet, fearless, and a natural leader. He was kept at Chickamauga and elsewhere in the South throughout the war, serving, after the Eighth was mustered out as lieutenant in the Two Hundred and Third in his eagerness to see active service. After the latter regiment was also mustered out he enlisted, on June 22, 1899, in the Engineer Corps of the Regular Army, and was sent at once to the Philippines.

Brown was the only man of the Engineers who went with General Young on the famous "hike" from a point near Manila through Luzon to Vigan, on the north coast. He won the highest commendations from his superiors, including General Young, for gallantry and for efficiency as an engineer throughout that most arduous expedition. All the maps of the route followed were drawn by him under almost inconceivable difficulties, and they are beautiful examples of field drafting.

Returned to Manila, Brown was put in charge of building a bridge at Paranaque. It is characteristic of him that he worked upon this bridge for weeks while so ill that he should have been in the hospital. He stuck to the work until it was finished, and thus made his death certain. Had he lived he would soon have received the commission in the Regular Army which he coveted.

CHAPTER I

The New West

$\mathcal{T}$HE UNITED STATES at the outset of the new century was an excited, ambitious country. In 1898 it had destroyed the Spanish fleet in Manila Bay and forced the Spanish army from Cuba. Through negotiations with Spain it acquired new territories in 1899, including the seventy-five hundred islands in the archipelago known as the Philippines. For America, the Philippines was essentially an uncharted land with seemingly unlimited potential. Complicating matters were the facts that the Filipinos had declared their independence and formed a government, had a seasoned army under Aguinaldo, and were willing to fight for their nation. America now had to crush that independence movement and occupy the country in order to, as expansionists argued, save the Filipinos from themselves. This was challenged by a strong anti-imperialist coalition in the United States, as well as many individual citizens, who argued that taking the Philippines was unethical and ran counter to America's cherished ideals of freedom and democracy (although it should be said that some anti-imperialists acted from racial considerations, fearing the addition of more nonwhites to the population). For all concerned, the coming U.S. adventure in the Philippines demanded a discussion of America's right to acquire land and govern people. Just a decade after settling its own frontier, it appeared America had found a new West to conquer.

The end of one century and the beginning of another was also an exciting, ambitious time for John Clifford Brown. He had quit an enviable engineer's job to serve as an officer in two volunteer army outfits and in June made the decision to enlist as a private in the regular army. These decisions were apparently against the wishes of his family and the advice of his friends, and he had to justify the choices to himself continually thereafter. Despite the criticism and uncertainty, he left Willets Point, New York, with Company B, Engineer Battalion, crossing the continent by train. Brown found the twenty-one-day trip exhilarating. He was a young man in uniform setting off on the greatest adventure of his life. He left San Francisco in July on the *City of Para* and, after a stop in Honolulu, reached Manila a month later. He had arrived in America's new frontier.

Brown disembarked in Manila at one of the critical junctures of the city's long history. Commodore George Dewey had taken the USS *Olympia* some months earlier, leaving the Philippines's largest city a hive of military and international activity in its wake. Manila Bay was a hodgepodge of European and American vessels. Incoming troops, diplomats, and carpetbaggers of all stripes were replacing the Spanish aristocracy and displacing Filipino aspirations for independence. Along the Escolta, the city's most fashionable street, bars and brothels competed with refined restaurants and bodegas. The *zarzuela* was shortly to be swapped for jazz. English would become the lingua franca, the language of instruction, and the desired speech of the city's upscale youth. The Stars and Stripes was flown throughout the islands. The American era had been born.

It was a difficult birth. Hostilities between U.S. and Filipino troops began on February 4, 1899, when disputed circumstances caused an eruption of violence in the Manila area. For weeks the two armies fought at close range on the city's outskirts, the result being the defeat of Aguinaldo's Army of Liberation, which caused its rupture and eviction to points north and east of Manila. Major General Elwell Otis, seeing that the seat of Aguinaldo's government and the bulk of his army were in the northern areas, set out to destroy Filipino guerrilla leader in March. The U.S. forces, usually consisting of state volunteer regiments, captured Malolos, the capital city. The Americans easily won confrontations at Calumpit, San Fernando, San Isidro, and other places in Pampanga and Bulacan provinces. The Filipino soldiers, who had defeated the Spanish just a short time before, became demoralized.

The U.S. victories were to some extent superficial, and the operation illuminated a number of weaknesses that would hamper the army throughout the war. While it was true that Otis and his state volunteer forces had captured major cities and chunks of central Luzon, very little of the area was actually occupied, much less pacified. Otis simply did not have enough troops to hold onto the territory. American casualties were light, but sickness in the ranks was catastrophic. The army's Medical Corps, just as it had been in Cuba, was poorly prepared for the onslaught of tropical disease and the maladies associated with deficient provisions. In many cases, doctors simply did not recognize or understand the illnesses affecting the men. Another dilemma was the inability to supply the front lines. For example, the U.S. strategy failed to take into account Luzon's marshy, flood-prone plains, where draft animals sank up to their bellies in mud. The problem of getting adequate supplies to troops in the field was never solved during the war.

When the *City of Para* dropped anchor in Manila Bay, Aguinaldo's forces were in Pampanga, shocked by the early debacles around Manila and Malolos, but hardly destroyed. The Filipino leader had assumed complete control of the government and military in 1899 after deposing Apolinario Mabini as president of the revolutionary cabinet and (presumably) ordering the assassination of Antonio Luna, Aguinaldo's rival as military chief and arguably the revolutionary army's most able general. Despite flirting with the idea of peace with the Americans, Aguinaldo decided to follow a more decisive course. He attacked San Fernando on June 16 and was easily repulsed. His troops, however, were not forced from the area. In August, General Otis concluded that he first needed to secure the railroad line between San Fernando and Angeles in order to crack the spine of the insurrection. Otis ordered MacArthur to execute the plan, and MacArthur did so by taking Angeles on August 16, but only after stiff resistance from the Filipino forces. Once again the Filipinos were driven from their positions, but they retained a strong presence in the area.

Brown's journey thus begins in a kaleidoscope of transition. His country has moved beyond the post-Frontier fugue and onto the international playing field. Some of its people were thrilled and impassioned at America's new manifestation of power; others were uncertain and troubled. The Philippines had been caught between two colonial masters, its sense of nationhood stunted by war and confusion. Within this historic shuffle is Brown: a cultivated, wealthy man who has shed his skin as a New York professional to become an army private. It was a magnificent, unsettled time, and looking at Brown's letters and journal entries written in the summer and early fall of 1899, it is easy to consider his trek across half the planet as wonderfully archetypal. He begins on the U.S. East Coast, the center of commerce and technology, and moves westward, ever toward his independence and destiny. He crosses the fields of Kansas—mindful of his associations with John Brown, slavery, free states, and the Civil

War—through what was once buffalo country, and ends up in vibrant, multicultural San Francisco. He then travels to one of America's new acquisitions—Hawaii, with its freshly deposed monarchy—and finally on to the Philippines. This exotic destination, with its decaying European architecture and decadent Spanish culture, was pregnant with possibility. First, however, the natives must be made to see America's moral and military superiority. Brown is a willing instrument for that enlightenment. Brown's westward journey is the nation's journey from North America into the twentieth century.

Dear Mamma:

You must not feel so badly about my enlisting. It is only for a few months anyway and I shall make out all right. I joined this morning and take this chance to give you my first impressions.[1] In the first place this Company B of the Engineer Battalion leaves for Frisco en route for Manila July 5th or thereabouts, as soon as it can get equipped for the Tropics. I have been put in a room in barracks with five other young fellows, three of whom were in Volunteers. The bunks are iron with springs and mattresses with sheets and pillow-cases. As a captain I never knew such luxury in the Volunteers. My five room-mates are all clean, nice young fellows. The food is unexceptional though plain and roughly served, though there are waiters and we have china to eat off of. For dinner we had corned beef and cabbage, bread and gravy and coffee. All nice and as many helpings as you wanted to ask for. For supper, bacon, lyonnaise potatoes, bread and gravy and lettuce salad with French dressing, coffee of course. You see I won't starve. Altogether I like it very well and am sure I will get on very well.

Address my letters to John C. Brown, Company B, Engineer Battalion, Willetts Point, N.Y.

At 9:15 lights go out. Reveille at ten minutes before six. So you see I do not suffer and you do not want to think I am. As for health and strength I was over the weight limit and the surgeon said I was absolutely sound.

Your loving son,
Jack.
June 22, 1899.

Dear Mamma:

You would be surprised to find how pleasant the life is here. The fellows are all intelligent, clean young men. The food is better than the officers ever had in the Volunteers and as well served. The work is not hard and I would be perfectly contented if I did not think you were needlessly worrying. When exactly we start I do not know. We have drawn our light clothes for the Tropics. The company is to be vaccinated tomorrow. The ranks are full one hundred and fifty men and we will probably start for Frisco soon. The men look at the service down there seriously but are all glad to go. C Company of this Battalion was in the Cuban campaign, serving all through it without the loss of a man either from wounds or sickness. We may do the same. I am going to send home from time to time letters addressed to me. I wish you would put them in my desk unopened. They will be nothing but rough notes which I may some time expand into something. Everything important I will put into my letters. The life in the barracks is as different from what I had imagined it as possible. Last night I was reading "Tom Brown at Rugby."[2] Most of the men in the room, there are ten of us, were writing. One was reading his Bible. I am sure if it had not been for the rifles and the equipments I should have thought myself in a dormitory at school. I imagine the Engineers are very different from the rest of the army.

Your loving son,
Jack.
June 22, 1899.

B Company, Batt. of Eng.
Willetts Point, N.Y.,
July 2, 1899.

Dear Mamma

We leave Wednesday morning at six o'clock. I believe when we get to Frisco we go on the City of Para, but that is mere rumor.[3] The life continues very pleasant and interesting and I am sure I am going to like it very much. The fellows are very enthusiastic about the trip and expect to do great things. All letters addressed here will be forwarded as soon as possible. I will write whenever I get a chance and will telegraph when we arrive. Don't worry, for everything will go all right and it won't be many months before I am back. The two weeks that have passed since my enlistment has hardened me up and I am in fine shape for the trip. I was very much obliged for the newspaper slips.

Your loving son,
Jack.

Somewhere in West Virginia,
July 6, 1899.

Dear Mamma:
So at last we are really off on our long journey. We are very comfortable, being in regular tourist cars which are you know just like a sleeping car but not finished so well. Them are only two of us to a section, so each man has a berth to himself with clean sheets every night. So it could not be any nicer. I am well and perfectly contented. Tell Phip I got his letter O.K. Pardon the haste.

Your loving son,
Jack.

St. Louis, Mo.,
July 7, 1899.

Dear Mamma:
Everything is going lovely and I am enjoying the trip across the continent very much. We have plenty of good food and as I wrote you our accommodations are excellent. Of course even now we are much farther West than I have ever been and so it is all strange and interesting. It is a wonderful trip to be paid for making. It is worth any sacrifice, or would be for I am making none but enjoying every minute. The men are quiet and well behaved. There is not half the bad language or horse play that there was among the officers I went South with when I was in the Volunteers.

Your loving son,
Jack.

Somewhere in Kansas,
July 8, 1899.

Dear Mamma:
This is certainly a wonderful trip. I am enjoying every moment of it. You
well know that I have always enjoyed traveling, but in my wildest flights of
imagination I never thought I should take a trip like this. Don't worry about
the discomforts, there are none. We have plenty of good food. Fresh bread
every day and as I wrote you before we could not be more comfortable as to
the car unless we all had private cars. Last night we stopped for coffee at
Ossawatomie. You remember that is where the John Brown of the Civil War
came from.[4] The whole town (I don't believe there are 4000 people in it)
were at the station to see us. Every one dressed in their Sunday best. It was
quite gay.

> *Your loving son,*
> *Jack.*

Somewhere in Colorado,
July 9, 1899.

Dear Mamma:
We expect now to get into Frisco either Monday night or Tuesday morning.
How long we will stay there I do not know, but I will write from there if I
get a chance. The ride across the prairies was very interesting, as we stopped
from time to time to run about and get exercise. Every one tried to shoot the
prairie dogs and coyotes, but without success. To-day we are in the Rocky
Mountains. I expect we will be in Salt Lake City by night. I may not write
any more till Frisco, as every one has used up all the paper and envelopes we
had provided for the entire trip. For some reason no one thought in advance
of writing from the train. It has been one of the most fascinating trips I have
ever taken and I have enjoyed every minute of it. One funny thing is the
hours. Of course there is nothing to do in the evening, so by seven every one is
asleep and every one is up by five or even earlier, when as was the case this
morning the scenery was interesting. I have written you every day but you

may not have got them all as one has to trust people at the stations to mail them. Am in perfect health.

Your loving son,
Jack.

Somewhere in California,
July 11, 1899.

Dear Mamma:
Our long railway journey is nearly over. We are only about one hundred miles from Frisco now and will probably be in at noon. It has been a wonderful trip and I can truly say that I have enjoyed every minute of it. It is a trip which I have always wanted to make, but I did not realize that I should some day make it at Government expense. I have written you every day, but some of the letters given to anybody at out-of-the-way stations may have miscarried. My health has never been better and I am in fine spirits. Don't worry.

Your loving son,
Jack.

Angel Island,
San Francisco Harbor,
July 13, 1899.

Dear Mamma:
Were you ever in San Francisco? Isn't it a curious place? I got a pass yesterday and went all over it. They have a fog here every day at this time of year. We are in barracks, seven miles from the city, on an island. It is a curious place, all a big hill, and looks like Capri, Italy. I would not take $5000 for the experiences of this trip. I believe we sail this afternoon on the City of Para, but I know nothing definite of course.[5] I will write from Honolulu. My health has never been better. Will you get a New York Sun for July 6th and send me the article about the Engineers going away? I should like to see it.[6]

Your loving son,
Jack.

On Board U.S.S. TRANSPORT,
City of Para,
July 18, 1899.

Dear Mamma:

We are now five days out and two days from Honolulu, where I expect to mail this. From Honolulu it is twenty-eight days to Manila, which is the next place I will have a chance to write. Life on a transport is not nearly as bad as my imagination led me to expect, and I imagine it is a paradise beside the torments which you are picturing me as enduring. Each man has a bunk to himself and there is plenty of fresh air. The food is really very good. Usually hash or bacon with coffee and fresh bread for breakfast. Stew or beans or soup with coffee and bread for dinner, and rice and apple sauce with fresh bread and coffee for supper. Not Delmonico's, of course, but good and wholesome. I have had all I wanted to eat and I have not been seasick either, though that is not strange as it has not been very tough and after the first day the sea has been as smooth as a mirror. There are 900 troops aboard, but she carried 1,200 on her last trip so you see she is not overcrowded. We are going to stop two days in Honolulu and will all be allowed on shore, a place I have always wanted to see. It is a very pleasant way to see the world and I should not hesitate to advise any one to take the trip. There is a Portland boy in our company, a fellow named Sawyer. I don't fancy him myself but he hunted me up, having seen those newspaper articles you sent me. I don't know who his parents are but he used to work in Hooper & Leighton's. I got the letter you wrote me on the 4th of July in San Francisco, just after I had mailed my last letter to you and just about an hour before we sailed, so it was like a last good-by. I was very glad to get it. I can't help thinking that it is much nicer to travel around the world this way than to stay at home, but of course I don't like you to worry all the time. There is really no need of it. We are taken the very best of care of. For instance there are eight army doctors on the boat. I forgot to mention that onions, cabbage and lime juice are issued it intervals. So don't worry. It won't be a very long time before I am back. Why I will have been in the service two months when you receive this. My health and spirits are of the very best. I hope yours are.

Your loving son,
Jack.

JULY 24

We sighted the islands about 6 A.M. on the 20th. It was amusing to hear the comments of the troops, some swearing that what others took for land was the smoke of a steamer, others that it was cloud. It was 1 P.M. before all doubt was settled. At about 3 P.M. we were off the harbor of Honolulu, making the dock before supper. The small boys swam off to the ship as she approached the dock and dived for nickels as the boys do at Naples. I think my first impression was a sense of disappointment as the islands were not as tropical as I had expected. After supper the wharf was crowded with hucksters who did a thriving business with the soldiers. The ship at once began to coal. No one allowed on board.

JULY 31

Ordered to parade at 9:30. There was an immense scramble to clean rifles which had not been looked at on the trip. Marched to the Palace, in front of which we stacked arms, and were then marched about four miles to the beach Weikeiki for a swim. It was during this march that I first began to appreciate the wonderful beauty of the place. Every house seemed set in a frame of dense foliage. Dates, cocoanuts, bread fruit, bananas, royal palms and banyan trees seemed to be in abundance besides many other trees and shrubs whose names I did not know. I was amused at our officers who appeared much more demonstrative in their enjoyment of the strange scenery than the men, who for the most part marched along stolidly enough. After a most refreshing swim we were all given liberty until 5 P.M., it was then about 11 A.M. I had about $3.00 and my two most intimates had nothing, so we walked back to town and had dinner for a quarter apiece, a five-cent cigar and a glass of beer. I made a few purchases and got shaved and a hair cut, bought a paper and then we had no money at all. On sighting the islands it had occurred to me that when I went to Washington to enlist I had gone on in the train with Mr. Arthur Sewell, of Bath, Maine, who made me promise to look up his son Harold, who was minister to these islands before they were annexed.[7] On inquiring at the store where I made my purchases I was delighted to find him a sort of popular idol, that every one hoped he would be appointed governor, etc., etc. Called at the American consulate and found him not at home though they telephoned to his residence. Went through the fish market, admiring the many strange and bright-colored fish, and then through the Palace, now used as government offices. At 5 P.M. fell in and were marched back to the ship. As I came over the side a note was handed me from Mr. S. asking me to call in the evening if possible. Before I could arrange to do that met him myself, he having waited nearly two hours for me. He was cordiality itself and would take no refusal. I must make his house my headquarters during my stay. He went to the ship's adjutant and got me a pass until the next morning. Drove me to the Club, where he put me up, and then to his house, which is on the beach a short distance beyond where we had our swim. It was, he explained, one of the old chief's places. The place is full of very tall cocoanut palms, which he tells me always denotes an old chief's place. Back of his house and right on the beach, so much so that at high tide the sea is not ten feet from you, is a gigantic haw tree, a tree the branches of which about ten or twelve feet from the ground spread out like in umbrella and form an impenetrable shade. There is a platform under it, it is lighted by electric lights and it was here that I met Mrs. S. and here with the addition of a Mr. Ervin, a wealthy sugar planter, that we had our dinner. It is truly a place to rave about. The sea lapping the beach so near you, while you can see it breaking in snowy masses on the barrier coral reef, perhaps four hundred feet outside. To the left, the beach, lined with similar places, stretches along for over a mile till ending in a curve, not unlike the Bay of Naples, it terminates in a rocky point, Diamond Head, which is the crater of an extinct volcano. Our dinner (it was a supper) was intensely American. Soup, broiled salmon, green peas, Rhine wine (it was preceded by cocktails), cold ham, potatoes, celery, champagne. After this course the only native dish was introduced and only for my benefit, an alligator pear. Why a pear unless for its shape I do not know, for it has an immense stone and is eaten either with salt or Worcestershire sauce. The flavor is unlike anything I have ever tasted but resembles a nut. It has a thick skin. Cigars and Hawaiian coffee. It may be fancy, or else contrast to the ship's coffee, but it seemed the most delicious I had ever drank. A comfortable bed with mosquito netting, for mosquitoes seem the only drawback to this earthly paradise. Was called at 5 A.M. as I had to report back to the ship. Saw the C.O. Major, who very graciously extended my pass indefinitely, but my Captain thought I had better sleep on the ship. Why I don't know. Had punctured a tire coming to the ship so had to walk, reaching there about 9 A.M. Found Mr. S. had waited breakfast for me. Had a swim and the luxury of a fresh-water shower first. Was ravenously hungry—Mr. S. insisted on my trying many strange (to me) fruits. Fresh dates, mangoes, which I found delicious pineapples, quite different from those we have at home, and the Australian passion fruit. Then an ordinary American breakfast to which I did ample justice. After a smoke, after my experience Havana cigars taste good, we went for a drive—I should mention that Mrs S. had a brother, Sydney Ash, who did the same thing I am doing, going out as a private in the 4th Cavalry. The grounds of the late Princess Kaliokallani are the most beautiful it is possible to imagine.[8] A most delightful drive which lasted until about 2 P.M., during which we saw everything in the town, including the Bishop Museum which we went through, seeing the priceless feather capes, helmets and, I have forgotten the name, but the things they wave at funerals. During the ride I learned much about the politics and economics of the islands and many side-lights and curiosities of history, of annexation and the war. Much that I do not care to write and which I hope I will not forget. Altogether the ride was most interesting, for not only were the surroundings strange, beautiful and interesting, but Mr. S. is a fascinating conversationalist and has been present at and taken part in some interesting and important incidents in these Pacific Islands. Mrs. S., who is in a delicate condition, did not appear at the midday meal, which is dinner. No strange dishes. Alligator pears made their appearance again. S. is very fond of them. Tells me it is an acquired taste. In the afternoon watched the natives and others riding in on the breakers on their surf boards and in their log canoes, which with their outriggers are the first I have ever seen. Cigars and a long talk, also introductions to native women and others (there is no race prejudice here) until I thought that as the ship sailed the next morning and as I might not be back for some time I had rather talk to him. For supper he had prepared a most unexpected and delightful treat, that is, the principal dishes of a native feast. In a native feast, which really bears some resemblance to our clambake, all the dishes are cooked in holes in the ground, for instance the pig, the principal dish, is placed in a hole, hot stones wrapped in palm leaves are placed inside him. The whole is then wrapped in palm leaves, placed in the hole, surrounded by hot stones and covered up. It is left some time, a day I believe, but it is needless to enter into a description which any book on the island will supply. Other dishes were crabs, fish, chicken, the luah itself, which is the leaf of the tarn cooked with cocoanuts and is not unlike our spinach, yams, big sweet potatoes, cocoanut pudding and of course poi, which with a little fish is all a native wants. Personally I did not much like poi, Mrs. S. gives it to her baby, but the pig seemed the most delicious thing I had ever eaten and I was not hungry either. Reported at the ship as she was reported to sail at daybreak. She did not, so on July 23d all the Engineers were given liberty until 12 M[idnight]. Went to S.'s, breakfast and a long talk. He wanted to do a lot for me, but I would take nothing but a few dollars, which being broke were much appreciated. Ship sailed at 4:45 P.M.

Dear Mamma:
I send you these few pages from my journal instead of a letter. They will give you a faint idea of how much I enjoyed the islands, owing to Mr. S., but it will be a faint idea as my emotions and experiences were too remarkable to put on paper. Those three days are numbered among the most delightful that I have ever spent and I start on our long trip much refreshed and invigo-rated. Please save these pages after you have read them and put them with the letters I have sent home addressed to myself.

Your loving son,
Jack.

AUGUST 1
The last week has been absolutely uneventful. The sky almost cloud-less, the sea perfectly smooth. The doctor who enlisted me at Wash-ington barracks asked me into his stateroom a few evenings ago and we had a long talk, with drinks and cigars.[9] He told me to come in whenever I had time, but I hesitate to accept favors which I can-not repay until so long. We passed a small British cruiser yesterday proceeding leisurely under sail. She is the only thing we sighted

since leaving Honolulu. The food, much to my surprise, gets better than ever. There is good variety, we had salt mackerel for breakfast the other day, and things are well cooked. I have an idea the men are beginning to find me out. They all know I was an officer in the Volunteers. There are two men from the 8th and one from the 203d in the company. Several have asked me why I did not try for a commission. Not knowing exactly how the men lived, I find many of them provided with little luxuries that I lack. All that can be remedied as soon as we get ashore.

AUGUST 2

A little excitement last night about 7:30 P.M. One of our men, Lile, got into some dispute with one of the crew. Lile got a knife and when they got them apart the man from the crew had eighteen stab wounds. It took 104 stitches to sew him up and he will probably die. Lile, who is now in irons, was not hurt at all. I think from what I hear it was Lile's fault. Washed my clothes this morning, the first time I ever did it. Was not much of a success, but I think I got some of the dirt out of them. It seems there is another fellow from Portland in the company, Paine, who lived on the corner of Chestnut and Cumberland. I notice more and more the unfailing kindness with which I am treated, every one seems to try to help. The sunset last night, I always watch them from the extreme stern where I am nearly alone, was the most beautiful yet. Course still due west.

AUGUST 4

The first land since we left Honolulu passed at 6:30 A.M. The smoking, volcanic island of Farrelone de Pajaros, the most northerly of the Ladrone Islands, Guam being the most southerly. Of course none of the others were visible. It seemed to be little more than a volcano. Yesterday afternoon at eight bells the machinery was stopped for a few moments. I do not know why. In spite of that logged 301 miles, an average run. The maximum has been 318. There is a heavy ground swell setting in from the southwest, dead against the wind. I hope it does not portend heavy weather. Showers again to-day. I suppose the rains are upon us. I must try and remember some of the stories my bunkie, old Oscar, tells me after our evening bath and before we are quite ready to go to sleep. I suppose it is his manner as much as anything which makes them funny, but the one of the "Old Sergeant and the details" was very funny, paper is too scarce to write it.

AUGUST 5
One of the colored Infantry died either today or last night. He was buried at three this afternoon (spinal meningitis).[10] I have always thought of a burial at sea as impressive. This was quite the reverse, the soldiers crowding the rail to see the body thrown overboard and apparently thinking the whole thing some form of amusement gotten up to relieve the monotony of the trip. I find I am getting to be known among the officers, whom I avoid as much as possible. When I am on duty it is quite usual to hear "Is that him?" Lieut. O[akes]. of "ours" made some advances to-day, asking me if it was true I had graduated from M.I.T., saying also they would give me a chance when we get ashore.

AUGUST 6
Sunday. A little incident, pickles for dinner. A sharp squall in the afternoon and another later which cleared the decks at 7 P.M. Found Oscar Japhet very low in his mind, some one had stolen his canteen and khaki blouse and that with the rain had filled full his cup of misery. I admit of course that a private's life on a transport is not exactly luxurious, but it is all so distinctly humorous if you look at it the right way that it becomes interesting and amusing.

AUGUST 7
It is interesting to note the development of custom. At first on the ship men wandered about aimlessly, now every company has a part of the deck which it considers its own. More than that each man has his place, which has by tacit consent become his and which he usually marks by leaving a blanket or a haversack when he leaves it. A new phrase which I do not think I have mentioned, "hand shaking," meaning to curry favor with the "non-coms." There is a lot of speculation as to when we will sight the islands. The special duty I have been on has developed into a perfect snap, owing to always reporting and a willingness to work. Sea smooth again, sky overcast.

AUGUST 9

When we came on deck this morning (6 A.M.) the Philippines were all about us. Shortly we made out Luzon itself, for we round the northern end. The islands are quite different from Hawaii. They seem as mountainous and rise as directly out of the sea, but the mountain tops of Honolulu or Oahu, to be correct, rise up brown and barren while these are covered with dense vegetation to the very summit. A square-rigged vessel in shore excited some notice among the men as rumor had been rife about a gun-boat of Aguinaldo's which was going to take or sink us.[11] All the morning we cruised the shore at a distance of about two miles. It was the first hostile shore I have ever seen, but I did not seem to feel any emotion except curiosity. The circumstances were not particularly calculated to produce emotions as it was showery, in fact our breakfast taken under the awnings which are pretty well searched by the rain was not enlivening, would have been a bit discouraging, but all know that there is worse to come and were uncomplaining. A rumor yesterday to the effect that the refrigerated beef had spoiled had a tendency to reduce my appetite slightly for one meal. I can find nothing wrong with any I have had, so today ate it again with a relish. The color of the water has changed to-day from that deep blue to a dirty green, so I imagine the water is not so deep as off Oahu, where the deep blue runs up to the coral reefs, a few hundred yards from the shore. Passed (1 P.M.) a lighthouse, the first sign of civilization. I don't of course know who holds the shore.

Dear Mamma:

They have just announced that we will arrive in Manila about 5 P.M. tomorrow, so I will seal this. I hope you will be able to make something out of these rather disconnected notes which have been written as the spirit moved and contain everything of importance that has happened since leaving the H[awaiian]. I[slands]. Please put them with the letters addressed to me when you have finished with them. And now that our long trip is so nearly ended (it will be five weeks since we left Willetts Point) let me assure you that it has been really a pleasant as well as a strange experience. I have seen a lot of the world, we are more than half-way round it. My health has never been better, the sea voyage agreed with me from the start, and I am in bully condition to tackle anything that may come along. I will try and telegraph you as soon as we land, but my duties may delay it. I can only hope that you have not allowed yourself to worry. As I have often written, the Engineers are seldom engaged. Besides the rainy season is nearly over, only about a month more. It will be over when you get this. I shall take the very best of care of myself and do not intend to drink, so I shall undoubtedly pull through all right. I will write as often as possible, but do not be worried if you do not hear from me, as the mails are apt to go astray and we may be miles from mail facilities. And so hoping you won't worry and with remembrances to all the family, not forgetting Scamp, I am

Your loving son,
Jack.[12]

AUGUST 10

Passed into Manila Bay, Corregidor island on our starboard, about 2 or 3 P.M. came abreast of a little village of thatch. Above it was the flag. I am not sentimental, but it brought a lump into my throat and a cheer from the transport. Then Cavite and then you could see the masts of the shipping off Manila. Then we made out the *Oregon*, the first time I had seen her.[13] It was raining hard and saw very little of the city.

AUGUST 13

Have been kept on the ship. The niggers left on the 11th and very glad we were to have them go.[14] The Cavalry got away on the 12th and then the ship seemed deserted. It was positively luxurious to have so much room. We thought we were going every minute and it has been pack and unpack continuously. Finally about 4 P.M. we were ordered into three canoes, which were taken in tow by a launch, and we left the *Para* after having been on her just thirty-one days. Passed the old fortifications up the Pasig River and finally disembarked about one-fourth mile from its mouth. About a two-mile march, it seemed much farther with knapsack, haversack and full canteen and one hundred rounds of ammunition in the belt, up the fashionable Luneta thronged with people, officers, civilians, Filipinos, Chinese and Japs, all driving, the women with no hats, across the wall and moat and finally halted in front of an old Spanish barrack, bamboo frames and walls of matting roofed with thatch. Each building about seventy-five feet long, raised about two feet from the ground, the beach at their back.[15] Some bargaining with venders for cigarettes, fruit and cakes. Mexican money one-half U. S., as is also, to my disappointment, Hawaiian money, which constitutes my sole wealth.[16] Coffee and corned beef (canned) before bed, blankets on floor. Slept sound and well.

AUGUST 14

Lieut. Oakes took me with him on a business trip.[17] All over the walled and outside city. Much impressed with the oddity and strangeness of everything. Water buffaloes and coolies carrying heavy boxes, four to a box. Diminutive horses. Wild-looking women with loose hair. Pretty little native children. Massive looking cathedrals, obsolete guns and fortifications. It all forms a curious medley in my mind. It seems that they are fighting on the north line, on the south line and between those lines and the city. A large garrison in the city, no one, citizen or soldier, allowed on the street after 8:30 P.M.

AUGUST 15

This is the winter season here, which accounts for the coolness which we all remarked. Not that it is not warm, but the heat is not unbearable and the early mornings, nights and evenings are cool. Cooking arrangements not yet straightened out. The water buffaloes, which they call caribous [*caribao*] here, have to be wet or they won't work, you see their drivers pouring water over them from small bottles. Yesterday for the first time they were kept off the Escolta, the principal business street. It is outside the walls. It seems the place where our barracks are is called Malate.[18] We have excellent shower baths which is a blessing. Most of the people, even of the poorer classes, are scrupulously clean. They do not wear much but it seems light and looks as if it had just been washed and pressed. They seem very slow about getting up our staff. It lies on the river bank, about three miles away, where it was unloaded and is not here yet. The Americans it seems have interfered with the use of broken-down, decrepit horses on the tram cars, which are now running with good though diminutive animals. Are not allowed away from quarters. Cummings, another Portland boy, who is in A Company, was down here last evening.

AUGUST 16

Teams pass to the left as in England. English sparrows here. I noticed a man fishing on the beach with a net the poles of which must
have been ten feet long. He spread them out and would then raise
the poles, finally taking out some little fish like white bait. The
Chinese carry all their burdens either on their heads or at each end
of a stick suspended across their shoulders. Their walk when thus
loaded is like an athlete walking on a track. Washed my clothes this
morning. Not that I like to do it, but as we are doing absolutely
nothing it kills time. Am bunking with Smith, a veteran of Santiago.
He is fertile in expedients and is always foraging. We are the only
two who take our meals in comfort, he having made us a little table
and seat in the shade of the barracks.[19] A good many mosquitoes at
night. Even as I sat here writing orders have just come in to go to
San Fernando on the north firing line. All is activity and bustle.

CHAPTER 2

Pampanga

*T*HE SPRING CAMPAIGN in 1899 showed General Otis that taking land from Aguinaldo's Army of Liberation was easy, but holding it and winning the trust of the local population was an entirely different matter. With the arrival of fresh troops that summer, Otis devised a scheme to annihilate Aguinaldo and his forces. Otis knew he had the power to defeat his adversary in open combat, but he was gravely concerned Aguinaldo would flee into the mountains and begin a guerrilla war. Hoping to avoid a partisan quagmire, Otis designed an intricate three-pronged movement: Maj. Gen. Henry Lawton's 1st Division would follow the Rio Grande first north to San Isidro then west to the Lingayen Gulf, flanking and sealing off Aguinaldo's escape route into the eastern mountains. Brigadier General Lloyd Wheaton would land on the Lingayen coast and block roads heading north while General MacArthur's 2d Division traveled northwest up the Angeles–Dagupan railway in an effort to push Aguinaldo into the pocket created by Lawton's and Wheaton's forces.

It was a sophisticated plan. As Brian Linn points out in *The Philippine War*, a key (and often forgotten) component of U.S. military doctrine was showing sensitivity to the local population. Benevolence was a critical operating term. Given this political objective, the military tactic of living off the land by U.S. troops was ruled out and, consequently, massive amounts of supplies had to be shipped from Manila. The Manila–Dagupan railway, which cut through Pampanga Province, anchored by the all-important San Fernando–Angeles link, became the centerpiece of the first phase of the operation. Once the damaged track was repaired, Angeles became the supply hub, thus equipping both Lawton and MacArthur's columns. With the Angeles project completed, engineer crews began making roads and bridges in the region safe for supply wagons headed north and west.

It was in this Angeles area engineering operation that Brown found himself in August, 1899. Hampered by Pampanga's weather and terrain,

Brown and the rest of Company B found the work excruciating. For the next few weeks, U.S. forces endeavored to repair the crucial railway line that connected various points north of Manila. Although the Americans controlled the cities of San Fernando and Angeles, they did not control the countryside. The result was that Filipino troops moved freely throughout several provinces. The American position was tenuous, and Brown often found himself working on guard details. In August, as preparations were being made to chase Aguinaldo north, Brown, who had some experience with a military sketching board while serving as a volunteer, was made a cartographer. His selection for the post set in motion what became the major event of his life. His job was to accompany engineer patrols into the field, usually on reconnaissance, and map the area. He often took the "point" while on patrol, an especially dangerous position. He enjoyed what he did immensely, saying, "I cannot imagine any work more suited to my taste than this reconnaissance."

Brown saw his first combat in late September. Reports suggested to MacArthur that Porac, a town southwest of Angeles, was the hub of insurgent activity. Using a two-column attack MacArthur drove the Filipinos from their trenches and took the town, pushing the defenders into the mountains. They never posed a real threat again. Brown's entry for September 28 may be the finest description of the battle extant. By the end of that day he had begun the metamorphosis into hardened campaigner.

Despite the efforts around Angeles, the scheme to catch Aguinaldo and destroy his army quickly became disjointed. Otis, with the railway still under repair, commenced the northern offensive in early October by sending Brig. Gen. Samuel Young with Lawton's cavalry arm to San Isidro, northeast of Angeles, by way of Arayat and Cabiao. Company B, under Lieutenant Oakes, took part in this offensive. It was assigned the back-breaking task of building roads, bridges, and ferries. After taking San Isidro, Young set his eyes on Cabanatuan in Nueva Ecija Province, where American and Spanish prisoners were supposedly being held. He indeed took the city, but found only Spanish prisoners. Moreover, the march had been dreadful, even for the more mobile cavalry. Despite the best efforts of Oakes and Company B, it became clear that the flooded terrain was slowing the Americans down considerably, and it seemed doubtful a linkup with Wheaton could be effected in time to shut down the mountain passes. Young suggested to Lawton that he be allowed to cut off from the main column and push north to meet up with Wheaton. Lawton, however, kept Young on a short leash, allowing him to make only short excursions to Talavera and Aliagra.

Brown took part in all aspects of this advance. He worked with Company B as an engineer and, after the San Isidro maneuver, was detailed to go on reconnaissance missions with the Macabebes (Filipino scouts) to sketch road maps. Brown left Company B to become an itinerant cartographer in late October. His only orders were to follow the advance on Aguinaldo and map its movements. The maps that he first sketched and later revised can be found in part four of the *Annual Reports of the War Department for the Fiscal Year Ended June 30, 1900*. His work in Pampanga is recorded on "Sheet No. 1, Road Map from Mexico to Cabanatuan."

A century later, Brown's road map can still be followed easily. As one drives north from Manila via the expressway or the older MacArthur Highway, the gray and black of Manila's concrete despair first gives way to Bulacan and then to the green of Pampanga's flat plain. Like Brown, the traveler will see thatched huts and men and *caribao* in the rice fields, although today the bucolic setting is blotched by countless billboards. Modern travelers will be impressed by Mount Arayat's domination of the landscape, as was Brown. If one goes in the rainy season, as Brown did, there is a serious threat of flooding. In the area bordered by the towns of Angeles, Mexico, and Santa Rita, a heavy rain will turn the plain into a lake. One need only see how saturated Pampanga gets to appreciate what Brown had to cross.

Pampanga is a province that knows misery. Brown notes that on the morning of battle in 1899 American soldiers joked, "It's either hell or Porac tonight." In June, 1991, hell came to Porac in the form of torrents of volcanic lahar created by Mount Pinatubo. The eruption buried a portion of the town under an incredible mudflow, killing nearly thirty people. Other towns in the area, San Fernando, Bacalor, Angeles, Bamban, as well as Olongapo in nearby Zambales Province, all suffered the volcano's wrath. Hundreds died. Rivers of lahar still flow during the rainy season a decade after the eruption.

Both San Fernando and Angeles, where Brown was stationed, are vibrant Pampangan cities serving as centers of provincial commerce. Angeles in particular has had a long relationship with the United States. It housed a military base at Fort Stotsenburg, which later became Clark Field. The latter was a strategic prize during World War II, and the anni-

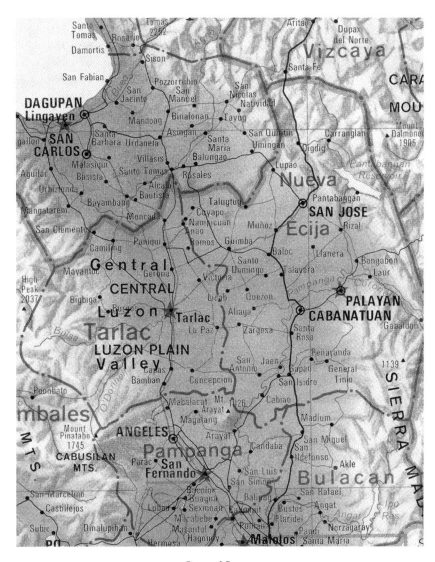

Central Luzon

hilation of the U.S. Far East Air Force during the first days of the war has long been considered one of the American military's greatest embarrassments. Holy Rosary, which Brown identified as the "largest church I have seen outside of Manila," had its roof destroyed by a crippled B-25 during a raid on Japanese-held Clark in 1945. The U.S. Air Force maintained a huge base at Clark until 1991, when Mount Pinatubo finally forced it to be abandoned. The air force left hurriedly and did not clean up any of the allegedly large toxic waste dumps. Filipino groups have been protesting ever since in an attempt to get the United States to pay compensation.

Brown took other roads and made stops at several places that would figure prominently in World War II. The Filipino and American prisoners of war who made the infamous Bataan "Death March" in 1942 were routed through Gaugua, San Fernando, Porac, Clark Field, and finally to Camp O'Donnell at Capas, near Tarlac in the province of that name. Some of the Americans later were transferred to a camp outside the city of Cabanatuan in Nueva Ecija Province. One of the most dramatic rescue missions of the war took place there in January, 1945. But in 1942, American soldiers were the vanquished, and they surely had a different view of the pastoral Pampangan countryside than did Brown.

Although Kapampangans stood alongside the road during the Death March and risked their lives to throw American prisoners scraps of food, such pro-American sentiments have not always been the norm in the province. During the war, the Hukbalahaps, an anti-Japanese peasant group, worked with escaped U.S. soldiers to harass enemy operations. After the war, however, communist Huks turned on the U.S.-backed Philippine government. Although the Huks were defeated, communism was not, and the U.S. base at Clark Field was a propaganda target for the Pampanga-centered Partido Kommunista ng Pilpinas (KPP). Student groups protested the presence of U.S. bases in the 1960s and this movement grew into the KPP's successor: the Communist Party of the Philippines, with its military arm, the New People's Army (NPA). The NPA assassinated several U.S. military retirees living in Angeles in 1987 and still operates throughout Pampanga.

Despite Mount Pinatubo and the NPA, several thousand Americans still live in Pampanga, the vast majority being military retirees in the Angeles enclave. By their own volition, they are removed from the Filipino social mainstream as well as from contact with other Americans, existing primarily on a lifeline woven from their retirement checks. The military presence Brown helped to establish in 1899 continues.

AUGUST 17
Left Malate at about 7 A.M. for the station, three miles' distance. Went in heavy marching order and was wet through with perspiration when we reached it, we having made no stops. Took train for

San Fernando. Outside of Manila the rice swamps extend for many kilometers. Most of them were under cultivation, but a fair proportion were not. Soon began to cross the niggers' (as the troops call them) rifle pits. Were very well made and were roofed in part with bamboo. At Malolus [Malolos], where the fight at the church took place, the pits were very numerous.[1] Also at Calumpit, the scene of Funston's exploit.[2] Were in what were apparently third-class coaches of the European model except that the division line of the compartments was only about breast high. In the rice fields the natives were planting the young rice plants. Reached San Fernando at about 1 P.M. sixty-six kilometers front Manila. Track guarded by detachments at important places. Marched to barrack, about five minutes' walk from station. Apparently the home of a planter, as outhouses and sheds were filled with sugar draining off. Had scarcely time to look around when Sergt. Casey said to me, "Get fifty additional rounds of ammunition and blanket roll and be ready to start in half an hour." Was ready and found a detail of twenty-five men and Lieut. Oakes. Captain was looking over the detail and threw some out. Was proud to be put in the first detail made from the company. Marched to the commissary and found we were going as guard to a bull train, 40,000 rations and ammunition which was going to the firing line, only six miles distant. "Load chamber and magazine." It gave me a little thrill to hear the order, the first time I had ever heard it save at drill. The train moved out, thirty-nine native carts and two mule teams. Was put into the advance guard, blanket roll on one of the buffalo carts. Typical village. All houses raised off the ground and built of bamboo. "Aggie" himself tried to take this town on 4th of July last, having previously sent word to the American commander that he intended dining here on that day.[3] He didn't, nor on August 4th either, and the chances are against his dining here for some time. So we soon came to rifle pits, very substantial they looked too. Here came our first taste of what was coming, for the pits were full of water which we had to wade. Here came our first breakdown and a delay of fifteen minutes, breakdowns and delays were so frequent after that that I shan't mention. All houses deserted. Rice fields not cultivated but fall of water, as we found to our cost, the road being straight across them. About 5 P.M. (we had nothing to eat since breakfast) we came in sound of the distant battle. (It was the 12th Infantry taking the town of Angeles.)[4] You could hear the crashes of the volleys and the occasional boom of a field-piece. Every one I think would have been glad if the train, which stretched out over a quarter of a mile, had been attacked. Our danger of course was from raiders and marauding parties. It commenced to rain now and we came to a stream breast deep and very swift through which we plunged and halted, waiting for the train to close up. I thought they never would get the caribous through that stream. Every one of the beasts laid down in the water, and beatings nor bayonets could move him till he was ready. Such language! Frantic officers, stolid Chinos (as they call the Chinese), the natives solicitous lest their precious beasts be abused and twenty-five wet, tired, hungry and thoroughly exasperated soldiers. We crossed three such rivers and the same thing was repeated at each one. At one we had a new experience. It was very dark now. The "point" suddenly challenged. Natives of course, two of them, loudly professing friendship. Spies I dare say, but orders are strict to treat all natives as friendly unless they are in uniform or have a rifle, so we let them go. We were not in a good place to be attacked, half the train on one side of the river, half on the other. We thought it had been raining before. It commenced now in earnest. I never saw such a rain. I was the point then, the most advanced point, the head of the train about three hundred yards in rear. I could feel the water running down my back inside my clothes, was cold and could not see ten feet in any direction. You may be surprised, but I was not at all anxious for the train to be attacked. We finally moved off and finally the moon came out and then fireflies by hundreds. Soon we came to the railroad. The insurgents had torn up about five miles of it, so we marched down the road-bed. Then we came to a cane brake and the damned buffaloes would not go on unless they had sugar cane. We called them sensible animals then, for we had been going since 5 A.M. without food and it was 11 P.M. then. Well, we finally got to San Angeles about 12 P.M., found our blanket rolls with difficulty, ate some hard tack and looked for a dry place to sleep. I found one under a table where the Signal Corps was taking telegraph messages from the firing line about a mile ahead of us. By great good luck I had a clean suit of underclothes in my blanket and so slept warm and dry.

AUGUST 18

Up at 6 A.M. and helped cook coffee and bacon. Started back at about 8. Immediately went through a brook waist deep, were going back a different way. Then got into the front wagon. Took off belt as hips were black and blue from the weight of the one hundred rounds. Hardly settled when "Out of that, men, natives ahead." Doubled for one-eighth of a mile, three other men and the Lieutenant. It was a native village and was in wild confusion, but as we ran in white flags began to appear in all the windows, so there was no fight and the empty train went through. Was a most picturesque village in a tropical thicket which almost hid the houses. Lots of natives. Women beating rice or grain with wooden pestles in large earthen pots. One native in a suit of bamboo which looked like thatch. That was last excitement. Reached barracks in time for dinner at 12 M[idnight]. Cleaned rifle and rigged mosquito net for bunk, blanket on floor.

AUGUST 19

Saturday. Breakfast 5 A.M. Washed clothes. The barrack is evidently the old house of a rich man, across the road is a broad river. Stone foundation. Only two stories, second almost all open with projecting eaves. The entrance to the rear wing, where my bunk is, is up a flight of stone steps decorated with large flowering plants in huge pots, through an arch that must have been part of an old church and looks at least a hundred years old. The grounds show that until lately they must have been well cared for. A thing that touched me, the beds are marked with the same kind of stone bottles stuck in the ground that my father used to mark the beds on the street front of the old house down town. The insurgents tore up the track between us and Manila last night, so there were no trains to-day.

AUGUST 20

The company being in the field stands no calls. Everything when one is not on duty is made as easy as possible. The only thing I do not like is breakfast at 5 A.M., which is before daylight. Breakfast to-day, oatmeal and syrup, coffee and fresh biscuit. Dinner, bacon and beans, potatoes and onions, rice pudding, coffee and bread. Supper, fresh meat, potatoes, coffee and bread. The water we drink is rain water, it rains every day, collected from the roof in large earthen pots that must hold over a barrel. It is filtered before we drink it. The sinks are across the street, over the San Fernando River. There is a well in the yard for washing. San Fernando, Province of Pampanga, about thirty English miles from Manila, about in the middle of the island from east to west. The railroad does not run across the island but to Dagupan on Bay of Lunganyen [Lingayen] on west coast. That is objective, I judge, of present advance. About seventy-five miles from Manila. Track not yet cleared (7 A.M.). Dagupan is about one-half way between Manila and north coast. About one-half of San Fernando has been burnt. Did my first looting this morning. Went into one of the deserted houses and took a native bed (bamboo) and carried it on my head to the barracks. One of our details just back was in a skirmish yesterday (no casualties).

AUGUST 21

On guard at the barracks. Difficulty in keeping awake, 3–5 A.M. Rare wood very common. The rough kitchen benches are made of beautiful mahogany planks, ten or twelve feet long and three inches thick. Also all the kitchen tables. All furniture moved from the house except a piano and some mirrors and pictures and some carriages on the lower floor, which was evidently used as a carriage house. As all the native huts are raised three or four feet off the ground on piles, I judge it has been found unhealthy to sleep on the ground. Troops are never put in tents but always in houses, native ones if the better class are not available.

Dear Mamma:

My health is as good as ever. Paper is simply not obtainable here, so you may have to wait for my next. I like the excitement of active service tremendously and would not have missed this experience for worlds.

Your loving son,
Jack.

AUGUST 22

Yesterday was called to officers' quarters. Found a number of non-coms there. Was asked by Lieut. Ferguson if I had ever done any work with the Cavalry sketching board.⁵ Said yes and blessed the impulse that had, at Camp Wetherell, prompted me to devote some time to its use. As I was the only private on the detail that knowledge may lead to promotion. Sergeants very gracious afterwards. Though I do not mention it specifically, it must be understood that it rains every day and night, sometimes continuously. Apparently nails are or were very scarce and labor very cheap, for all the furniture is mortised and dovetailed together. There is a native mill in our room which I judge was used for grinding rice or corn which must have taken years to make. About eighteen inches diameter, twelve inches high. All of *[the four drawings that originally appeared here are no longer extant]* solid stone except pivot A which is metal and handle B which is wood and which goes clear through. I imagine it is of native manufacture. The beds we have looted are all the same, built of bamboo, no iron whatever entering into their construction.

[The three drawings that originally appeared here are no longer extant. Their captions follow.]

P Side elevation   Top view
But I do not think I have given much idea of it.

AUGUST 23
Was sitting on my bunk killing time. It was pouring outside, when I heard the sudden hurry in the barracks which always denotes that a large detail is going out. "In five minutes at the latest." Now I did not have to be told that I was on that detail for I had been idling around for three days. My blanket roll was packed so it did not take long to prepare. Fifty men under Lieut. O[akes]. was the detail. Were loaded on to flat cars with Chinos laborers, where we learned that the niggers were taking up the track near Calumpit. Steamed down the track about six miles, where we found the break but no niggers, some rails had been taken out and the road bed dug up, but the enemy, 300 (estimated), had been driven off by a detachment of the 6th Artillery, who got there first from Calumpit. Leaving the Chinos to repair the track we pushed down the track to Calumpit, three miles further down, and made our headquarters in the empty freight house. Took all the blinds from the station to sleep on. Coffee

and hard tack, canned corned beef and then details were sent up and down the track. Curious sensation walking down the track in the pitchy darkness with a detail of four or five men, knowing there are 300 insurgents in the neighborhood who are anxious to shoot you and who may be laying behind the next clump of cane or behind the rice paddies for all you know. Was out twice during the night, 10 to 12 and 4 to 6 A.M. Nothing happened except a few scares, no shots.

AUGUST 24
Slept nearly all day when I was not eating. Country around here a vast marsh of rice fields. The town is about a mile away. The bridge (railroad) across the Rio Grande (the largest river in Luzon) at Calumpit has a caisson 120 feet down. It cost the company one-half a million dollars. Rebel trenches at Calumpit very strong, faced with iron one-half an inch thick. If the niggers had any sand could never have been dislodged. The bridge was saved from destruction by the persuasion of an Englishman resident in the town who owned stock in the railroad. Gen. Luna, who commanded the niggers, having collected dynamite to destroy the bridge felt he must use it, so blew up the church in lieu of something better. Out once in the night, 10–12.[6]

AUGUST 25
Dawned clear but soon clouded. The men who did not bring the mosquito bars could not sleep for the insects. Had mine and was very comfortable. A rumor that they were tearing up the track sent a detail down in a hurry. My curiosity that leads me to volunteer on such work will get me in trouble some day. Was a false alarm. While we were at dinner, about 12 M. [noon], saw a detachment of six men and a Sergeant of ours "hiking" down the track. They were to relieve six men of the detachment. I was one. Took train back to San Fernando. The daily train only one being run a day.

AUGUST 26
It was map sketching they wanted me for. About 8 A.M. Lieut. Ferguson, myself and one man as guard started out on the road to Mexico. Beyond the outposts started to map. Went as far as where the river crosses the road at La Gudi (deserted). Lieut. F. much pleased with my map. Started me alone to map the line of the in-

surgent trenches beyond to the west of the Mexico road. Trenches are deserted, but this was in the enemy's country and beyond our outposts. Met him and his guard at Carmen, another deserted village. Dinner. "Follow the line of trenches till they end, then strike for the railroad." He took the guard. Rice to my knees. After about two miles began to meet natives, not pleasant, smiling faces but the reverse. I had never seen a map of the country, my sole geographical knowledge was that the railroad ran about north. Finally struck a bull-cart trail that gradually grew into a road. Around a turn suddenly came face to face with a native who at once went down on his knees and laid a large knife, eighteen-inch blade, at my feet. Was puzzled. Could not carry the knife. Decided that if he had wanted to stick me he could have done it. Motioned him up. Started to follow me. Did not like that. "Vamoose," and laid my hand on my revolver belt. He vamoosed. By this time knew by the sun it was 5 P.M. Knew by Mt. Arrarat [Arayat] I was miles from San Fernando. Did not know how far from the railroad, struck a river, across it could see men with rifles. Did not know whether Americans or not. Bore to the south. Saw an outpost. It was the 17th at Collulit (where the bull trains go). They said there were no American troops where I had seen the armed men. Supper with the 17th. Walked back to San Fernando, six miles, over the road I had thought so dangerous (it was) when I came with the bull train. Darkest night I ever saw. San Fernando about 8:30 P.M. I walked fast.

AUGUST 27
Back to Collulit to join my map to the railroad. Had a guard. Warned us at the outpost that the niggers were round. Had driven in the outposts at Angeles, and at Collulit they had three companies out for them. Saw the rebels same place as yesterday. Guard did not want to go on. Did. Came back the San Fernando road. Mapped about one-third of it when the rain became too heavy. Passed native villages, some inhabited with scowling natives, some deserted. Passed abandoned barricades and sand-bag forts, and finally, about 5 P.M. were glad to strike our outposts at San Fernando.

AUGUST 28
Same thing. Same territory, only between the road and the railroad.

AUGUST 29

Consolidating the maps into one. Not very accurate but the best in existence of the country. Four miles wide from Bacolo[r] through San Fernando to Mexico, and running to a point at Collulit, six miles north. All northern portion my work.[7]

AUGUST 30

On map from 6 to 8.30 A.M., when I, our map being done, am leaving for Gen. McArthur's headquarters to draw some maps for him. Health never better. Was tracing a map in Gen. McArthur's headquarters. Put in a hard day's work at it, harder than I ever did for the N. Y. T. Co., but did not get it done. The General seems a young man, but T., who served with him when he was a captain, fifteen years ago, tells me he must be nearly sixty.[8] In my reconnaissance work I get a very good idea of the country, which is surprisingly rich and fertile. The soil seems to be a sort of loam mixed with sand. At least my shoes are always full of sand when I come back from a "hike." A great number of streams which are very rapid, so rapid that it is difficult to ford them when they are waist deep and yet the country is flat. I judge the San Fernando River is affected by the tide as it seems to rise periodically.

AUGUST 31

Muster and inspection of arms at 7 A.M. Cannot begin work at headquarters until 9 A.M., worked until about 11 A.M. when orderly came down, "Captain wants you." He was going to send out a reconnoitering party of twenty men and a Lieutenant and wanted me to make the map. Started at 12:15 P.M., marched four miles to Mexico (had mapped it previously) where we started the map. Then commenced the worst march I have ever made. The Lieutenant told me we were going to the enemy's outposts and drive them in, but we did not get there. It is no exaggeration to say that of the five miles we marched to the north of Mexico (on the right bank of the San Fernando River) we waded four miles in water which varied in depth from ankle deep to shin and in places the men would disappear entirely. What makes the road so bad is that the irrigation ditches have either been broken or burst and the water runs off in the road. We were way beyond our outposts. Mexico is a good two miles

beyond them, and the natives, we passed through two large inhabited villages, Bicetre Tanglela and Sapote, were very humble and
gave us bananas and cigarettes, everywhere displaying the white
flag. It commenced to rain and rained with tropical intensity, but
we kept on until Mt. Arratrat seemed less than a mile away and San
Juan, our destination, was estimated about a mile distant, but it was
5 P.M. and we had orders to be back by dark. Two men had played
out on the march out, which was cruelly fast, and now we turned
back more began to play out. In one place where the water was
waist deep a man laid down and said he had rather die than take
another step. He was dragged along. Men began to throw away
ammunition, so a short halt, the first, was called and I washed the
sand out of my shoes. On again, reaching Mexico after dark and the
barracks at 9 P.M.

SEPTEMBER 1
Spent the entire day drawing the map we got the data for yesterday.
It seems we were within a mile of San Jose, where there are 500
rebels. We were eight miles beyond our outposts. Had a very interesting talk with Lieut. F., W[est]. P[oint]. '97, who gave me much
information about the enemy's position and our plans, not available
to every private.[9] I cannot imagine any work more to my taste than
this reconnaissance.

SEPTEMBER 2
San Fernando is beginning to wear quite a business-like aspect.
When we first came here it was quite deserted save for the troops,
but since then the Filipinos have been coming back, last week a
bullock train of thirty carts, each with a family. Shops are opening
and the regimental band plays occasionally. Of course a good half
of the town, including the stone church, has been burnt and troops
are quartered everywhere. Detachments are constantly passing.
Cavalry, their horses looking like elephants in comparison to the
native horses, in fact every branch of the service. Since seeing other
houses of the better class here I have changed my mind about the
arch leading to the rear wing of our barracks. It seems to be a common feature. The second floor, I have seen no buildings higher, is
the living floor, the first being used as carriage sheds, store rooms,

etc. The yard or court is evidently used in dry weather for meals or for lounging and it is to beautify that, that such an elaborate stairway (outside) leads to the, in our case, kitchen.

SEPTEMBER 3
Sunday. Nothing to do. Wrote a number of letters. Borrowed Root's "Topographical Sketching" from the Captain and spent most of the day reading that.[10] After supper, about 5 P.M., one of A Company's detachment came in with a "bino" jag and insisted he had seen armed niggers digging a trench, so a detail was sent out, but he had not and is now in the "jug."[11] A mail from home the 2d. Letters were dated July 19th. Came on the *Indiana,* which brought some 720 recruits. Since I have been doing this sketching the men have decided I am in for a commission. I notice a difference in their treatment which I can ascribe to nothing else, a touch of deference, an eagerness to do small favors, etc. I am sorry, as I would prefer to be a private as long as I am compelled to be.

SEPTEMBER 4
Rain continuous. Spent the entire morning on Root's book. If this keeps up I shall soon master surveying. Not that it is so extremely difficult. The men are eating large quantities of fruit, chiefly bananas which seem to be the only kind ripe. Also many are boiling down the sugar which is stored here in great quantities and making molasses from it, of which they eat enormous quantities, some drinking it. The result of all this is that some eight or ten of them have been sent to the hospital with diarrhea. It is noticeable that they all blame the climate. I do not notice any difference in the ration. It is the same, I am sure, that is furnished the troops in the States. The 51st Iowa came in from Collulit this morning. They are about the last of the State Volunteers out here and expect to go home in a few days.[12] We furnish a headquarters guard this morning. I mention these things to show the variety of duty we are capable of. The detail I was on is still at Apalit.

SEPTEMBER 5
Was on the early morning "hike" that goes three and one-half miles down the track to meet the patrol coming up. Was waked at 4 A.M.

and started at 4:30, after bacon and coffee. Was raining hard. Two weeks ago I should have felt nervous thrills as we passed the outpost and stepped off into the pitchy darkness. Felt nothing except a slight annoyance at being waked so early. The rain soon stopped and we were treated to a splendid sunrise. Natives began to go to work in the rice fields, swimming their caribous up the numerous streams, the while sitting on their backs quite naked. Children squalling in the village of Santo Thomas quite like America. Many birds, some quite like those at home. One bird like the kingfisher, one like the chippy, a plover, herons of several kinds and a number of finches. Met the patrol six kilometers down. All well. Reached the barracks at 8:30 A.M. Drill started to-day, 9:30, 4 to 4:30. The reason, the men had been straggling too much from the barracks. I have had little to say of the natives who have come into the town in great numbers. They are small, brown people, very straight from carrying weights on their heads. Not pleasing to look at. All smoke constantly, men, women and children, and the women chew betel nut. They all wear very few, loosefitting clothes and seem to be pleasant, good-mannered, moral people. I understand their besetting sin is gambling and that few ever become rich. The Chinos are everywhere and are great friends of the Americans and enemies of the insurgents, who always when they catch one put him to death with every conceivable mutilation. All the dirty and manual work of the army is done by Chinos, who get, I believe, twenty cents a day.[13]

SEPTEMBER 6
On guard at Gen. Wheaton's headquarters.[14] Gen. Wheaton being at Collulit, the guard was only three men, myself acting Corporal. By a curious coincidence we all three had served in the Volunteers, Lehman in the 71st New York, Wyer in the Volunteer Engineers. It was a beautiful night and one of the finest places in San Fernando, so that after we had shut the iron entrance gates it was like sitting under grandma's porte-cochere. There was not a breath of wind not a cloud and the stars shone with a vividness I have never seen equaled. I was "on" from 10 to 12. In the perfect silence all sounds seemed magnified, the hum of myriad insects, the occasional stir of the foliage seemed like distant musketry. Then I heard a native baby cry

and the low tones of the mother. It must have been a quarter of a mile away and it restored the scale of noises. You could hear the horses stir in the Artillery lines in Square de Sagasta. It was altogether perfect and I never knew two hours to pass more quickly. On again from 4 to 6 A.M. and saw the night pale into the dawn and the day break quickly. Was relieved at 11 A.M. to draw a map at Gen. McArthur's headquarters. They had just captured a ladrone, or thief, from a band of about forty. They got him in the territory I made reconnaissances over alone and otherwise, so the danger was not wholly imaginary. He was armed with an old Remington, the "pull" of which was so strong as to make it impossible to shoot straight, one of the long knives or "bolos" and a dark lantern. He expected to be shot every moment and the guard were handling and laughing at his equipment, saying "boom, boom, poco tempo," which means shot presently. He was a young fellow and stood it rather well, though you could see tears roll down his cheeks.[15] He was turned over to the provost and will be put at work. Any one at home who believes these people capable of governing themselves has only to come out and he will be sadly disillusioned.

SEPTEMBER 7
Spent the morning at Gen. McArthur's headquarters tracing a map. It seems that that ladrone captured yesterday belonged to the native regiment that deserted Spain to fight for the insurrection. More natives in the town every day. It is significant of modern times that the only matches obtainable here are safety matches which are made in Japan. It seems strange that after joining the army to be rid of desk work I should have so much of it to do. I shall ask to be relieved if it threatens to be permanent. I think, and it is this that keeps me cheerful at it, that I will be sent out on the reconnaissance and get my chance again the next time there is anything risky on. I do not like the rear when there is a chance for adventure. We furnish train guard and two outposts now. The 51st Iowa marched away for home yesterday. This is McArthur's division. He has Wheeler (Fighting Joe), Lawton and Hall for Brigadiers. As far as I can place them the regiments are: the 9th, 12th, 17th, 22d Infantry, A Artillery, 4th Cavalry, B Engineers and Bell's 36th Regiment of U.S.V. Drew most of the afternoon for the Captain.

SEPTEMBER 8

Forenoon, drew. Had pie for dinner. Have had it several times now. It is curious how good it tastes. Afternoon, drew.

SEPTEMBER 9

Guagua and Santa Rita were attacked last night. They are only three or four miles away and the firing, rifles, machine and field guns, was plainly audible. As usual, the insurgents were repulsed. Have not heard our loss. Drew till 9:30 A.M. The Q.M. Dept. is building the railroad and is doing it very badly and slowly. Have not got to Angeles yet and it is only twenty kilometers from here. Never think of preparing a bridge until they get to the stream. Bringing the Chino laborers back here from beyond Collulit to meals. No one knows why they do not let the Engineers do it.

SEPTEMBER 10

Was on outpost last night. Outpost is an easy guard, from 6 P.M. to 6 A.M., four hours off, two hours on, and the next day to yourself. It is not pleasant to sit out there waiting to be shot at, for they have been firing on the outposts steadily for a week. Last night however was perfectly quiet, not even any rain, whether or not it was their licking of the night before that kept them quiet I do not know. The mosquitoes however were worse than my wildest imagination ever painted. I wore simply a chambray shirt over the upper part of my body, as usual, and it was no protection. I had not been on post five minutes before all sense of danger merged into a prolonged cuss at the mosquitoes. Company badly drilled, talking on outposts.

(It is the same moon, dear mamma, but we see it some hours later.) We used a freight car to sleep in, all the cars and engines are European model, having shelter tents, blankets and ponchos. My first four hours in could not sleep an instant on account of the mosquitoes, but sat up and smoked. The head net, blessed invention, kept them off my face, but they bit through the shirt. The next time I came off, by sleeping between the doors in the draft got asleep. Not a shot was fired oil or at any of the outposts. Almost continuous and very vivid lightning during my first trick, very little thunder. Drew clothes. When we drew clothes at Willetts Point I followed the advice of some old soldiers and drew very little. It did not occur to me at the time, but they were thinking of my "finals" and the saving in clothing allowance. The result was I felt the need of underclothes. Determined not to repeat the mistake, my knapsack is now filled to bursting. Luckily it won't break my heart to throw things away.

SEPTEMBER 11

I think the rainy season must be near its last stages.[16] In the last week it has only rained occasionally, mostly at night. The roads are drying up. The wind comes occasionally from the northwest, which indicates that the monsoons are changing. Here the wind blows always from the southwest in the rainy season and the northwest the rest of the time. The typhoons come when the monsoons are changing. Nothing all day. Studied "Root's," a great resource. Had some washing done, fifteen cents. I am beginning to know the wily Filipinos. Last time they charged fifty cents.

SEPTEMBER 12

Up at 4 A.M. Beefsteak, bread and coffee and down the track to meet the patrol north from Apalit. A lovely morning and a beautiful sunrise. Sergt. Carroll, the "torpedo expert," had the detail.[17] He insisted on talking to me all the way and finding I could meet him on his own grounds grew personal. It seems he has been in the service twenty-five years and has a son twenty years old. He came out here on active service because he lost his wife last February and the associations at the Point were painful. Incidentally, he is hated in the company and is accused of cowardice on two occasions already, though of this I know nothing as I was not present on either occasion. He is an agreeable talker and told me incidents about almost every officer in the Engineer Corps. All this when we were beyond our outpost, which had just been fired on from the direction in which we were marching. Back at 8 A.M. and found a nice breakfast of oatmeal and milk, coffee and bread. The last time I came in from that "hike" I had difficulty in getting a cup of coffee, but there has been a change in the kitchen, the man who laid down on our twenty-mile "hike," Hawkins, being cook. Corp. Rees is examined for a commission on the 15th. He is a nice fellow and has a brother who is a captain of Engineers. The Corporal has served two years and six months and is older than I am.

SEPTEMBER 13

On the guard at Gen. McArthur's headquarters. A quiet, uneventful guard. Some interesting talks with some of the old soldiers. One, Breen, who has been in eleven years, told incidents of barracks and fields that remind one of the books of King. Stories of the women, the officers' wives and daughters, it was very interesting. The junior Sergeant of the company, Lowenseu, he has been in eight years, sat up with me nearly all my tour talking about himself. I give an outline. Living in San Francisco, of a family very well to do, he ran away when fourteen and spent some years on the South Pacific, between Australia, Tahiti, Honolulu and the "Coast." Had some money left him, traveled, reached New York, lost all he had and "took on." He made the night pass very quickly. Letters from mamma and Blue on the 12th dated August 6th.[18] My letters from Honolulu had just been received.

SEPTEMBER 14

Took my rifle apart, the first time since the day after the "hike" with the bull train, though have oiled it after every trip. In very good condition. Took over an hour. Since I received the ten dollars a couple of weeks or so ago I have felt like a millionaire, for the majority of the men, we were last paid at Willetts Point, spent all their money in New York on a last tear, and few if any had a cent after leaving San Francisco. A loan of fifty cents has been very gratefully received and is a favor I have kept for my most intimates. You can get very fair cigars six for ten cents and very good, well-made ones four for ten cents. Cigarettes are thirty or sixty for five cents, depending on the size. The cheapest are about the size of those in the States. There is a curious jargon the men use for communicating with the natives, who, speaking Pampamgan, know only a little Spanish. For instance, "Sabe jawbone?" means "Will you trust?" A great many of the natives trusting for bananas, etc., till pay day. I saw a native child "hanging on behind" one of the curious two-wheeled carriages, quite like in America.

Walked down to the market, which is across the bridge by the square. I should judge that there were two or perhaps three hundred women squatting on their heels before the large flat baskets. As they and their customers were all talking at once it made quite a buzz and quite reminded me of the times I have wandered around the markets with my father. There seemed a great variety of things to choose from. Live chickens, some in coops of basket work, some with their feet tied tight together. Eggs of various kinds, though I saw no hen eggs. Several kinds of fish, a number of which varieties were flopping around and out of the baskets, some kinds were dead and some dried. There were many kinds of shrimps, some small and some as large as our lobsters with their large feelers much longer than their bodies. Many kinds of nuts or fruits, though I think this is not the season for fruits. Some vegetables, the ever present leaf that the natives chew with their betel nuts. Dried caribou meat, of course tobacco in all forms. A variety of cooked dishes, like pies cooked on banana leaves. I have yet to see a soldier who would tackle any of the cooked dishes and a soldier will try almost anything. Rice, coffee and sugar of course, though I was surprised to see what I took for corn. Perhaps the most interesting thing was to see alive a number of varieties of game birds, snipe of various kinds and birds even smaller than our sandpeeps though similar. There was much bargaining and adding this and taking out that from the measures. Some of the purchasers had maids with them to carry the plunder, but the majority were of the poorer class, which is I imagine the first invariably to come back to a captured city that has been burnt and looted. The costumes would be a bit startling in the States, but we have got quite used to them here. A bit of cloth wrapped around the body forms the skirt. The bodice is a light gauze wrap or else a loose sort of Zouave jacket. It rarely meets the skirt in the poorer classes and there is an embarrassing vacancy until, as I say, you get not to mind it. Most of the natives go barefoot, but those who can afford it, I judge, wear a sort of Chinese sandal. I have yet to see stockings or indeed any hint of under garments on a native. And the square was noisy with the drill of a light battery of which the horses were mules.

On the guard again at Gen. McArthur's headquarters. Was orderly, so got the night to myself. All the troops here were paid today. Some $20,000 dumped into the town that has not seen a pay day for years I guess since it belonged to Aggie, when our troops were paid last June. I expected to see a wild time, but beyond the gambling in barracks saw none. The men are all buying absurd things. One of our men came back from hospital where he has been suffering from dysentery, his first act was to eat all the native candy he could get and of course was soon sick again. There was a card in the paper to-day from the postal authorities saying they were only able to recover thirty bags of mail from the three hundred on the ill-fated *Morgan City* and that all mail which reached San Francisco between August 1 and August 10 was lost.[19]

Sunday. A lot of gambling in barracks. I cannot help thinking how much better it would be for troops in the field if they were not paid. The pay days in the Volunteers linger long in my memory. Of course if the men want to send their pay home the chance should be given them, and the men should either have say a dollar a week for tobacco, stamps, etc., or those things should be issued from the company fund and charged to the men, as our Captain did on the transport. It might be objected that the tear will be so much bigger when the men do get the money, but that could be arranged for by withdrawing the regiment to be paid from active service. It cannot add to the efficiency of the men to gamble all night and do duty the next day, and I have seen them do it even on the firing line, nor do I see how it can be prevented with the companies split up and separated, some in one house, some in another, moreover some of the non-coms are the worst gamblers. Almost all the men have squared up their "jawbone." The sentiment of the company is strongly against cheating the natives. When we first landed the men, judging entirely from what they had heard in the States, were loud in their denunciations of the country. Now almost all admit it is a fine country. Personally I, and I think all thinking people here agree, cannot help seeing that the country will amply repay the States for their trouble in subjugating it. The man who stuffed the native candy yesterday is back in the hospital. All the men to whom I had lent money, some ten dollars, paid me, much to my surprise it must be admitted.

SEPTEMBER 18
This gambling in the army is a funny thing. In a banking game it is the thing to cheat the banker, if you can, and in poker if you can do your opponent in change or by not putting in your full bet no one seems to think it odd. Some of the men are broke already, absolutely busted, every cent of their two months' pay gone. I happened to notice yesterday that one of the long benches had been split and repaired. Now in the repairing the oddity came in. Instead of nailing a cross piece on the bottom, as we would do in the States (it was a rough, ordinary kind of a bench), a piece had been let in.

[*The two illustrations that appeared here are no longer extant.*]

The wood is so hard that an ordinary knife makes little impression on it, so the cheapness of the labor that makes such work possible can be imagined. Got bored this morning. Capt. Sibert, who has been made Chief Engineer out here, having gone to Manila, leaving Lieut. Oakes in command, took "Root's" with him, thus depriving me of a great resource. Tried writing out problems in geometry from memory. Killed several hours at it. Good mental gymnastics, splendid practice and makes the time go very quickly. It is an occupation that is always available in leisure hours. There are signs that the advance will soon begin.

SEPTEMBER 19
Lieut. Oakes broke six firstclass privates, two for cowardice, the others because he thought some of the second-class privates were better men. One of those broken, Schweitzer, who has been in the company office, is nearly broken-hearted. He sat at the side of my bunk after I had turned in and told me his troubles with a pathetic little catch in his voice for nearly an hour. He seems a simple fellow, but has ambitions for commissions. I woke up some hours later and he was still turning and muttering. His mental state reminded me of some of my New York experiences and was very

instructive. The insurrectos sent in a deputation to-day, one lieu-tenant-colonel, two majors and five buglers. It is said they came in to arrange about an exchange of prisoners. It is said that they have twelve of our officers and some thirty privates. In trading these natives are like the Europeans, asking much more than they expect to take. Unfortunately the average soldier, who is just as happy broke as when he has money, usually pays them what they ask, which demoralizes them. It has not rained very much for the last ten days, but it started in last evening and has rained steadily ever since. People who should know say it rains until December. I for one should not care if it proves no worse than the last month, which I have really enjoyed.

SEPTEMBER 20
Guard at Gen. McArthur's headquarters. Troops keep arriving and officers are rejoining their commands. The advance cannot be much longer delayed. The Cavalry and Infantry who came over on the *Para* with us got here to-day. In spite of the fact we hated the col-ored men on the ship, it seemed good to see the familiar faces. Gen. Young arrived. When I was a captain I used to be very careful about the use of the word class, thinking the men might be sensitive about it. To my surprise its use is very common. Nothing is more usual than to have a man say to me, "Of course for one in our class." Mail from the States. All my letters from Honolulu seem to have been received. Another ten dollars from Phip. Rained hard all day. It looked odd to see the native women with large bundles on their heads, bare feet and few clothes carrying modern umbrellas. The town has completely changed. About twenty shops have opened and you can buy anything you desire. So much for American pro-tection. The town was deserted when we arrived.

San Fernando, P. I.,
Sept. 21, 1899.

Dear Mamma:
As you must have seen before this, the life out here is much pleasanter than we had any idea of. You notice I have not had any of the hard, dirty work you anticipated. On the contrary the various duties, the constant change of

scene and duty, the excitement and the knowledge that you are doing your
duty makes it the pleasantest life I have had. I know it seems funny to you
that I like it, but I really do. I am always more than glad to get your letters.
Tell me more about your speeches. I am much interested in them. Please ask
Phip to add the North American Review *to the list I have already sent. By*
the way a letter to any one in the service of the Government only needs a
two-cent stamp, not a five-cent one.

My health continues to be all that any one can ask.

Your loving son,
Jack.

I have been in the service three months today.

SEPTEMBER 22

On the "hike" down the track to meet the patrol coming north. Another beautiful morning and sunrise. Even in the country you see ten natives to one you would see a month ago. A new resource yesterday. Found a Spanish geometry, find I can read it, of course I have no dictionary, fairly well. My knowledge of French and Latin helps and also the context. Worked at my Spanish geometry all day. The train was attacked between Angeles and Collulit and two men killed and some wounded.[20] As a result our train guard, recently withdrawn, is on again. Took my usual bath, put on clean clothes and turned in. It commenced to pour. I was just thinking how comfortable I was when "Turn out there. Everybody out." Luckily I always make a point of knowing where my things are and so was down in the first ten, which was all the men they wanted in spite of the excitement. The rain was fearful, the lightning vivid and blinding and it was like wallowing in the darkest closet, only occasionally you would go up to your waist in mud. A short wait at headquarters and then with two Signal Corps men we started to find a broken telegraph wire between here and Bacolov [Bacalor?]. Sergt. O'Donnell in command. You couldn't see a man if you had hold of him, and we were told that the wire had been cut to draw us into an ambush. I was pleased to have the Sergeant say at the last outpost, "In case of attack Brown will assist in directing the movements and the firing." And I a second-class private. I had the advance, the point, and a terrible march it was. Suddenly I heard something in the road not thirty feet ahead. "Halt" and then the clatter of a mounted man retreating. "Halt, halt or I fire," the movement ceased. "Who goes there?" and then the frightened answer, "Friends." "Advance one to be recognized." "One I said." The darkness grew blacker but I could see nothing till the horse pushed his nose into my face. It was Gen. McArthur's native interpreter and some friends. One of the Signal men said he recognized them and we let them pass, though what they were doing out there at that hour passes my comprehension. Well we were on the road to Bacolov from 7 to 1 A.M. and finally found the break. It lightened considerably about 10 P.M. but the rain never ceased. Slept very well, having put on dry clothes, and am O.K. now.

SEPTEMBER 23
Cleaned my rifle, which was thoroughly wet and dirty. Slept. Last night it was so dark that after repeatedly losing members of the party we went in single file, each man holding on to the man in front of him. A lightning flash would enable you to see plainly the road for half a mile and then you could see less than before.

SEPTEMBER 24
Sunday. Worked at my Spanish geometry all day. Corp. Rees was up from Manila. It seems he has not yet been examined for his commission. I got two letters from mamma and one from Nan, which came on the wrecked *Morgan City*. They were a little rubbed, but legible. They came on the 22d inst.

SEPTEMBER 25
Spanish.

SEPTEMBER 26
Guard at McArthur's.

SEPTEMBER 27
It is said we move today. The men are all packing up. Undoubtedly the advance cannot be much longer delayed. One of our reconnaissances, escorted by a detachment of the 24th, was driven back on

Mexico yesterday. The niggers behaved very badly. Ordered out to protect the advance of the Artillery.

Even before breakfast rumors of the approaching move began running through the company and some of the more nervous men in the company began packing up their things. About 9 A.M. the list came out. Sixty men were to be ready to start at 12 M [noon]. Lieuts. Ferguson and Houton, Sergts. Casey and O'Donnell. We were divided in two details. I was with Sergt. O'Donnell and Lieut. Ferguson. Promptly at 12 we moved out in regular advance guard formation, four double bull carts carrying rations and spare ammunition. At twenty-five minutes after two we were in Bacolov, where one of the details went to San Antonio, we going on to Santa Rita, the extreme left flank of the army, reached there at 4:30 P.M. and were at once ordered to the outpost to build a bridge and repair the road for the Artillery to advance the next morning. Worked until dark, in which time our detail, thirty men, had built a bridge thirty-five feet long, strong enough for a battery, and about a hundred feet of road. Supper in the dark and bed. We knew then that the attack on Porac would take place the next day.

SEPTEMBER 28

Up at 4, breakfast and started about 5. The big square at Santa Rita gradually filled with troops and bull carts.[21] Eight companies of the 9th. One 3.2-inch gun from the 3d Artillery. A little mountain gun and two troops of Cavalry with our detachment made up our column. The 36th (Bell's) one gun, a troop and our other detail the column which started from San Antonio. Gen. Wheeler was in the square quietly directing things when we got there.[22] The troops were very quiet, being sleepy. An occasional jest. The favorite one seemed to be, "It's either Hell or Porac to-night." It was very picturesque with the last quarter of the moon and the old cathedral. Promptly at 5:15 A.M., the time set the night before, the column started. A battalion of the 9th, then us, then the guns, then the other battalion of the 9th and the Cavalry escorting the train. Gen. Wheeler and his staff leading. Our bridge held all right. Gradually we left the houses filled with cheerful natives. Then came scowling ones, then the houses all had white flags. The sun was up then and it was getting hot. The road though was good. Now the houses by the road were deserted. A man dropped out from the company in front and lay panting by the roadside. It was 8:30 now and suddenly four shots came from the fields to the right. The other column had struck the outposts. "Quicker now, men," and for thirty minutes the pace was killing. Then came a halt. The road bent away to the left by a large tree. At the tree was Gen. Wheeler surrounded by his staff all dismounted. Gen. Wheeler was directing the deployment of the Infantry. The leading battalion deployed as skirmishers to the left, the other to the right. The guns and fifteen Engineers, myself included, went down the road. Each battalion kept one company as support. There was no reserve. It really reminded me of maneuvers. There was a little shouting at first as the alignment was corrected and then the lines moved forward with the precision of a review. Down the road was a rifle pit about 1,200 yards away. At this rifle pit the guns were told to fire. Now the firing commenced everywhere and the bullets commenced to hum overhead. Leaves and twigs began to fall in the road. Gen. Wheeler directed the guns to open. A wounded man came by on a stretcher. I thought the guns would never open, which I suppose was due to excitement. "You need not hit any particular picket in the fence, any picket will do," I heard the battery officer say and then the guns spoke. "Engineers at the guns," and Sergt. O'Donnell and ten of us raced forward. "Sling your rifles and help us get these guns forward," and grabbing hold of trail and wheels we shoved the big gun forward about one hundred yards, when they fired again. Twice we did this and then little circles of dust began rising from the ground in front of the gun. "Run forward a few of you and see where those are coming from." Sergt. O'Donnell, myself and two others ran forward. "Look out," and we flung ourselves into the bushes and the guns fired over us. Forward again, we were now about two hundred yards in front of the gun and then it was easy to see where they were coming from. Little puffs of smoke came from the trench and you caught momentary flashes from the trees at each side of the road. Did I duck? Of course I did, though I had intended not to, and the Mausers and Remingtons whistled overhead. We were firing now at the trees where the sharpshooters' platform could be plainly seen. We kept moving forward, occasionally lying flat as the guns fired. I saw a shrapnel shell from the mountain gun burst in the tree about six feet under the sharpshooters. Wounded or not I don't know, but I never saw people get out of a tree sooner. They seemed to fall from branch to branch. Now a shrapnel burst over the trench and we all ran forward, only to be stopped about one hundred feet from it by a bamboo entanglement. Here we fired two volleys and then tore it down and rushed to the trench. Except for a dead Filipino it was empty. A good deal of blood and empty cartridges, mostly Remingtons. When I saw the trench I wondered why the Filipinos had ever left it. It was on top of a ravine and was six feet deep. Cheering now on right and left, where the firing was incessant. The stretchers were running back loaded. The Sergeant sent me up the tree to the sharpshooters' platform. I could see the lines moving steadily forward, firing as they went, and Gen. Wheeler and staff back on the road we had just come down. When I came down the line had gone forward and I had to run to catch up. That run took about all the strength I had left. Found the guns halted on the ravine to the right, they could not get down. Moved to the left at a trot and finally got down. Still volleys and cheering, but few shots humming overhead. I heard the boom of what the Artillery officer said was a smooth bore, but the shot did not come anywhere near us. My tongue was hanging out now and I could not have doubled to save my life. It was ten o'clock. Suddenly we turned a corner and thank goodness there was a clear mountain stream. The guns plunged through. It was waist deep. I stopped and drank about a quart, nor did I see anybody cross without doing likewise. A few volleys away to the right. Up the opposite bank, round a corner, and we were in Porac. Laid down in the shade. Troops came pouring in. Then the gun that was with the other column. We had got there first. Gens. McArthur and Wheeler with their staffs. A troop of Cavalry and a pack train of ammunition. The firing stopped. Men began to come by with captured guns and men. Remingtons, Mausers and even old guns with one-half inch bore. They had also found the instruments of the Filipino band. Evidently they left in a hurry. I had fired five shots and had not used my magazine. So I was pleased to find I had not lost my head. Our loss was five men wounded and five or eight overcome with the heat. Filipino loss, forty or fifty killed besides those they carried away. Dinner at one, a bath in the stream and then we went out and built a road up both sides of the stream and cleared a ford. Supper and bed, quite tired.

SEPTEMBER 29

Up at 5, at 7 started for Angeles as train guard. Every one went except two companies left so as to hold the town. About an eight-mile march. Had to repair the road and build two bridges. Reached Angeles about 1 P.M. Quite hot and dusty. The insurgents' outposts are about five hundred yards from Angeles across the river. The railroad is running as far as Angeles. The bridge (railroad) across the river has been destroyed. There is the largest church here I have seen outside of Manila.[23]

SEPTEMBER 30

Breakfast at 7, the most leisurely meal since we started. A detail was sent out to cut blocks to raise the locomotive in the river. About eleven the Lieutenant [Oakes] came in with a list of the men that were to return to San Fernando. Every one was furious as we had the best men and the best Sergeants in the company and had hoped to stay together. I protested to the Lieutenant about being sent to the rear. He told me that we would soon be at the front again. Then I tried to get Lieut. Wooten to take me in his scouts in which Sergt. O'Donnell is assigned. He said Lieut. Oakes wanted a man who could sketch and do other things I could do and some could not, and with that I had to rest content. But we did not get off that day anyway. All the Generals in the island were here (Angeles) to-day, Otis, Lawton, Wheaton, McArthur and the rest. A short truce, during which time the insurgents gave up some American prisoners. The result was we could not get a train and had to spend the night here.

OCTOBER 1

Sergt. O'Donnell came to me and said he was doing all he could to have me assigned to the scouts. Left for San Fernando at about 8 by train, arriving there about 10 A.M. I could not help thinking of the day we left Manila and took our first bull train to the front. Angeles had just been taken and the railroad ended at San Fernando, twenty kilometers south. Found the company headquarters, and the majority of the men were to be sent back to Manila but that forty men, including myself, were to remain here to accompany the advance. Was gladder than I can write that I was to stay. Worked for two hours over my rifle, which was filthy. Bed, and the mosquito netting was much appreciated after sleeping for four nights in native huts.

OCTOBER 2

Spent the day in doing "bunk fatigue," which literally translated means doing nothing. The rest of the company got up to Manila at 3 P.M. There is one thing I have noticed ever since we have been here, but have not thought of mentioning, and that is the tree which attracts the fireflies. It is bushy and resembles in form and size our oak. At night there are millions of fireflies around it so that it looks like an exaggerated Christmas tree. The effect on a dark night is very beautiful. Saw a bird trap in the rice fields near Bacolov that struck me as very ingenious. A bamboo pole and string were the materials. The branch [*illustration that appeared here is no longer extant*] A was pulled up to B and fastened lightly by means of the twig C. Now the slightest weight at C was sufficient to spring the trap. The string, spread into the form of a loop, is drawn quickly against the pole and the bird is caught by the legs. At D a live bird is fastened to serve as a decoy. The great trouble on our little expedition was the bugs. Of course we had to sleep on the floors of the native huts and were in consequence quite overrun with all kinds of insects. It did not interfere with sleeping as one was usually quite ready to sleep when he got a chance. It was with a great sense of relief that one realized last night as he tucked in the mosquito netting that one was in an insect-proof bunk. The quarters are very roomy now with only thirty men here.

OCTOBER 3

While I was sitting here writing the colored Infantry was drilling in extended order across the river. After the drill one of the men came down and jumped into the river drowning himself. They have just got his body. One did the same thing Sunday. I guess they have been driven hard since they misbehaved.

OCTOBER 4

Guard last night at the company quarters. A clear, moonless night. One gets much time for reflection on those still, undisturbed night watches. A pontoon drill under Sergt. Carroll, who is in charge of our detail. It is rumored that a pontoon train is to be sent up here, a light outfit for advance guards. I was amazed at the simplicity of the drill. There are no orders, every man must know just what he is to do. The hitches, no nails are used in the bridge, are simple and easy to make. Very interesting. The niggers cut up an outpost at Santa Rita night before last. Three men knifed. It is supposed they must have been asleep as they did not fire. If they were they deserved all they got.

OCTOBER 5

The reason for the taking of Porac is now clear to me. It was not a general advance, as first supposed, but a straightening of the lines and clearing out the seat of the raids on the railroad.[24] It was held by 1,000 men. An advance [*original map no longer extant*] from Mexico will give us a straight line through Angeles (pronounced An-hay-las) instead of the angle formed by Santa Rita, Angeles and Mexico. The little tin clads come up to Guagua, about twenty-five miles from the Bay of Manila. Every one practicing knots. I find that my yachting has taught me all those in use here and some more. While on the road from Bacolov to Santa Rita saw the natives making rope from bamboo. I do not know of anything that is not made of bamboo in this country. It is hard to imagine a more useful plant. On my map I have exaggerated the distance of Santa Rita, Bacolov and Mexico from San Fernando. It is only about one-fifth the distance to Angeles. Pontoon drill again this morning. The only knots required are the baulk lashing, the side vail lashing, mooring knot, fisherman's bend, bowline, bowline on a bight and running bowline, timber hitch, half hitch and clove hitch, wall and midshipman's knot. Not a very large or difficult requirement. Got quite sentimental on some rather sad stories in some old magazines until I happened to think that we soldiers who are probably doing our share of making unhappiness are as cheerful and contented a set of men as one ever sees. Yet probably if written up properly some of our experiences would undoubtedly sound pathetic. So I decided not to waste sympathy. This is the laziest spell I have ever had. There is no officer with our detachment and save the short pontoon drills we are doing nothing but "bunk fatigue." No rain save the slightest showers for a week.

OCTOBER 6

There are funny types in the company. One of the oddest because so out of place is Rummage, a boy not eighteen and with the beauty and delicacy of a girl. He must have been very well brought up for his manners are good. He has a chum about his own age, but a boy from the streets of New York. As is natural under the circumstances, R.'s education in wickedness is progressing rapidly. Both are very willing, are great favorites, R. being much moreso. In fact there are some of the men who are actually jealous of R., and do all in their power to stir up quarrels, the result being that the two (they are only children) spend days without speaking to each other, and then are apparently better friends than ever. It is a curious and not pleasant sight to see this pretty boy swear like the most hardened soldier. Our outposts here were attacked last night and some insurgents killed.

OCTOBER 7

The charm of these days is something that will linger long in my memory. The weather has been perfect, reminding one of our most perfect Indian summer days. Of course it is warmer, but not much. Beautiful, cloudless days, with the faintest kind of a breeze. Then for some days our detachment of forty has had absolutely nothing to do but answer reveille at 6:30 A.M. It is probably the calm before the storm, but as Dolan, an old Irish Corporal, said yesterday, "If this is war let us never have peace." It is a very busy little town now. All the houses occupied and new ones, nipa huts, going up on the site of those burned or destroyed. There are a great many shops. In some you see the native tailors squatting on their hams busily work-ing on their sewing machines, which are not so different from ours, except that they run by hand instead of by foot; in some are barbers; a great many are restaurants. In one of these I saw a sign, "Fride American oysters." But the greatest number are notion shops, where one can buy anything from bananas and cigars down to pens and tooth brushes. Then there is the market, so you can readily imagine the interest one can find in wandering round this picturesque old town. At such moments it is hard to realize that our outposts, hardly a mile out from the town, shoot or are stabbed almost every night. I believe lack of trains and mules is delaying the advance now. The culinary arrangements of the natives are very simple. They will cook their rice, vegetables, and perhaps some fish or cakes with less wood than an American cook would take to kindle her fire. The fire is built in an earthen pan, on top of which is placed the pot or dish containing the things to be fried or stewed. Am continuing my work on the Spanish geometry.

OCTOBER 8

Sunday. One of the men cut my hair and shaved me. I am more and more struck with the willingness of the men to help each other. Of course there are men who are unpopular and who have hard times, but the company is always ready to help even them if they are in serious trouble, while a man who is liked can always be prepared to receive anything he lacks or happens to fancy. Money, tobacco, matches, clean underclothes, anything that any one has is always at the disposal of any one who is liked. It is really touching at times, for these things while of small value in the States are sometimes invaluable here where it may take months to replace them. I have been very much interested in watching during the last week the construction of a native house. It is about thirtyfive feet long and about twelve feet wide. Every bit of it is bamboo and not a [*illustration that appeared here is no longer extant*] nail enters into its construction.

It is, moreover, perfectly water tight, being roofed and clapboarded, if it is allowable to use the term, with the nipa palms. To do this the leaves of the palm are sewn in strips about a foot [*illustration that appeared here is no longer extant*] long and from eight to sixteen inches wide, thus. After one piece is fastened in place another is fastened on top of it in the position *a b.* The roof is given a very steep pitch and the eaves are overhanging. [*The illustration that appeared here is no longer extant.*] The rooms are divided by weaving in split bamboo. The vertical strips are put in very close together. On this is fastened a closely woven mat of split bamboo. It took six men about ten days to finish this house. The man in charge said he would sell it to me for forty pesos. Labor is worth twenty cents a day.

OCTOBER 9
It is curious to see how the men spend their time. Some gamble, but very few because most have lost or spent their money. The wandering about the town is mostly done after supper (5 P.M.) as it is cooler. Some of the men, almost all, play some game of cards, solitaire or something of that sort. The non-coms and a few of the men read old magazines. The arrival of the train at 1 P.M., with Manila papers and news in general, is an event. The men sit round and tell stories, stories of their experiences and stories they have heard. The days pass quickly. I have my Spanish and write a good deal. We hear the remainder or bulk of the company is on the south line near Imus (pronounced E-mus, with the accent on the E), held in reserve and not engaged. There must be two or three thousand natives here. There were hardly twenty-five on the 17th of August.

OCTOBER 10
When things happen in the army they happen quick. Lieut. Oakes came up from Manila yesterday afternoon, and shortly it was rumored that we were to move soon. Later he sent for me for some things about maps, etc., and told me he thought we would move on the 11th. At 12, midnight, orders came for us to go to Mexico in the morning.[25] Reveille was at 5 instead of 6:30. Knapsacks were packed and sent to Manila. Our detail of forty now has only haversacks and a blanket roll. We are attached to Lawton's column. Whether it is a brigade or a division I do not know. He is coming up from the south line. The advance on Tarlas [Tarlac] is evidently to commence. The campaign is supposed to last three months, which leads me to suppose that we will go clear to the north end of the island after crushing "Aggie."[26] Part of the detail started about 9 A.M., with the bulk of our tools. I started about 1 P.M., as part of an escort to the remainder of our tools. Uneventful but hot march to Mexico, a bath and supper, the last of the detail coming in about 6 P.M. A bird, I suppose it was, screamed for about an hour in the middle of the night, much to the discomfort of our sentinels.

OCTOBER 11

Up at 4 A.M. An extra hundred rounds of ammunition was issued. Our column, Gen. Young, consists of six or eight companies of the 24th Infantry, the six-gun battery of the 37th Infantry, and the 4th Cavalry. Found transportation short and had to turn in over half of our tools. Every company turning in something. All these things delayed the start. Finally moved at about 8 A.M. As soon as I knew that we had to "tote" our haversacks and rolls I knew mine was too heavy, but it was too late to change then. Some threw their rolls away, others hastily tore their rolls apart and discarded boots and blankets. Started out at a killing pace which moderated after perhaps thirty minutes. Very hot. The hardest march I have ever made. Santa Ana about 11 A.M., very nearly played out. Five of our detail had dropped out, and about twenty of the colored Infantry. Quarters and dinner at 1 P.M. Were ordered out again to fix the road for tomorrow's advance. Escorted by a company of Infantry and some Cavalry which drove in the insurgent outposts while we built about 200 feet of corduroy over a mud hole, using bamboo for stringers and crosspieces) and the natives' fences and underpinning of houses for covering. Dirt on top of matting. Back at dark, supper and bed, very tired.[27]

OCTOBER 12

Up at 4. Tore my blanket in two and abandoned my shelter tent, which I have never used. Started at daylight for Aryat (R-at) [Arayat]. Insurgent outposts not replaced so we were not bothered. After had built some 200 feet of corduroy the road was passable for the light guns and Infantry, which passed us and soon became engaged. It was over very quickly and the town was ours. Our loss was four Infantry men wounded. The insurgent loss was heavy as shells were thrown into the town. Three companies of the 22d came up from Candaba, arriving just after the Infantry had been through the town. The gunboat *Laguna de Bay* also arrived, for the town is on the Rio Grande, the largest river in the island, which is here about 1-8 of a mile wide. With customary stupidity the insurgents did not destroy the bridge, though the town was fired either by our shells or the insurgents and about one-eighth of it destroyed. Our work on the road was just commencing, for the train must get through. At 12 M. [noon] we had dinner by the roadside, and then work again. Tearing down fences and houses, cutting down banana trees and bamboo, carrying hay, anything to fill up the mud holes. It was the hardest day's work I have ever done. It was about 5 when we finally got into the town, in time for a bath in the river before dark. To explain the state of the roads it must be borne in mind that it is only about ten days since the rain stopped, and while the roads are dry on top the wheels of the heavy wagons cut right through. We were assisted in our work by details from the Cavalry and by about fifty Macabebes under Sergeant Casey.[28] After the fight natives began to drift back, and they were impressed, so that at the end we had thirteen of these also working. Altogether built about half a mile of corduroy.

OCTOBER 13

Aryat. Just two months ago to-day we landed in Manila. Further exploration of the town (the expedition is stationary to-day, waiting for rations it is said) corrects some of my impressions. We did not cross a bridge last night. On reaching the road the river bends sharply back on itself, making a turn sharper than a right angle. It seems to be a town as large as San Fernando, but of a different character, lacking the solid stone business center, though having fine residences (we are quartered in one, having driven out the owners) it has more the air of a country town. It has a very large market, where a great many different kinds of fishes are for sale, all alive as seems to be the custom. We are not more than a mile from Mt. Aryat, an extinct volcano which rises abruptly from the plain to the height of over 800 meters (about 2,400 feet), but like all mountains here covered with trees from top to bottom.[29] Very beautiful it is in the early morning light or when the sun is sinking. Angeles is on the other side of the island, about fifteen miles away. I judge a good many natives left before the fight, but some still remain. The insurgent force was about 2,000 men, some of them armed with wooden guns of which we found quite a number. There does not seem to be any money in the town, it being impossible to get change for the smallest piece of money when you try to buy anything. Cannot buy any cigars or indeed any form of tobacco. About two hours later all these things could be bought. Helped dig a sink. Soil very rich to a depth of more than five feet. Enlarged a map for the Lieutenant which a Corporal had made on too small a scale.[30]

OCTOBER 14
Went all over the town correcting a map made by one of the Sergeants. Combined some maps. Visited all the outposts which are very near the town, in it in fact. This must be due to the fact that the insurgents have no artillery and are looked down on as insignificant opponents. Made a number of maps and began to understand the situation. We are about fifteen miles northeast of San Fernando, on an east and west line with Porac and Angeles, with the mountain (Aryat) between us. Rations come up the Rio Grande, which blocks our advance, being (I measured it with a Pratt range finder) about 150 yards wide. When the flying column came south through here last May they came from the old ferry to Aryat. That road is not impassable, and to-day the men are out building a [*original map no longer extant*] trail ferry about the edge of the town. I staid in to draw maps. The Signal Corps got the telegraph into the town from Candaba last night.

OCTOBER 15
Heavy firing last night. I don't know where nor why. Outpost firing is such a common occurrence since we left Mexico that no one notices it. The troops now here are eight companies of the 24th, three of the 22d, two of Macabebes, they are on the other side of the river, the battery (Astor's mountain guns) from the 37th and I think a troop, and several troops of the 4th Cavalry, in all nearly 3,000 men. Rained last night. I find my adjectives fail me when I try to describe the beauty and charm of this country. It is the garden spot of the world. That will have to cover it. I do not think the natives have any more heart in the fight. It is a common sight to see their officers beating them to make them stay in the trenches. The Macabebes are for us and are enlisting in as large numbers as can be allowed. After a fight I have an idea that they scatter to their homes and do not join the insurgents again unless forced to. As more and more territory passes into our hands the native army diminishes. Their

ammunition is very short and poor. Most of their powder they make themselves. Not one-half of their army has rifles. The detail is working on the ferry. I think it will take a week to complete.[31]

OCTOBER 16
A hard day's work at the ferry, mostly shoveling, fifteen minutes on, fifteen minutes off. Gen. Lawton arrived on the gunboat. This is the 1st Division, fifty men from the 4th Cavalry.

OCTOBER 17
Still on the ferry. Gen. Lawton spent most of the day there personally hastening things. Got rope across and ferry running and ferried across a battalion of the 22d before dark.[32] [The illustration that appeared here is no longer extant.] Dotted line shows excavation. Trail ferry.

OCTOBER 18
Started from Aryat. Delay as was natural at the ferry. Stockman in command of bull carts. Caught the detail at old ferry, three and one-sixth miles on San Isidro road. Marched till 8 or 9 P.M. and camped in barracks, seven miles from Aryat, the insurgents had used the night before. On post from 2 A.M. till 5, when breakfast and start. 22d and Macabebes had a skirmish and fifty insurgents captured.[33]

OCTOBER 19
Cavalry and mountain guns went by in the night. Raining hard. No dinner, very sleepy. 24th passed, we working on roads, then a battery from the 4th Artillery. Caibao [Cabiao] at 5 P.M., having only made four and one-third miles since 6 A.M. Delay due to roads, which were terrible. Chicken stew for supper, chickens stolen.

OCTOBER 20
Reveille at 4 again and more hard work on roads and bridges.[34] Artillery and Infantry behind at Caibao. Dinner en route. San Isidro (Ys-e-dro) at 4 P.M., six miles. Is larger than San Fernando and is on the Rio Grande. Was taken yesterday. Wash in river, first for four days. Thirty-one miles, about, northeast of San Fernando.

A halt in the muddy road between Arayat and Cabiao.
Courtesy Harper's History of the War in the Philippines, 1900.

OCTOBER 21

Reveille at 4 A.M. and breakfast by moonlight. Daylight at 5:30. Detachment was marched back to Caibao to strengthen a bridge. The old guard, three men and myself, were left here, I to consolidate the route sketches of the march. Was very glad. Bought chickens, so we are living like kings after eleven days of the field ration. The country is quite different from San Fernando, being higher and drier and cleaner looking. Nights quite cold. Had to walk about sharply the night I was on guard on the road to keep warm. Natives seem friendly and cheerful, which coupled with their unwillingness to stand in a fight leads me to suppose they have little heart in the fight. The only casualties when we took this place was a man from the 22d killed by a shell from the 37th, an unfortunate occurrence. The natives, on the other hand, being driven into the river, lost heavily. The battery from the 4th Artillery just got in, 5 P.M. one is short on rations. I think there will be a slight delay here. More tobacco and wood other than bamboo and less cane and rice here abouts. Bulls stolen from fields by our forager, Baume, to replace

Cavalry horses being ferried across the Rio Grande at Arayat.
Courtesy Harper's History of the War in the Philippines, 1900.

and strengthen our tool train. About sixteen miles northeast of Aryat and thirtyone or forty from San Fernando. We did not get a map of country from Santa Ana to Aryat. Chicken, fried, and fried bananas for supper. Detachment got back about 8 P.M., having built a bridge two miles from town.

OCTOBER 22
We are early discovering a use for the banana tree. It makes an excellent thing to fill mud holes in the road, being very bulky for its weight and easy to cut down. We sacrificed a good many groves of them on the road up here from Aryat. Naturally the owners protested a bit, but "c'est le guerre." Lieut. Oakes having discovered by sending me on a message that I could ride started me at 8:30 A.M. to bring up Sergt. Casey and his Macabebes, two miles south of Caibao. Had a delightful ride down in the cool of the morning. Made the eight miles in about two hours. Was a wretched pony. Country looked

so fresh and beautiful that it was hard to realize that three days ago the army was fighting its way up on the road I was riding back on alone. Passed two bull trains bringing up rations and the guard of the ferryboat. We have to cross the river again here, being poled up. River too shallow for gunboats. A hot ride back, reaching here about 3 P.M. The detachment working on the ferry. Signal Corps got the telegraph in today. Are thirty miles southeast of Tarlas [Tarlac]. Caibao, which I did not see at all when I was there before (we got in at dark and left at daylight), is merely a collection of native huts with a tumble-down church, the poorest I have seen over here. It is not on the river and is surrounded by and partly built on a marsh. The object of its existence is a mystery to me. It was on the marsh two miles south of the town that we were so delayed by mud and water on the advance. I saw no sign of hostility on the part of the natives, most of whom had a cheerful word or a smile as I passed. A number of natives filling up mud holes. Evidently they would rather do it themselves than have us use their banana trees and houses. Roads still heavy, but easily passable. A light shower last night.

OCTOBER 23

The detachment still working at the ferry, myself doing nothing in quarters lest more maps should be wanted. A quartermaster on a casco shot and four privates wounded in our rear last night. It was in this town that the insurgents had Lieut. Gilmore and thirteen other Americans confined, barely getting them out as we came in. Some of the men went over to the jail, a massive structure as this is a considerable town, to see the inscriptions they left on the walls. Poor fellows, I suppose they wanted the world to know something of their fate. The writing was mixed with hieroglyphics, so the natives would not think it a message.[35] It is my impression that we are on a big turning movement. I have no idea of our objective of course. If, as we seem to be doing, we are establishing a chain of posts as we advance the insurgents, when we close we will have no place to run to save the China Sea and our fleet. We have two batteries, twelve guns, a large force of artillery for our numbers, something more than a gun to 400 men instead of the usual one to 1,000.

Rain. The detachment working on the ferry. The boat was poled and hauled up here last night. Yesterday I made a map of the town and so know it thoroughly.[36] The main town is along the bank of the Rio Grande for about a mile and is one-half a mile wide. Native huts extend about a mile further in both directions, up and down stream. In the center of the town, opposite the church, is a walled enclosure one quarter of a mile square containing large stone buildings. I think it was a convent. It, like everything else, is in a state of ruin. It would be interesting to know how long since this town has been in the hands of the natives. As it is thirty miles from the railroad, it may have been years since the Spaniards held it. I was wrong about Lieut. Gilmore. It was last May when the flying column came through here that he was here. The inscriptions on the walls of the prison are still here however. Sent off some mail yesterday (have had no letters for over a month). As they may not go through will repeat some dates I do not care to lose.

LEFT	ARRIVED
San Fernando, Oct. 10	Mexico, Oct. 10, 4 miles
Mexico, Oct. 11	Santa Ana, Oct. 11, 5 miles
Santa Ana, Oct. 12	Aryat, Oct. 12, 5 miles
Aryat, Oct. 18	Caibao, Oct. 19, 10 miles
Caibao, Oct. 20	San Isidro, Oct. 20, 6 miles[37]

The town contains some fine houses, though most are in bad repair. No glass except for mirrors is used in this country. The only glass I have seen outside of Manila was in a house, the finest in the town, in Angeles.[38] We are on a long "hike." The Lieutenant asked me last night if I had sketching materials for one hundred miles. Some talk with the Lieutenant, who is thinking of sending me to Manila to ask Capt. Sibert for more Engineers. As there are three bridges to build in the next seven miles, I could easy catch up with the advance. He also wants fifty Chinos. It seems that the last man who tried to bring them up lost them at Calumpit. Had some of the most delicious bananas to-day I have ever eaten. Raining hard.

OCTOBER 25

The river was singing when I went to sleep last night. To-day it has risen eighteen feet and is flowing bank full. Up before daylight and started at daylight with one other fellow for the lower landing at Caibao. Pony back of course with rifles, ammunition and a day's rations. Caibao at 8, lower landing at 9. Found the Chinos we went down to bring up had not arrived, so waited. The country with the river bank full looked quite different from the last day I tried the same ride. About 1:30 the gunboat came along towing the casco with the Chinos, did not stop so we rode four miles to the next landing. Had our supper there, cooking our bacon on one of the native fires. It was 5:15 before the gunboat got up there. Did not stop and so we came on to here, reaching here after dark. While we were at the upper landing the launch on which Major Howard was killed came down the river. It was an ambush of course and the Major was killed at the first fire. His only words were, "Keep her going. Whatever you do, keep her going," thinking apparently only of the safety of the stores the launch was towing.[39] The Nordenfeldt gun on the launch jammed, as is usual I believe.

OCTOBER 26

The river has fallen greatly. I noticed a great many more men around the country yesterday. When we marched up it was all women and children, now the men are coming back. There is a good deal of Indian corn up here, the yellow kind. The grinding machines are huge stone affairs, worked by the women and children, with a wooden frame which is suspended over it. The ferry being under water has been abandoned. The detachment is now preparing the timber for a trestle bridge. I seem, since the advent of our new "top sergeant," to be a sort of privileged character reserved for map drawing and expeditions like the last time. River still deep enough for the gunboat. She has not got here yet, but I don't think it will belong. Bright and pleasant, as was yesterday. The natives here do my washing, underclothes, socks and towel, for five cents, and it is very well done. Company bought a calf yesterday, so we are to have roast veal for dinner. There is a large storehouse filled with tobacco in the town. The men are taking large quantities. When rolled up it makes very fair cigars. Can buy plenty of cigars here and the Japanese safety matches. Is a drug store in the town, so we are quite well fixed. The little notions and dry goods which at San Fernando came up the railroad from Manila are of course absent. Changed the plan about the ferry, and all hands worked pulling it across the river a mile from quarters. Completed at dark.

OCTOBER 27

Up at 3 A.M. and breakfast. Twenty-two men, the Macabebes, accompany the advance, I also made the map.[40] I started at daylight and caught the advance at the ferry. Pushed forward and advanced with the scouts, who were from the 22d. Road good, but bridges all down. Passed the Engineers about one mile from the ferry repairing a bridge. An attack expected at the river Tubio, but there was none. I fell in the river making a bridge for the scouts. Got it built finally. Two guns in the river where a dugout upset. Natives got them and returned them. Engineers came up as we passed. As we passed through Tuboatin [Taboatin] natives told Maj. Ballants [Ballance] the insurgents had trenches across the next river. Could have ripped us at the Tubio. Continued to accompany the scouts. At 12 M. [noon] the scouts fired four shots. (I forgot that earlier the gunboat stirred them up and the leading company of the 22d fired at the insurgents as they ran up the bank of the Rio Grande. The gunboat, the *Laguna de Bay*, crackled and roared for thirty minutes.) Went forward and peeped through the grass. There sure enough were the trenches across the river, not three hundred yards away. Could see the niggers plainly. No firing after the first shots. Sent for the mountain battery of the 37th and sent two companies of the 22d to flank the trenches. This was not a success, as they could not get across the river, though we did not find this out till later. (Inclose some notes I took during the fight, which lasted till 1:35.) We had a man killed and one wounded. I don't think we did the insurgents any harm, though they finally ran away. Why I don't know, as we had to cross the river on rafts which took half an hour to build. It would have cost many lives to have crossed under fire. Men in the battery not very brave. The river was tributary to the Rio Grande and the fight was about a mile from the latter. I was lying down about ten feet *[illustration that appeared here is no longer extant]* from the guns. No more excitement. Santa Rosa at 5:15 P.M. It was amusing to see the guns go across the river on rafts. Horses swimming. Banks thirty feet high. Santa Rosa on the Rio Grande, a comfortable country town, good houses, all of wood and bamboo. Ten miles almost due north of San Isidro. This seems more than 10 miles.

OCTOBER 28
Santa Rosa. Every organization here, the 22d, the battery and troop of the 37th and Gen. Young's escort, ate their last rations for breakfast. About half a mile from the town is another bridge down, river not fordable, but it is the lack of rations that is delaying us. Here too the insurgents had trenches, but they did not stop in them. Our outposts are across the river. Here, as at the river above the skirmish, the temporary floating bridge was not taken up nor was the wire stripped from the telegraph poles, as it was a few miles from San Isidro, until the scene of the fight. The road is a splendid turnpike and the fine, substantial bridges look as if they had been suffered to decay or else destroyed years ago when the Spaniards were here. Every organization has a detail out foraging. The trains must be halted at the skirmish, where the river is fifty feet wide and about eight feet deep. The old bridge was thirty feet above the present level of the stream. I am having a delightful time, going anywhere I like, my orders merely being to accompany the advance and map the road. Of course at a halt I have nothing to do. The men are always ready to share their rations. Letters from home the night before leaving San Isidro. Read them today, my first chance. Swept the cracker dust out of my haversack for dinner and reboiled the coffee grounds I had used for breakfast. Assigned to F Company of the 22d, with whom I had been staying, with the sergeants' mess, for rations. Foragers came in with mutton and rice, so had a fine supper, though without salt. One-half of each company sent back to bring the rations from the last river by hand. Was issued three days' rations to last four days. Nice fellows, the sergeants of F. All were with the regiment in Cuba.

OCTOBER 29
Macabebes came up the other bank of the river. They are a success. The Tagalos [Tagalogs] cannot be trusted and are mixed with Lowe's

scouts, who are part civilians, part men detailed from regiments.[41] They found two dead Filipinos where we had our fight, but the twentyone shots fired by the Artillery killed none. The *Laguna de Bay* killed a lot. An interesting talk with Capt. Ballants, who is acting Major of the battalion (F, 1, A, K,) of the 22d with us. He was next me in the advance.[42] All officers very kind. Am having the time of my life. Was told by the Adjutant General there would be an advance to-day, but it does not seem to materialize. A burning town in the mountains, some twenty miles away, very impressive and a bit awful. The Signal Corps get the wire in this afternoon. There must have been three miles of wire (insurgents') still up. The view back of the town is beautiful, perfectly flat for perhaps twenty miles to the verdure-covered mountains, not all woods, but no bare places. Lieut. Oakes came up. Sent for me and seemed pleased with the work, but rebuked me for being so far forward in the fight. Some of the officers had told him.

OCTOBER 30
Started out with a scouting party of the 22d, but Lieut. Oakes saw me and told me to go with Lieut. Batson and his Macabebes.[43] Marched out to Sunicap, where we crossed the Rio Grande in bancas and plunged into the swamp. Lieut. Batson and myself the only white people in the party. Soon lost our way, frightful walking, grass eight feet high. By beating the guide his memory became better and we found the road after an hour's hard work.[44] After going a short way to Ahaga [Aliaga?] turned towards Cabanatuan. The Macabebes march so fast I had difficulty in making my map and keeping up. Insurgents fired the grass, but we reached the river before the fire reached us. Crossed the river again and were in Cabanatuan, where we found the party from the 22d, who had had an easy march. No shots. Is a larger town than Santa Rosa, with a large church and ruins of a much larger convent or something of the sort. The 22d found the telegraph were up all the way. On our side of the river it was down. We found a large coil of the wire thrown in the swamp. Bridges all down on our side and road evidently little used. Cabanatuan at 11:30, four miles. Borrowed a horse from Lieut. Henry, 22d, and followed the Cavalry back to Santa Rosa, which I reached just as three companies of the 22d and two

guns were coming out, so joined them and mapped this side of the river.[45] On this side a beautiful road, well wooded and very pretty. Bull carts got up, so F is having company mess, so rations no longer bother us.

OCTOBER 31
Cabanatuan. Beautiful wood work in convent and church. Macabebes captured an insurgent signal officer, but no firing on outposts last night.[46] Decided I had been out long enough, so walked back to Santa Rosa alone. Reported to the Lieutenant, who told me to finish up the maps. Detail now increased to seventy-five men working on bridge at Minotula River, just outside the town. Spent the evening in the Lieutenant's quarters, talking and smoking cigars. He tells me this march, if not stopped by peace, will be more famous than Sherman's march to the sea.[47]

NOVEMBER 1
Command started at 7 A.M. and made an easy march to Cabanatuan.

NOVEMBER 2
Cabanatuan. Reveille at 4 A.M. and a detachment sent north towards Talevera to build a bridge. I went along to make a map and returned. Found rest of detachment had been sent back towards San Isidro, to make the roads easier for teams. An order from Gen. Lawton published to-day saying the success or failure of the expedition depended upon supplies and urging care and economy. Evidences of hasty flight of insurgents along the road I traveled this morning, shells, old mortars and bells thrown by the roadside. In the convent here was found a reloading outfit. A Spanish prisoner, brought in to-day, says the insurgents are out of food and ammunition. I am left here to go with scouting parties whenever possible to map.

NOVEMBER 3
Reveille at 5 A.M. Accompanied the detail as far as the bridge, and then with three men from the 34th as escort was sent on to Talevera, eight miles, which was captured by the 1st squadron of the 4th Cavalry. An arsenal here, many rounds of Hotchkiss ammunition and seventy-five sacks of American flour. Just as I came in a detail of

twenty men from L Troop and some scouts from C Troop were ordered out on a scout. I went with them one mile northeast through a jungle and then we came to an open savannah about half a mile wide. The men were deployed as skirmishers and the advance taken up. About one-third of the way we were fired on, from four places in the wood in front. Fire returned, black powder the insurgents used, and the advance continued. Insurgents fired say twenty shots and then ran. Their camp in the edge of the woods was left in a hurry. We found chickens, pigs, rice, sugar, six bulls and four carts. Took everything we could, including the bull carts and loads, and destroyed the rest. Returning with D Troop coming out as a reinforcement. About two miles from Talevera. Messing and quarters with D of the 4th. They came over on the *Para* with us.

NOVEMBER 4

Talevera. A bull train with guard of one hundred men attacked and one man killed on road which I came over yesterday. This was about 4 P.M., November 3. Got permission from the Lieutenant Colonel of the 4th Cavalry, in command here, to take my three men on a reconnaissance to Santo Domingo, three miles to the west.[48] Did so. This town was visited by Cavalry a few days ago. Is a native village pure and simple of about one hundred houses. When the insurgents abandoned it they left fifteen wounded in the church. Visited these. Found our men on our return dumping the captured ammunition in the river. We are hot on their trail. If our transportation holds out and our communications not interrupted this will be a striking blow. Rained all the morning. This is the extreme front of the army. The town was a very important capture. A moulding room, fine tools, dynamite bombs, some twenty [*illustration that appeared here is no longer extant*] or thirty stationary grenades, some old Spanish cannon, brass, bronze bells, and some eight or ten wooden guns bound with wire. The Spanish guns, muzzle loaders, seem very old.

NOVEMBER 5

Talevera. Col. Hayes sent for me last night and asked some questions about my reconnaissance. This is a delightful detail. I am my own boss and going when and where I please so long only as I keep up with the advance. I miss my blanket roll, but have slept in a horse blanket the last two nights. The troop is living well, though on short rations. I have eaten caribou stew and a vegetable that is not unlike our squash and is very good when boiled and thickened with flour. Ammunition is what the squadron lacks. Natives coming back to the town. The three men of the 34th with me are Wright, Douglass and O'Brien. Couldn't move as all bridges and ferries in our rear are washed away. Took the three men and made a reconnaissance to Calipahan and a mile a half further on the banks of the Talevera. Returned, as I judged from actions of natives I was to be attacked from the rear. It would be hard to imagine pleasanter soldiering than this. Of course there are hardships, such as not having my blanket roll and in consequence having no change of clothes. But the absolute freedom from all restraint, the power to go where you please, is indeed in this beautiful country charming. Then as this mapping is something the men do not understand I am treated as something extraordinary. The officers are very kind, furnishing me with all the information they can and helping me in every way possible. There is a marked difference between the Regular officer and the Volunteers. The two officers of the 34th now up here impress one as a poor sort of noncom. It is nice for me in one way as I ask and get escorts which I would not dare ask for from a Regular. If this detail depends on working faithfully I am sure I shall hold it. Light showers all day. Permanent squads in D Troop as in the 22d. It works very well and is, I am sure, the best for field service if not for all cases.

NOVEMBER 6
Talevera. Scout with five men of the 34th (Dorrington's scouts) to Santo Domingo, then north to Baboc [Baloc], seven and one-half miles, and back to Talevera by Calipahan, in all scout twelve or thirteen miles. Between Santo Domingo and Baboc (a village of perhaps thirty houses) took two bolos and three hundred bullets from a party of natives. Also took three furloughs from insurgent army. Let them go as I did not care to be bothered by prisoners. Road from Baboc to Calipahan in fearful condition. A hard day's work. Dinner at Baboc. Ate the bacon I have had in my haversack since October 29, was in good condition.

NOVEMBER 7

Was awakened this morning at 4:20 A.M. by bullets tearing through the roof and the noise of heavy firing.[49] Then the troop stable guard fired their revolvers for an alarm, so for a moment it seemed as if the insurgents were in the town. The troop poured out into the street and formed with the Mausers overhead sounding like a tense telegraph wire struck by a hammer. Our outposts had not come in and were not firing, though the insurgents were firing heavily. An insurgent bugler, the finest I have ever heard, was blowing marches and the bolo charge and the insurgents were yelling like demons. Still no firing yet from our outpost down the river road. At this time I located the dipper and the north star for the first time since I have been in the island. Then our outpost and B Troop poured in volley. (They had let the niggers get within a hundred feet of them and killed two, left on the field, and wounded a great many with the first volley.) The niggers, who evidently thought they had captured the town, screamed and ran. Our firing stopped, we are very short of ammunition. The insurgents commenced again at a distance. The first streak of dawn D Troop thrown out to the right as skirmishers, I went with them. Advanced to the river half a mile and halted. No more firing anywhere till Dorrington's scouts crossed the river firing a few shots. Barracks again at 6:30. The two dead insurgents were fully equipped with mess kits, Mauser rifles and belts. The first of our men to get to them took their money pouches. One of them gave me one of the copper cents. Our casualties were one horse killed and two wounded, all shot on their picket line. Ate our last ration for breakfast. Brought in yesterday some beautiful vases six inches high and some thousands of cigars found in the jungle. The cigars were issued to the men. Immediately after I had finished writing details from Troops I and B were sent out to Santo Domingo to reinforce the scouts. I went. Two of the bridges had been torn up and at one the insurgent rear guard had attempted a stand. Santo Domingo looted by our men. The only thing I saw that I could carry away was a bottle of ink with which I am writing this. Mine gave out yesterday. A lot of powder was found and exploded. Through some one's blunder a man from the 34th was killed and one badly injured.[50] Back at 1 P.M. Took a bath and washed clothes, the first time since November 1 that I have had time. An attack of "dobie itch" in consequence. They keep bringing in dead Filipinos. One wounded one, now dead, said they came from Tarlac. Bull train with rations and ammunition came up, also F of the 3d Cavalry, Batson's Macabebes and Gen. Young.

CHAPTER 3

Northern Luzon

*I*T BECAME QUICKLY EVIDENT that Otis's tri-part entrapment of Aguinaldo was mired in the Pampanga mud. Given the terrain and the time frame, Lawton feared he would never be able to rendezvous with Wheaton in time to close down Aguinaldo's escape routes. However, as Lawton pondered how to link up with Wheaton, news arrived that Aguinaldo was planning to shift his capital northeast from Tarlac to Bayombong in the mountains of Nueva Vizcaya. For Aguinaldo to achieve this he had to use the mountain pass at San Nicholas in eastern Pangasinan. Young, seizing the moment, offered to take part of his cavalry, the 22d Infantry under Ballance, the Macabebe Scouts, and a mountain battery to move on San Nicholas, as well as the nearby pass at Tayug. To enhance mobility Young would cut his men from their supply train, believing they could live on the barest of provisions. Lawton, with trepidation, agreed. In early November the eleven-hundred-man force set off from Talavera.

Aguinaldo was clearly a better fugitive than a military strategist. Unknown to Young, he dispersed his army and canceled his plan to resettle in Bayombong. Rather, with his family and staff in tow, he turned west into La Union Province and then up the coast of Ilocos, eventually cutting east into Abra. This was a bold, desperate move, and the chase of Aguinaldo that ensued is one of military legend. Even if he had not done this, it seems doubtful that Otis's plan would have succeeded. Wheaton had problems landing his supplies at Lingayen Gulf, and a typhoon delayed the deployment of his troops. Young, after a quick march across much of Luzon, waited for him at San Nicholas, the rendezvous point; Wheaton, however, still had his forces concentrated in the San Fabian area. The trap, as Otis envisioned it, would never have materialized.

It was at San Fabian, a coastal town in Pangasinan, where Brown, who had crossed Luzon with Young, joined up with the 3d Cavalry and traveled north after Aguinaldo. At that point, the U.S. command was unsure

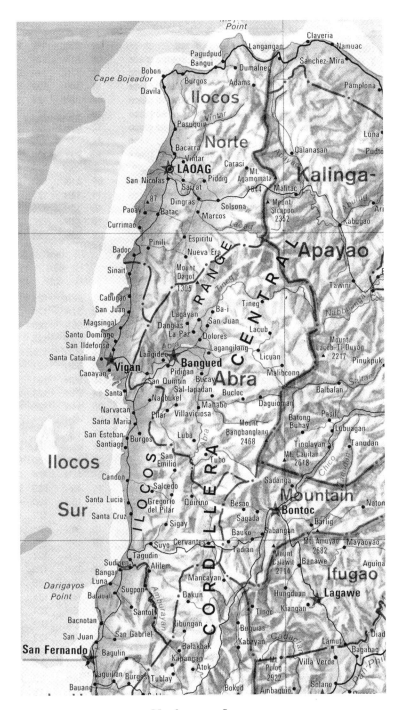

Northwestern Luzon

in what direction Aguinaldo would flee: north up the coast or back east across Luzon. It was also assumed that Aguinaldo had split up his army and Young wanted to prevent the rebel forces from reorganizing in the nearby mountains. Furthermore, Young and other commanders were deeply concerned about the American prisoners being held by the experienced and competent Gen. Manuel Tinio and his men, known as the Tinio Brigade. The Filipino leader, after a disastrous attack on Vigan, deployed troops to fight delaying actions for his fleeing president at Tangadan Pass. At this isolated aperture in the Benguet range, Young's troops drove the Tinio Brigade from its mountain trenches. While the U.S. forces celebrated a conventional victory, one that Young called "more like war than anything I have seen in these islands," the Filipinos evaporated into the mountains and launched a protracted irregular conflict.

One need only see the central and northwest portions of Luzon to appreciate the incredible march Young's forces endured in their attempt to defeat Aquinaldo. It was one of the most arduous and yet unsung operations in U.S. military history. First north from Talavera to San Jose, then northwest across the island, Young's troops were forced to fare with little food and water, poor equipment, and, for many, no shoes. The weather was dreadful and the terrain even worse. Fever and dysentery were common. Rest came for some at San Fabian, but for others the hike continued due north. With the sea on their left and the spine of the Benguet and Abra Mountains on their right, Young's men were trekking into uncharted territory with no source of supplies other than an occasional appearance by a navy gunboat or transport ship. Not the least of their worries was the local population. While Brown saw a land where the people were tired of war and compliant with U.S. rule, he and others underestimated the intensity of Filipino nationalism. They failed to comprehend that while U.S. troops were being welcomed into towns with handshakes and brass bands, many of the same folk were supporting Tinio and his men. In fact, in 1900, the year Brown left the supposedly pacified northern Luzon, U.S. officials considered it to be the most troublesome area in the Philippines in terms of guerrilla activity.

Brown's road maps offer cartographic testimony to the difficulties faced by Young's "flying column." Nine of the ten maps Brown drew that appear in *Annual Reports of the War Department for the Fiscal Year Ended June 30, 1900*, volume 1, part 4, relate to the journey from Cabanatuan to Bangui. The map devoted to the battle at Tangadan Pass is also almost certainly his work. Comments such as "deep mud," "2 to 3 feet of water in road," and "bridges would not support wagons" bear witness to the hazards encountered during the column's march. More importantly, the maps are all very accurate—no mean feat given the circumstances.

The landscape today would still be recognizable to Brown. In fact, one traveling along his route will see similarities that produce a decidedly eerie feeling. The country between San Jose and Tayug is magnificent. Like Brown, one can smell the fried bananas and *bagoong* in towns like Villasis. The beach at San Fabian is just as glorious under the swaying coconut palms, although today's traveler has the luxury of numerous resorts from which to choose. San Fernando in La Union Province bustles with commerce, but now its role as a port is minimal. Saint Christopher's in Bangar's plaza is impressive, as are the Spanish churches in Agoo, Paoay, Vigan and other towns along the way. The stone culverts Brown saw along the roads are still there. The old stone lighthouse built by the Spanish atop the hill at Nagpartian is a local landmark. Sadly, however, the response to a 2001 call for public support for its upkeep was mixed and its future as of this writing was not assured.

Two stops along Brown's journey are particularly noteworthy. Tangadan Pass, where Brown witnessed his largest battle, became the site of an intense engagement during World War II. Tangadan Mountain, which by that time had a tunnel through it, sits astride the highway near the Abra–Ilocos Sur border southeast of Vigan. It was the hub of Japanese resistance in northwestern Luzon during the last year of the war. The area is a series of hills and ridges, many of them quite sharp, which guards the entry to Bangued and the Abra Valley. Much like Tinio before them, the Japanese had emplaced numerous defensive positions from which they controlled the line of fire to the south, southwest, and southeast. During March and April, 1945, U.S. forces secured the fortress-like area, eventually ending all resistance. Vigan, Bangued, and the rice-rich Abra Valley were freed of Japanese occupiers. The fall of Tangadan sounded the death-knell for the Japanese on Luzon, just as it did for Aguinaldo a half-century before. Today, one need only stand on the highway near Narvacan and glance at the foreboding range to the east to understand the Tangadans' immense strategic value.

Bangui Bay also deserves special mention. Touted for decades as the next great tourist destination in the Philippines, it has not and may never meet that expectation. Indeed, it remains virtually unknown. It is simply too far and too difficult to reach. This is unfortunate; once one arrives in Bangui, the serenity that Brown found is immediately apparent. The air is so fresh that it intoxicates. It is frankly astonishing to sit on the beach at Bangui and read Brown's entries of December 18, 1899, to January 2, 1900: the pastoral images of the *bancas* fishing off the coast, the *caribao* toiling in the brilliant green fields, and what he calls the "arcadian" people working in the shadow of the mountains and within earshot of the surf are all still there. It is heady stuff, and it is easy to understand why Brown, exhausted from the hike north, says at Bangui, "I am happy to be alive."

There would be differences in today's northern Luzon, of course. Buildings, both commercial and private, are almost uniform in their concrete and tin, an architectural combo that postdates Brown. Because of Brown and those who came after him, many enterprises carry a distinctly American influence. In a roughly half-mile stretch in Cabanatuan there is the Wesleyan University, the Harvard Institute of Technology, and the Texas Hotel. Bangui is likewise typical: there is a store named "Drexel," there are indications that the Jaycees have been everywhere in the town, and there are ceremonial plaques showing the assistance the United Banguiarians of Hawaii. It should be noted that the Ilocanos of this region, known for their hard work and frugality, were much sought after as laborers in the sugar fields of Hawaii. Consequently, Ilocanos have, over the course of a century, made a substantial contribution to the Hawaiian Islands, Alaska, and California. While Brown would probably not be surprised at the American influence in the Philippines (he witnessed the early signs of it), he would certainly be shocked at the Filipino impact on the United States.

✣

NOVEMBER 8

Two columns left Talevera. One, Batson's Macabebes, Troop F 3d Cavalry and Gen. Young, went by Hacienda al Vale [Hacienda del Valle], striking the main road about one mile below Bo San Jose.[1] I went with Gen. Young. The other went by Santo Domingo, striking the road at Baboc. It was the fact that I had been over the road to Baboc that determined my going with Gen. Young. A hard march and no excitement. San Jose, not the Bo, about 2 P.M., fifteen miles. The other column got in about an hour later. Captured a few rifles, some Hotchkiss ammunition and dynamite. A poor wooden or rather nipa church and some two hundred native nipa huts. Just after supper (no dinner) firing commenced at the outposts and continued intermittently all day. Slept in the open, sharing the blankets of a man in D Troop who worked on the hold detail with me on the *Para*. A bright, clear night, luckily, but cold.

NOVEMBER 9
Troops A, B, D, L of the 4th started out at seven. I went with them on foot. After going six miles commenced to rain hard and I had to stop work on map. Rode bare back the lead horse of Troop B to Puncan fifteen miles from San Jose. An up-hill road through a wonderfully beautiful mountain country with numerous streams and brooks. Finally going through a canyon we heard the advance guard engaged and soon after came on the little village of Puncan of which I saw little save a stone church, being busy "nestling" a pony and bridle and saddle.² Captured here five rifles and some insurgents, one of whom was wounded. Two miles northwest of Puncan crossed a river and took a trail for two miles leading north. It proved to be the wrong one. It was frightful in places. So turned back and retraced way to river, then northwest for four miles and west for one, reaching Caraglan [Carraglan] after dark, about 6:30 P.M. Pony fell with me three times, but I was not hurt. It is impossible to give an idea of the richness of these grassy ridges over which the road led. No trees save in the surrounding mountains, but for miles and miles a carpet of short grass. At times our whole column, four troops in single file, was visible as it wound up and down and around the ridges. A ride which made one forget hunger, rain and fatigue. The most wonderful grazing country I imagine in the world and absolutely deserted, not a hut outside of the towns.

NOVEMBER 10
Scout with details from B and D Troops two miles and up the hills. A beautiful plain Caraglan lies in, five miles by one mile, surrounded by hills. Mountains back of the hills save to the east. Cut an insurgent telegraph line running northeast and southwest. It is thought that the line runs between Tarlac and the new insurgent capital. I forgot to mention yesterday that up in the mountains are trees that look like our pines. In fact the mountain scenery is very similar to the White Mountains. All the streams look like trout brooks, but I

do not know whether the water is cold enough or not. Cut rice for my pony, who is a poor kind of a beast with one hip knocked out, but he saved me a weary march yesterday and may again. Go to sleep now as soon as it is dark and up and breakfast before daylight.

NOVEMBER 11

Caraglan. It is pretty cool up here, not very tropical. One is cold with one blanket at night. There are cocoanuts and large palms growing everywhere, bananas also and some of the palms we have on the piazza at home but growing very high. We are practically living on the emergency ration now. By itself I do not think it would do, but the cooks put caribou meat and rice in it and when you add your hardtack you have a substantial meal. All the hardtack we have by the way is what was issued at Talevera and brought up in haversacks or saddle-bags. Another large capture of cigars yesterday, which resulted in every man getting ten. Some very good houses here, a thriving little settlement but absolutely deserted. An important thing happened this morning. A band of some 180 men armed with bolos and having some two or three mounted officers in uniform came in and gave themselves up and were disarmed. They say there are more behind and a few squads were sent out. I would have gone, but having been told by Col. Hayes that no movement of troops would take place to-day I was washing my only suit of underclothes and of course could not get ready in time. I have an idea that the backbone of the insurrection is broken. Some beautiful Toledo blades among the swords and knives which I would have taken had it not been so impossible to pack it.[3]

NOVEMBER 12

Caraglan. Most of the men very nervous last night, thinking the surrender of the bolo men a ruse and alarmed at an exposed position twenty-five miles from supplies and the army. Just at dusk a detail sent back on the 10th came through with two days' rations packed on their saddles, the men walking. It is to last us four days. This is said by the bolo men to be a great game country (it certainly looks it), though inhabited by rude tribes who fight with spears and bows. The huts here are filled with skins of deer and sheep. The bolo men say they were afraid to stay out longer in the hills. Had a good rest yesterday. The emergency ration is both palatable and filling. Has rained every day since we left San Jose. One wonders at times what is going on in the world or anywhere outside of our column. It is the only drawback to a delightful experience. Cut rice grass for the pony. I saw monkeys running about the trees on the road up here. I don't think I mentioned that when we came in here we released two persons, a man and a woman, the one from the pillory and the other from the stocks. They said their son had just been shot because he would not join the insurgents. This paper was looted at Talevera.

NOVEMBER 13

Left Caraglan at 7 A.M. with Troop B. Headquarters of the 4th Cavalry and the prisoners. A bright day and I got a good map of the country. We crossed one brook about fifteen times and one river six times. I had turned over my broken-down pony and got a good one. Stopped at Puncan one hour for dinner, but as I was with the point we were not notified but munched a few hardtack. Got to San Jose after dark, about 7 P.M., and found to my surprise a good supper waiting, of macaroni and apple sauce, the first time I have had enough since leaving Talevera. A hard day's work through a beautiful country.

NOVEMBER 14

San Jose. A lazy day. Occasional showers, no sunlight. Last night, as usual, I slept in my clothes, sans boots, which was unusual, and as usual was cold in the early morning. Some movement of troops. Gen. Lawton and a troop of the 3rd went to brigade headquarters, which has been moved to St. — thirty miles to the northwest, since I left here. I did not go as I cannot work in the rain. Two Cavalry men got into a fight at dinner and fought it out, but it was not an interesting fight and I was just getting square for my week on short rations so did not pay much attention. Caribou [*caribao*] stew. I find the meat very good, though of course you cannot tell very much about it in a stew. When we came down the mountains yesterday noticed a bunch of cattle grazing about two miles away. It is certainly the finest grazing country in the world. These islands are certainly a treasure. No one who has only seen the rice swamps around Manila can realize their magnificence. Would like to get some news from home, but see no chance of it for weeks. The men in the column behind me shot a deer yesterday. It was eaten today and said to be very nice. I did not get any so cannot say.

NOVEMBER 15

Rain, also rained continuously all night, which means all the rivers are up and I dare say all the bridges and ferries down in our rear. Troops moving to the front all night. The cursed rain keeps me back. I can't sketch in the rain, but I shall go forward trusting to luck soon as I think the end is very near. It has been a wonderful campaign. No one in the States will ever know what the regular enlisted man has cheerfully done and endured. Well planned it was to keep Aggie amused on the railroad with his gorgeous uniforms and magnificent edicts while suddenly this column was launched at his flank and rear. I imagine that even after we started he thought the condition of the roads and the absence of bridges would keep us back, until too late he found that nothing could stop the regular U.S. soldier. News came from the front late last night that his personal baggage and machinery of the government has been taken. With the Cavalry in the mountains he must either fight, surrender or disperse his army. I think he will do the latter.[4] I wish I could get forward. Started with bull train of 22d, 37th, 34th at 1 P.M. Raining hard. Half a mile from the town ran into a morass and were four hours making a mile, breaking the record as all other trains had taken eight or twelve hours. Was dark then, but pushed forward to a mythical town said to be eight miles away. Was so cold my teeth chattered and had to get off the pony and walk to keep up the circulation. At 10 P.M. made a reconnaissance forward two miles and finding no town the outfit camped. Raining hard and cold, no fires, no blanket or poncho, nothing. Ate some raw bacon and hardtack, found a hummock and creeping under the lee of a bush went to sleep.

NOVEMBER 16

None the worse for the experience I cooked some bacon, made a cup of strong coffee and started again in the rain over the worst roads I have seen in the islands which is saying a lot. Used a box compass and notes for the map. Got into Lupas [Lupao] about noon, when the Lieutenant in command of the train hearing another train was stalled in the mud a mile or so out decided to lay over until morning. Plover and other game birds in great plenty along the road. A comfortable meal and smoke with my old friends of F Company, 22d. A greater contrast from last night cannot be imagined.

NOVEMBER 17

No one in our house had a watch, so we got up at about 3 A.M. and cooked breakfast. What a delicious breakfast it was, the bean soup we had for dinner warmed over and fried canned bacon which is just as good as ham. I ate all I could stuff and went to sleep again. Started with the same bull train, but the train of Lowe's scouts passing it I went on with them. They moved faster than any bull train I have ever seen, but were soon passed by the pack train of the same organization and I hiked along (on the pony) with them. Passed through — and St. Quinlan [Quintin] at a trot, so saw nothing of them save that they were both fine towns.[5] A rich country and more populous than I have yet seen in this island. Tyuke [Tayug] at 12:30 P.M. Quartered and messing with the scouts. Roads fearful, mud to the pony's belly. Capt. Ballance and a battalion of the 22d moving on Dagupan from — .[6] Passed some large trees full of the largest bats I have ever seen or heard of.

NOVEMBER 18

Left Tyuke with Lowe's scouts about 7 A.M., arriving St. Nicholas, three and onehalf miles, about 8:30 A.M. It is certainly a most beautiful country, houses everywhere and beautiful rice fields, beautiful verdure-covered mountains on right and front, apparently about three or four miles away I was at the other side of those mountains when I was at Caraglan. Some of the bolo men we captured up there are now serving with the scouts.[7] The white men in the scouts (half are Tagalos) are not very military but I think effective. It looks strange though, to one used to the formalities of the regiments it is not altogether pleasing. This place is about twenty miles from Dagupan. Gens. Lawton and Young are across a river, about three miles from here. That is the front. We can't get across the river, which has risen, so have camped here.[8] No blanket last night, am getting used to it. Slept comfortable. Seized the opportunity for a bath and washed the clothes I have on, the only ones I have had since leaving Cabanatuam. Worked for an hour separating ground coffee from hardtack crumbs in my haversack, they got mixed on the road up here. Learn something every day. That won't happen again. Crows (or are they ravens?) are the commen bird since we were at San Isidro. Saw as many as thirty species of birds on the road from Lupas [Lupao] to Tyuke.

NOVEMBER 19

Had the most vivid, sensible dream last night I have ever had, about lots of things I have not thought of for months and some events of daily occurrence. Oppressed me so much I made up my mind I would be killed today. Did not however prevent my riding with the "point" as usual. Left St. Nicholas about 8 A.M. (Still with Lowe's scouts) and marched (I on the pony) ten and one-third miles to Binalowen [Binalonan] through San — and Bo San Filipe.[9] A populous country with few jungles and much cultivation. The towns are larger and richer than those around Manila and the people more intelligent and apparently more educated. It is God's own country. Crossed two bad river crossings, one where Lieut. Lunar was drowned (Rio Agnow) [Agno]. We were pulled across on rafts by native ferrymen, an interesting sight. Road fairly good and the sunshine enabled me to use the sketching case, which is much easier than a box compass and note-book. This is the Province of Pangasinan and the natives speak a different language front the Tagalos (whom we are fighting) and from the Macabebes.[10] Mountains about five miles from our right, giving beautiful days. To-day's march was west, the first time since we started. We are only six hours from Dagupan. Cows on the road, the first I have seen here. No sooner had we arrived than my friends, the Sergeants in F, 22d, saw me and, it being dinner time, they brought me over a fine mess of boiled caribou and rice. As the rest of the scouts had nothing to eat till supper you can imagine I appreciated it. Gen. Lawton came in at about 6 P.M. We hear Dagupan has fallen, that the insurrection is practically ended but that Aggie escaped with a hundred men. That Gen. Young and a troop of Cavalry is hot on his heels and that Aggie is shot but not killed unfortunately.[11] The 22d tell me that one town they came through welcomed them with a band and cooked meats.

NOVEMBER 20

Left Binalowen about 11 A.M. with Maj. Ballance's battalion of the 22d (A, F, L, K) and marched (I on pony) thirteen miles South, through Ornatuna [Urdaneta] to Vassalis [Villasis], arriving there 4:30 A.M.[12] The battalion is living on the country and half the men have no shoes. No one in the army (Lawton's division) except the Cavalry have blankets or ponchos now. Road very bad, for miles is water waist deep and deep mud at intervals. Road lies through rice fields, which the natives are harvesting, with many small barrios or collections of huts. Drank the milk of green cocoanuts, which are six times as big as the ripe ones and hold about a quart of cool, fresh tasting, colorless liquid. A very populous country. Natives seem glad to see us and bring us sugar and rice. Are much bigger towns than those around Manila, but without the stone buildings.

NOVEMBER 21

I shall really be sorry if the insurrection is indeed ended. I have really enjoyed the hardships, the excitement, the change. I am convinced this is the healthiest climate in the world. We have been "hiked" about in mud and rain, sleeping on the ground without blankets feet and clothes almost continually wet, and yet the men, notwithstanding short rations, are not sick. I do not think I have ever been in better health.

NOVEMBER 22

Vassilis. Native market in full blast. I bought bananas, fried and au natural in enormous quantities for the expenditure of about ten cents, also rice cakes which are very good. Started out with the scouts to the west. All maps show a road west to Malasisqui [Malasique] and all the natives say road does not exist. We went three or four miles through swamp and rice paddies, through T—, a mere collection of native huts, to —, merely six or eight huts in a dense thicket. Every day I think the road the worst I have ever seen, but this was fearful. No dinner and pony pretty tired. Scouts badly played out.

NOVEMBER 23

Vassalis. A damp, foggy morning, a little rain last night. The people about here are a simple agricultural people, who have taken little or no interest in the war and only want to raise their crops of rice in peace. I think they are naturally cruel. I saw them kill a bull yesterday and it was sickening. There are fine cattle hereabouts. All about here they are gathering rice. You hear them pounding it in their rude wooden mortars until very late at night. Left Vassalis at 1 P.M. with Capt. Ballance's battalion, 22d Infantry, and marched thirteen miles back to Binalowen, arriving there at dark (about 6 P.M.) a pleasant ride for me as having already mapped the road had nothing to do but ride the pony and enjoy the scenery and brief sunset. American methods sadly needed in the rice fields, where all the work of harvesting, being done by hand and "bolo," is very slow and laborious. These people (Pangasinans) have never been in the insurgent army.[13]

NOVEMBER 24
Left Binalowen (same organization) and marched eight miles west to Manawag [Manaoag], a small town. A delightful ride for me through a beautiful country. Lots of rice fields and cocoanuts and saw tomatoes and corn growing besides lots of castor beans. Capt. Ballance, who commands the battalion, much interested in the map and had his interpreter give me the names of all small towns and rivers. A battalion of the 33d stationed in Manawag and they are enough to make a man sick. They had marched sixteen miles and had one skirmish and thought they had ended the war and were already (having been here less than three weeks) preparing to go home. "Why," one of them said, "for four days we have had nothing to eat but bacon and hardtack and coffee." That to men who hadn't seen any rations for weeks at a time and had been skirmishing and fighting since October 10.

NOVEMBER 25
An easy ride through San Jacinto to San Fabian, ten miles. The coast and rations at last. A splendid bath in the surf, which came rolling in on a sandy beach. To the right mountains and rich vegetation, to the left towards Dagupan the coast was misty and indistinct. A beautiful picture with a transport rolling and pitching and alive with signals in the distance. This town is about ten miles north of Dagupan, the northern terminus of the railroad. I have marched

and ridden over two hundred miles through mud and rain since October 10 when we left San Fernando and the railroad. Forty-five days on short rations, with no clothes but those a man had on and since I left the company no blanket or poncho, yet I have enjoyed it, which is lucky for my work is not over. I must go back again to the company and begin again. Bed with the roar of the surf in my ears and a bamboo mat over me so that I slept warm for the first time since I left the warm saddle blankets of the Cavalry. The pony is really getting fat, he was a mere bag of bones when I got him. Well has he carried me over about one hundred miles, through mud up to his belly and across river with rocky bottom and swift current and he with no shoes, like the battalion I have been with. No shoes. Poor old battalion. The men have marched and fought without complaining up to the limit of human endurance. Today nearly half of them are on sick report, literally played out.[14] I think I deserve a day's rest myself. I am my own boss now. I have left the company and may take a day or so lay off.

NOVEMBER 26
San Fabian. A glorious sunny day. Washed all my clothes and myself. Another glorious bath in the surf of this beautiful Bay of Linganean [Lingayen]. Hunted cocoanuts and drank their milk. Some of them hold two of our tin cups full of milk. Shall send some letters home from here if I get a chance. I have been carrying them now in my sketching case since Cabanatuan on November 2. Stuck some twenty sheets of this paper together with flour paste for use in the sketching case. They have not got Aggie yet, though the chase is getting hot.

NOVEMBER 27
San Fabian, a beautiful place. Tall cocoanuts and large, graceful palms with leaves twenty and thirty feet long. Watched them, fascinated, as they waved in the ocean breeze between me and the brief tropical sunset. The glow of the firelight from the campfires all made a perfect picture. Then too there was no mud, a thing one has lived in for days. Nights cool and nice to sleep if one has a covering. My bamboo mat does nicely. Found the 3d Cavalry was sending a wagon train forward and that the 22d was to stay and refit. Hated to go, to

leave the comforts of a permanent place and take up the "hike," but felt I ought, so started at 3:30 P.M. and moved north with wagon train and detail of twenty men from Troop F, 3d Cavalry, under Lieut. Ripley.[15] Along beach for the entire distance. We made about three miles before camping for the night. Glorious sunset across the bay. Slept in the open. My bamboo mat, which I use for a saddle cloth by day, is a great institution. Slept warm, every one else complaining of the cold.

NOVEMBER 28

As I sit here just after sunrise it is hard to imagine anything finer, the surf to the left and the hills, a few hundred feet away, rising some two hundred feet abruptly. A pleasant ride along the beach with fishing villages not so unlike ours, then inland over a road that might, save for the difference in architecture, be through Deering. Pretty hot in the middle of the day, but delightful at morning and evening. Camped at sunset about two miles beyond —, having been in the saddle all day and only made twenty miles.[16] A beautiful sunset over the beach, only a quarter of a mile away across the rice field. Cooked my bacon and boiled my coffee, finishing just at dark. Slept under a native hut. Very cold, but kept warm. Many Frenchmen up here, French flags flying everywhere.

NOVEMBER 29

Started at daylight and just had time to cook my breakfast, having got up at 4:30. Another pleasant ride, though hot and tiresome. Reached San Fernando [La Union] a little before noon. Is on the sea with the ruin of a dock. Are unloading supplies from a steamer in small boats. Are about thirty-six miles north of San Fabian. Haven't had time to wash or take off my boots or leggins. Pony standing it well. While I was writing the above we were expecting to move right out. However, in a few moments orders came to remain all night. Swapped the pony, which was an old one in wretched condition, for a fine little beggar. Gave ten dollars to boot. Might have stolen one, but could not make up my mind to from these friendly natives. Is a good beach, about two miles long, with a stone foundation and a pile extension which apparently used to go out to deep water, the beach deepens very suddenly, but is destroyed. The wreck of a large steamer up the beach about a mile from the pier. Had a splendid bath. Have got the dobie itch, a sort of skin disease, very prevalent up here, due to mud and no change of underclothes. Is not a troublesome thing. This used to be a fine town, has a lot of stone houses. Was shelled and the 33d burned part of it by accident.[17] Also part of it seemed to have been destroyed some time ago. French flags flying here also. Stone church, government building and prison around the plaza. Four hundred paces from the plaza to the pier. Hills green with bushes and trees all around the town, perhaps seventy-five feet high. No one here when we got here but sick men, but eight companies of the 33d came in about 4 o'clock. A beautiful road coming up between sea and mountains. They say anything that grows in the United States will grow round here. Not very hot except in middle of day, with beautiful mornings and evenings and cold nights. Some more of the wooden cannons captured in the trenches which line the bills around the town. Will have a house to sleep in tonight, a great luxury. In spite of the hardship one cannot help enjoying the beautiful country and the quaint old towns.

NOVEMBER 30

Through the guard being forgetful the detachment had to rush to get breakfast. As it was I was the only one who made coffee. On a good pony the day's march was a positive pleasure. A cool, stiff breeze made the riding delightful. At one estuary two or three hundred natives were fishing with large nets, making in the clear sunshine and dancing water backed by the green hills a picture such as one seldom sees. At a halt at about 12, to let the train close up, I ate my Thanksgiving dinner with good wishes for the family at home. A splendid green cocoanut, full of milk and with soft meat, and the last of my hardtack was the meal. In the afternoon the wind grew stronger and the cultivated fields were replaced by bush and cactus. To stand on some promontory and watch the coast, the road lies along it the entire distance, white with the foam of the breakers, the spray blowing far inland, was grand. Left the train at a native ferry a few miles below Namacapan and came in with Col. Hare of the 33d and staff, arriving here about 5 P.M. Train not in at 12 P.M. Had no rations or quarters, but found a hospital steward and a Cavalry man, whose horse had played out, keeping house, and they took me in, fed me with meat, rice and coffee, had a bath, plenty of blankets and was fine. Had my clothes off to sleep for the first time since November 3 at Cabanatuan. A good town, fine church and good houses.[18]

DECEMBER 1

For breakfast the three of us ate two fried chickens, a dozen fried eggs and a pot of rice cooked dry, native style, all the coffee you could drink. The best meal I have had on the island. "Hiking" over these fine roads in this beautiful country in fine weather in pursuit of a beaten enemy is another thing altogether from toiling through mud waist deep in pouring rain. This is a pleasant jaunt and is very enjoyable. Started about 10 A.M. and rode ahead of the train four miles to Bangar, crossing the River Bangar one mile from the town on a native ferry. The train was delayed for hours at the ferry, so for two or three hours I was the only American occupant of the town, where I was creating an immense sensation and was surrounded by a crowd of twenty or thirty. Finally, about 4 P.M., the 33d came in. They were met by a band and cheers. Now the sun sets here about 6 P.M. and at 4 the light is soft and beautiful. The old moss-covered stone cathedral, the tree-covered plaza with the soldiers and the white clothed natives, it was all beautiful. The train pulled in about 5 and we went on a mile further, camping just at dusk. Am assigned for rations with Owens, the Cavalry man we picked up at Namacapan, and the Commissary Sergeant of the 22d, who is with the train, also a civilian clerk in the quartermaster's department. Fried chicken and fried potatoes for supper and very good it tasted. Slept in the parlor of a wealthy native, sharing Owens' blankets.

DECEMBER 2

Started at daylight and marched twenty-two miles for Cundoon [Candon]. Fearfully hot, not a breath of wind. Felt it worse than any march yet. Passed first through Tequidin [Tagudin], coming into the town over a long and difficult ford, the fourth or fifth already. It is only about 8 A.M. All the inhabitants working in the immense fields which surround the town and which extend from sea to mountains, about five miles in width and miles long. All church property seems surrounded by ruins, giving it a picturesque air, and all towns in need of repair. Next came Cebilla [Sevilla], a poor town on the coast, with a nipa church and only about one hundred native huts in a straggling settlement. Then Santa Cruz, and here came a native band in uniform preceded by an immense white flag. The population gathered on the plaza to welcome us and had water for the men and rice for the horses. Stayed here for dinner, the band playing all the time, sometimes native airs and sometimes tunes from operas that I knew. Bought cigars (I must smoke twenty or thirty a day) and sugar. Next came Santa Lucia, with the biggest cathedral I have seen outside of Manila, and another band and more welcomes. Stopped only a minute, which time I put in changing the paper on my sketching case, then a tedious march through a beautiful country with fine cocoanut groves, reaching Cundoon about 4. Were delayed at the outskirts of the town by a bad bridge and did not get in until dusk. Found troops here, some of the 3d Cavalry and 33d Infantry. Some one kicked over our coffee just as it was made, causing much profanity. Fried potatoes, bacon and coffee for supper. Slept in a large building with some disabled soldiers. A fine town, the plaza especially fine, the cathedral setting back in a little garden. Many stone houses.

DECEMBER 3
Left Cundoon at daylight (Sunday), a beautiful morning. After a short time mountains appear on our left for the first time after leaving San Fabian, and we cross through a rocky pass and a bad road, coming out suddenly on Santiago with a church and convent, or whatever the buildings next to the church are, perched on a rocky hill like a feudal castle. Another band and more welcomes. Only a short stop and on again to San Esteban which is on the coast again. More stone buildings. No halt. The road from here for a few miles is beautiful beyond words. Honolulu is nothing to it and more than that I can't say. High rocky coasts with deep bays and inlets and wonderful vegetation. Made Santa Maria at about 12 and Gen. Young at last. I have been chasing him since I lost the advance by going up into the mountains with the 4th Cavalry. Started out with the General immediately. He seemed glad to see me and so did his Adjutant General. Lieut. Smedberg invited me to attach myself to his escort which I gladly did.[19] Owens, who has been bunking with me, be-

longs to headquarters, so I have plenty of blankets again. Marched four miles to Narlocean where we were met by a band and assigned to fine quarters with the General. Slept on a bunk for the first time since leaving San Fernando on the railroad.

DECEMBER 5

Started at 7 A.M. and marched about three miles, when we left the highway and went up a very bad trail into the mountains. Soon found the insurgents strongly intrenched on Tennadin Mountain [Tangadan Pass].[20] I went forward to sketch the position and found Gen. Young and his Adjutant reconnoitering from a shady knoll about a mile from the first trench. The General explained the position and disposition he had made with his troops, making me use his field glasses to see better. About 9 o'clock, a long wait while the troops, three troops of Cavalry and some two companies of the 34th, were taking their positions. I smoked and even slept a little and the General told stories about the Civil War and wished for Artillery, for you could see two or three lines of intrenchments up the hill and a redoubt at the top. Gradually the beautiful morning light gave way to the glare of noon and still no shots, though the insurgents were working like beavers on their trenches and their officers sitting in the shade on top of the hill which was about 300 feet high. The first shots were fired at 2:05 P.M. in an attempt to capture the insurgent outpost, an attempt that failed, though the outpost was driven in. At about 3 the troops, except the Infantry which had been sent on a long detour to prevent the insurgents' escape, having reached their positions the firing opened heavily. Thinking it would soon be over I left the General and walked down the road about half a mile in order to complete my sketch before dark. Bullets were flying overhead which I did not mind, but when they began to cut the grass and bushes near me and to sound as if they had blankets tied to them (those were the ricochets) I got into a ditch with considerable promptness. I found I had inadvertently got in advance of our skirmish line which was on the plain on both sides of the road. Firing heavier and more continuous than I have ever heard. Had a fine view of the trenches which were above me and straight ahead. Was perfectly safe as long as I staid in the ditch, and as I was out of sight of our men, and where I had no business where I was. I staid there smoking cigars. The sun began to get low and still our lines did not seem to be getting very much further forward. About 5 P.M. heard the welcome sound of the Infantry behind the insurgents' position, and, fearing to miss something, came out of my ditch and walked down the road, not slowly either, until I came in sight of our troops when I assumed an air of nonchalance and leisure. Firing very heavily and the wounded began to drift to the rear. The sun sank and I thought for a moment they would stand us off. A battalion of the 33d arrived and were held in reserve, losing a man, shot through the head, a good half a mile behind us. Got the lower trenches but the redoubt still held out. It got dark and thinking ourselves no longer visible got on our horses just in time to have Mausers cut the air above us. Got off our horses at the General's order and watched the light flashes come up the hill. A brand new moon about ten degrees above the horizon. Soon heard the yells of the men as they charged trench after trench and finally about 7 P.M., after an hour and a half of darkness, prolonged and continuous cheering. They had got the redoubt. "Well," said the General, "that was and is more like war than anything I have seen in these islands." Mounted and rode through the darkness over a horrible trail, expecting to have the pony break his neck or mine every minute, to the entrenchment where the General by means of bugles and hollering, got reports from his troops now scattered over five miles of very rough country. Very nice to hear the reports from the mountain tops repeated time and time again in the perfect stillness. (The bugles had blown attention.) Eight men wounded and one killed were our casualties, "Don't bother about the niggers tonight." Soon the hum of talk broke out everywhere, the men camped where they were and fires were lighted everywhere. Very picturesque. We rode back to the first barrio (about a mile), where the General found a house. So did Owens and I, who bunked in with a native family who cooked us a fine supper of chicken and rice and vegetables before we went to bed. Bed about 11 P.M. The battle of Tengadin Mountain.

DECEMBER 6
Left Lungar, which is the name of the little Bo where we spent the night, and rode down the trail three miles to the river, crossing where we left the main road, and halted for breakfast. Started again at 9

and rode some fifteen miles through Santa — to Vigan, the second biggest town in the islands.[21] About a third of the way the road, passing along the beach between the mountains and the sea, was wild and interesting. The rest through a shady plain was not. Noticed though the wells and watering troughs were large and exactly like those we see in illustrations of the Bible. Dead insurgents in the road and river just before coming into Vigan and found that they had stood off a desperate night attack the day before.[22]

DECEMBER 7
Got up late, having been wakened twice by heavy firing on the outposts. In the afternoon a reconnaissance to find some trenches the insurgents had been said to be building. No trenches there. Sailors and marines are helping garrison this place. Was sent, with two privates as escort, back to Tengadin Mountain to make a more complete map than was possible under fire.[23] Reached there at about 4 P.M., late to make much more than a beginning. Slept in the same house as before. The two privates with me very nervous and begged to go back five miles further to camp. Would not do it.

DECEMBER 8
Got up an hour before daylight, breakfast and started for the trenches which were so strong as to make it seem impossible to take them, the one on the summit is at least 400 feet above the plain across a trail that is all but impassable for a horse. A half a mile further on is a field intrenchment a good profile with trench and firing platform and sodded slopes. This was taken the next morning. Dead insurrectos in the woods, not a pleasing sight. The Cavalry rode back to join their troop and I rode back to Vigan, eighteen miles, alone.

DECEMBER 9
Drew clothes, which I sadly needed, and drew (no pun intended) the map of the battlefield.

DECEMBER 10
Left Vigan at 6 A.M. with Troops A and H, 3d Cavalry, commanded by Maj. Schweigert [Swigert]. Troops reduced to a total of ninety-

four men by the campaign, should have two hundred and forty. Passed through Botni [Bantay?], San Idelfonso, Santo Domingo, Masignal [Magsignai], La Pot [Lupog], Saboogan, into Sinite [Sinait].[24] With the exception of Botni, which is just across the brackish stream from Vigan, all the towns were large, having a good number of stone dwelling-houses and many streets with stone culverts. The highway is the ruin of a fine macadamized road with ditches and stone culverts. Many magnificent and decorative stout bridges over the streams. On one I noticed the date 1849. Altogether it was a fine day's ride, the little pony going well, and much enjoyed. I am messed and quartered with the battalion Sergeant Major and so got a good room and bunk in the church buildings. Got a government saddle and saddle blanket while I was with brigade headquarters, so am comfortable and can carry clean clothes. Every one expected a night attack, so slept with my boots and revolver on. Twenty-one miles.

DECEMBER 11
Left Sinite at 7:15 and had an easy ride to Batac [Batag], eighteen miles.[25] I always ride with the advance guard, so escape the dust. Reached Batac, coming through Badoc and leaving Pauai [Paoay] on our left, about 1:15. A courier here overtook us and so we left tile wagons and main road and struck for the mountains to the east of the town.[26] Rode across rice paddies, very rough riding as any one knows who has ever seen a rice field, and finally followed up a creek bottom till about three miles from Batac we, the advance party, suddenly turned a corner and were right on top of five insurgents with rifles. The surprise was mutual, but American nerve beats tropical every time and we bagged three, leaving two escaped. It was dusk now and Maj. Schweigert ordered a camp, there happening to be a little plateau on our right plenty large enough to accommodate our reduced troops. Surrounded by hills, but the insurgents have not "sabe" enough to know the advantage that gives them. Slept in the open, bunking down with a little trumpeter attached to headquarters. Owing to the proximity of the insurgents slept with revolver and boots on.

Started at daylight and went up the creek bed, a steep and difficult trail, until the guides said the insurgents were right ahead.[27] Troops dismounted, leaving the horses on another little plateau, and then forward on foot for perhaps a mile, trail steep and difficult, when the firing commenced and soon became general. Troop, deployed. I accompanied the skirmish line of K Troop. Insurgents plainly visible and bullets singing overhead, some twelve volleys firing, much firing from A Troop on our left. Country fearful for fighting (we were well up in the mountains), being much cut up with almost perpendicular ravines and water courses. Finally rested. Pretty well blown, on the top of a little hill, firing still continued, and commenced to write up my notes, regarding the whole affair as a joke, when word came that a man in A Troop was killed. Poor fellow, he was buried where he fell with five insurgents, not buried, to keep him company. It were easy to wax sentimental was there time. A considerable wait while the horses were brought up (I came near losing my pony who broke away, as it was I chased him much nearer the insurgents than I cared to go and much further than I would had he not had all my rations, the blanket I had been so long without and clean underclothes strapped to his saddle), then forward again for another mile, when we were fired on again from ambush and lost another man killed and one wounded. Finally the ambush was discovered and the men run out. The rest is not pretty reading, but it seemed natural enough at the time, when men had been toiling and fighting (it was now 3 P.M.) in the broiling sun all day. When the men in ambush, they were in a cave, were located they were rushed and ran, threw away guns, etc., and turned weeping saying, "Much amigo, you amigo," —bang, the last from a revolver. When it was over there were three "good" insurrectos, and incidentally a man had a carbine broken off short at the stock. Another hasty burial, and then a climb as straight up as it is possible to go for a thousand feet and then three miles along the ridge top, commanding two as beautiful valleys as it is possible to see. The trail was frightful, horses falling and rolling, and hot and tired men swearing, and officers hurrying the little column ahead. It was sunset when we began to descend into the little town of Banne [Banna], some 1,000 feet below us and three or four miles away. The artist that painted the sunset in the mountains that grandma has in her gallery was a genius. I thought of that picture a thousand times and will own it, if money can buy it and I get out of this alive, to commemorate this day. Reached Banne at dark without the expected fight and in ten minutes the dead were forgotten in the bustle of watering, grooming, cooking supper and bargaining for eggs "eclog" in Illoco, in which province we are. Slept in the schoolhouse without boots or revolver.

DECEMBER 13
Left Banne, a small mountain town, at 7:15 and marched eight miles to Dingrass [Dingras], a large city. What lies the Spaniards told about these islands. Where we were told to expect wild, fierce natives we find fine turnpikes, rich, prosperous cities and a population that care less about this so-called insurrection than the average New England farmer. Every one in the fields harvesting rice. It is almost incredible, but every spear of rice is picked separately and by hand. Imagine the task! Left the main road at Dingrass and followed a rough road towards Piddag [Piddig]. About half-way caught a fine road and the rest was easy. Eleven miles from Banne. Quartered with headquarters in the church buildings. After supper, bacon, hardtack, coffee and scrambled eggs, it was dark, but the moon was visible flooding the valley with light and showing up the picturesque, tree-buried town and the distant mountains. A band came up to serenade the Major and with it a crowd of white-clothed natives. They played well and I sat in one of the deep stone windows listening to them for an hour or two. It was too beautiful to be real, like a scene from fairy land or some beautiful stage picture. I really wondered what I had done to deserve such happiness and beauty. Every one felt it. It was the most perfect evening imaginable. Just as I was wondering whether I would not be shot to pay for it some one came up with the pleasing intelligence that the little pony had run away, so I had to turn out and hunt him, which I did for over an hour without success, only stopping when the outposts came near shooting me once or twice, which was partly due to it being unusual for any one to wander about at that hour and partly to "bino," of which the town was full. I was sorry to lose the little beggar (my feet were only four inches from the ground), but I suppose he was

tired of his job and I don't blame him as he had all the weight to carry that a big horse has. A Troop sent off with the 37th bull train.

DECEMBER 14

Left Piddag with K Troop and headquarters at 7 A.M. and marched eleven miles to Laoag, passing through San Miguel. Reached Laoag, the capital of Illocus [Ilocos] Norte, at 10 A.M., where we staid two hours. This town, which is only a few miles from the seacoast, has been previously occupied by the marines. Drew three days' rations and left Maj. Schweigert there as Military Governor of Illoco Norte. Pushed on with K Troop, Capt. Hunter, making fourteen miles more, passing through Baccarae [Bacarra] and Pasuquin, both large towns, finally camping on the beach about four miles north of Pasuquin, having made twenty-five miles to-day.[28]

DECEMBER 15

Started at 6:40 A.M. and marched twenty-five miles to Banqui [Bangui], passing through Salona [Solsona?], a small fishing town, passing a lighthouse which marks the northwest corner of the islands, turned south for the first time since leaving San Fernando, Pampanga, and then due east up over the mountains (some 2,000 feet) on to an elevated tableland, to the little town of Nagpartian, where we stopped to cook coffee.[29] On again till we descended sharply on to the settlement of Banan, and then on to Banqui, which we reached at 3:45 P.M. Found the town held by marines and Gen. Young on the *Wheeling* in the bay.[30] The country to-day wild and chiefly chaparral.

DECEMBER 16

A much appreciated lay off, a bath and clean clothes. I have plenty since leaving Vigan. The General sailed to the south. Ate dinner off a table for the first time in months. Heard our first news of the war in the Transvaal.[31] This little town of Banqui is a pretty place with a tree-covered plaza surrounded by a few old stone buildings. We are on the north coast of the island, where it is cool all the time in the shade and only hot in the sun in the middle of the day. It is like our October at home. The *Wheeling* left some papers and magazines here and I enjoyed the luxury of reading in an armchair, with nothing on hand to worry me, for the first time since leaving home. Am messing with the Sergeants, so all I have to do is to groom and water my pony.

DECEMBER 17

After I had gone to sleep last night was awakened by whispered orders to put on boots and be ready to turn out at a minute's notice.[32] It seems that the Presidente of the next town had sent in word that a party of insurgents had just passed through his town moving this way. Our little troop of forty-eight men is up here to head off the enemy retreating northward. Nothing came of it but another night in boots and revolver. No mail for over two months and no chance of getting any for heaven knows how long. Accompanied the Doctor in a house-to-house search after incriminating documents which we did not find. Did find a pair of American leggins (by the way, at our last fight the insurgents had American leggins, uniforms and mess kits, presumably taken from the American transport wrecked at San Fernando de Union), which we promptly confiscated as well as some blank paper which we took and of which I obtained a good share which I sadly needed, this being my last sheet. Took a bath in the surf and admired the curving beach backed by the mountains. The notes of the birds about here suggest the Maine woods very strongly. There is a bird whose call is so like the alarm note of the robin as to bring visions of home up with startling distinctness, also a bird which I have never seen with a note like the black-throated green warbler, and one similar to the hermit thrush. Some strange, wild-looking natives came out of the mountains today, naked except for a "G" string.[33] Read the October magazines and the *New York Sun* containing an account of the race for the American Cup.' The most restful, luxurious day I have had since I have been in the army.

DECEMBER 18

Banqui (Ban-key). Another lazy day with no duties except to eat and water the pony. Read a good deal and wrote. Am speculating now as to where and how I shall spend Christmas. Now speculating is a foolish thing for a soldier to waste time on, but I have not forgotten my Thanksgiving dinner, when I threw prudence to the winds and recklessly ate the whole of my hardtack (about a double handful of crumbs) with a cocoanut. That was an indiscretion I should have paid for by going supperless to bed was it not for Owens, whom I ran across as I was disconsolately wandering about Nammacpacan some four hours ahead of the train to which I was then attached. It was the beginning of a very pleasant friendship. The orders for horse exercise have suddenly been changed and the troop has turned out in a hurry, too quick for me to go with them, leaving only a guard. The church bell rings violently and the ringer is arrested. I go out with the troop. The falsest kind of a false alarm and I soon return.

DECEMBER 19
Banqui, province Illoco Norte. I don't think I have mentioned the old Sergeant (Lanney, twenty-two years in the service) who has made my lot such a comfortable one since I have been with K Troop. He is Remington's beau ideal of a cavalry sergeant. To see him at the head of the column, he always had the advance guard and I always ride with it, is a delight to the eye. Thin and wiry, he seems a part of the horse, the best in the troop, by the way, he rides. Long service on the Indian frontier has made him cautious, and the advance guard is run as an advance guard should be run, to the discomfort, openly expressed, of the men who are apt, unless the enemy is seen, to look at the advance as an opportunity to "rustle" and a freedom from the restraint of the column. He took a fancy to me and so I share all his privileges, of having my meals cooked, dishes washed and the pony fed. Also I always get good quarters, sleeping next to him, and listen for hours to tales of the frontier and the army in the old days "before the war," a phrase which has shifted its meaning forward some thirty years. The *Wheeling* and General Young appeared in the bay at daylight with orders, but what they were I do not know.

Shall I, now I have time, describe a day's march, any day since the rain stopped on November 17, Infantry, wagon train or Cavalry they are all the same, only at the end of a day with the Cavalry you have more miles to your credit. Well, the bugles sound first call about an hour before daylight and you get up instantly, for the time is short enough at the best. First the pony must be fed from the supply collected the night before and then you make your little fire, boil your coffee in your tin cup and fry your bacon in your mess pan. The first streaks of dawn are visible as you commence to eat, eating everything, even the grease, in which you hastily crumble a few hardtack (three is a meal). Daylight comes with a rush in the Tropics and you barely have time to saddle up before the column moves. For an hour or two it is dreamlike, cool and the country of surpassing beauty, then it gets hot and hotter and the monotony of counting the pony's steps, the only means of accurately gauging distance, becomes wearing, until finally about 12, in a town if you are lucky, in the open if you're not, the column halts. If you are with Cavalry coffee is cooked, if you are with anything else you don't but hastily munch two hardtack, so as to have four for supper, and eat some native sugar or a few bananas. Then on again, it growing cooler and cooler, until the order is given to camp for the night. Sometimes this is at 4 o'clock, sometimes at dusk, sometimes after dark, in a town or settlement or in the open fields. Now at whatever hour it is the first thing is feed for the pony, which I buy if the natives are handy, in the Cavalry the buying is done for me, or cut in some convenient rice field. Then the supper, which is breakfast over again, is cooked and eaten, and then all except the unfortunates whose turn it is to do outpost roll themselves in their blankets, in a house if one is near, on the ground if one is not, and sleep the sleep of healthy, tired men, to wake and do the same the next and the next day, and so on for weeks, as these rough and necessarily incomplete notes must show. This is the eighth province I have been in, Manila, Bulcan [Bulacan], Pampanga, Neueva Ecija, Pangasman [Pangasinan], [La] Union, Illoco [Ilocos] Sur and Illoco [Ilocos] Norte, in the order in which I entered them.

DECEMBER 20
Banqui. If I ruin my health out here, it is perfect now, I will do it by smoking which I do incessantly, cigars being plenty, cheap, you can get twenty for ten cents, and very good. The result is I am seldom without a cigar between my teeth. The beach here is not like that hitherto met. There are no cocoanuts, their place being taken chiefly by trees full of delicious mandarin oranges which are

not as picturesque, and the hills which rise all about and in places out of the bay have not the luxuriant growth of trees. It is more like the chalk cliffs of England, minus the chalk. On the bay native fishermen work all day in heavy canoes hollowed with infinite patience and skill from a single log. Three men cannot lift one and being narrow they would not stay upright a moment were it not for outriggers of the useful bamboo. Very little return they seem to get for their labors. I have discovered one fact in natural history new to me, that is that bananas cannot be ripened on the trees, where they run to seed, but must be picked green and ripened artificially. This, by the way, I learned at San Fernando Pampanga, but have had no time to write it till this welcome lay off, which I only get because situated as we are forty miles from the nearest troops I can't get back and the troop isn't going forward. An insurgent officer came in to see about surrendering his men, the same that gave us our alarm a night or so ago. I do not know what conclusion was reached. He left any way after about an hour's talk with the Captain. A slight shower this afternoon, the first drop that has fallen since the rain ceased so suddenly on the 17th of November. A slight earthquake shock last night at 11:20. This phenomena of earthquakes accounts for the ruinous condition of so many fine stone buildings which, in the majority of instances, have had no repairs since this fine country became unsettled some six or ten years ago. I do not remember saying anything of the Spanish troops (prisoners of Aguinaldo) that we, commencing at San Isidro, have been releasing at every town we took. Sometimes by ones and twos, finally as the insurrection waned by hundreds. Of their extravagant expressions of joy, hugging and kissing each other or any one who would let them. I was very sympathetic at first, but when a Spanish Major or Colonel stole four days' rations from Owens and I at Vigan and we had to beg, borrow and steal for just that period, I kind of lost interest and all sympathy, which they never deserved after surrendering to such poor fighters as Aggie's boasted army turned out to be. Why, if they had been any good (the insurrectos), well, there would be no one in Gen. Young's column left alive. We have no real right to be here, we ought all to be dead by side of some mud hole or impassable ford, as we wandered in the jungle, or by some mountain pass.

Bangui Bay. Courtesy Joseph P. McCallus.

DECEMBER 21

Banqui. The laziest kind of a lazy life, but very enjoyable after the haste and bustle of the last ten weeks. There is magnificent surf bathing here. We live well on chickens and eggs, an addition to our regular ration, which is much appreciated. Of course I do not imagine for a moment that these things are paid for, but they taste as good as if they were. Also we have goats which make good steaks and stews. At present we are out of bacon, which complicates the culinary operations as grease is lacking. It is true that hogs are plenty, but they, being the scavengers of this island, have habits so openly disgusting that even the natives do not eat them unless caged and fed for some time previously. I happened to see in the papers a discussion as to whether a certain officer carried a sword on a certain occasion. Certainly not. I have not seen one in the army outside of Manila. Even the Cavalry have discarded their sabres. Rain all last night and this morning. I devoutly hope it does not last.

DECEMBER 22

Banqui. The *Wheeling* steamed into the bay about 4 P.M. yesterday, bringing the pleasing intelligence that Gen. Tinero [Tinio], the same who gave us our scrap at Tengardin Mountain, was moving on the town with 1,500 men.[34] We have forty-eight. They evidently thought the crisis acute for they tried immediately to land sailors and marines, a thing the tremendous surf and darkness soon put a stop to. They kept the search-light playing on the hills all night. Personally I refused to get excited and got my usual good night's sleep, which anxiety has only kept from me twice since I have been here. Once, the first night at Aperlit, last August, and the other recently, when the young troopers kept we awake most of the night we spent alone on the battlefield. They were sure their last hour had come and after talking about it for hours, once even seriously considering (they would have done it had I not shamed them out of it) saddling up and riding for their lives, they ended by making me nearly as nervous as they were. It is of interest to note that a day or two later, while I was still at Vigan, one of those two shot the other, while drunk on "bino," during a dispute on their courage. A glorious Indian summer day. Sent some mail, including a report to my Lieutenant, by the *Wheeling*.

DECEMBER 23

Banqui. I was thinking last night how extremely lucky I was. I would not take many thousand dollars for the last months. Had I been an officer I could not have seen as much as I have on this delightful detail, drifting from one command to another but always keeping up with the advance. It has been glorious. Word came with the *Princeton* of Gen. Lawton's death.[35] Every one extremely sorry. Perfect weather. It is a pleasure to be alive. The accounts of the fighting in the Transvaal are beginning to reach us. A war worthy of the name. Also reflections of our own campaign, but all so distorted and untrue as to be unrecognizable unless the names of regiments are distinctly given.

DECEMBER 24

Banqui. The day before Christmas. Even the most unimaginative are picturing what is going on in the States. Last Christmas I was at home and I can imagine very exactly what is going on. The papers we are getting from the war ships speak of the insurrection as over. I can't say whether I am sorry or glad. One thing I am glad of, that I came in the ranks with the Regulars and not with a commission in the Volunteers. A bath in a pool in a bamboo thicket with hard, sandy bottom and cool, limpid water. What folly to talk of the Baths of Caracalla. How flat seems the memory of the swimming tank at the University Club. To-day being Sunday the natives all came in to church in considerable numbers. The fresh, clean costumes of the women were really quite attractive. A good many men also went to the service in scrupulously clean costumes and with handkerchiefs on their heads, so folded as to form a sort of crown, the top of the head being bare with a point sticking up behind.

DECEMBER 25

Banqui. Christmas in the Tropics. A glorious fall day without the chill that fall brings in the latitude of New England. The natives made here a great ado about Christmas Eve, sitting up till long after 12 to watch a little theatrical performance which was played in front of our quarters. It must have been a very funny play as the audience screamed with laughter, but of course the dialogue was in Illoco so we could tell nothing about it except by the actions. I judge the play was not dissimilar, by that, from those performed at country fairs by strolling players. At midnight there was mass in the old stone church and much ringing of bells and playing of the band. In the midst of it all, land and ominous, two shots from the outpost. Instinctively you reached for your revolver and waited for the volley that follows the discovery of an approaching column. It did not come and "I guess the outpost saw a ghost," with which the incident closed. Every once in a while the Presidente would translate a joke on Aggie or the wane of the insurrection. I noticed they were always received with applause and laughter, though it is not hard to imagine that in some cases it was a little forced. To-day again the town is full of the bright holiday costumes of the women coming to church, to which, by the way, they are summoned by a brass band and drum corps, which plays in the intervals when the bells are not ringing. As I write, with the sound of the singing coming in at the open windows, we are quartered next to the church, you might easily, if you cast no glance at the surroundings, imagine yourself in New York, but as to

Christmas, no effort of the imagination can make it seem anything like that. One of the marines is a Salem boy who has often been to Portland. He having known people there whom I have never heard of makes it a bit awkward at times, but my inventive faculty stands me in good stead. Did I mention that the Sergeant Major of this squadron, we left him at Laog [Laoag], was an old Portland boy named Reese. In talking to the Doctor off the *Wheeling* last night I was surprised to learn that there was no blockade of any of the coast until last September, that all these cities then held by the insurgents were allowed to trade with the world with perfect freedom, that American men-of-war have been ordered out, and have gone, of ports where vessels flying the American flag were discharging cargoes. It was remarkable the number of people that were in the church, remarkable too the silks and satins the women wore since when we first arrived every one was more than poorly dressed. The soldiers and sailors were all out to watch the natives and the natives were crowding round to see the soldiers, so it was very gay. Then the Presidente took his "Principals" and all their male and female relatives in to call on the officers. A box of hardtack was opened and distributed to the crowd. The natives are very fond of hardtack. They would rather have it than money, and so they jostled each other and scrambled, men, women and children, making a very lively and bright-colored scene. Then we came in and ate our Christmas dinner, which was a mutton stew with hardtack and coffee, with fried bananas and sugar for dessert. In the evening the Presidente gave a dance in his house. Just as I was turning in, bang, bang, bang, three shots in rapid succession from No. 2 outpost. Not hearing any answering shots I was going to bed, but the little naval officer became at once tremendously excited and caused the bugles to blow "assembly" lights put out and the crazy sailors to "man the windows." I noticed in one room that it did not occur to them to throw back the glass windows so I did it, dreading the shower of glass. Of course it was a false alarm. Luckily the dance was not broken up, the shots not being heard there.

DECEMBER 26
Banqui. Nothing exciting happened to-day unless you count the official flagraising which took place this morning, the troops, sol-

diers, sailors and marines being drawn up and presenting arms, the populace shouting, "Viva." Later the crazy sailors succeeded in burning up their signal station and a belt or two of ammunition. Sailors are all very well at sea, but they are like the Volunteers the moment you put them on shore.

DECEMBER 27

Should any one ask what I have to do, pocketed in this out-of-the-way spot, the answer is delightfully simple. Nothing. I have not a single duty. It is true that I water and groom the pony, but I need not do that. He is mine and if I wish to turn him loose and get another when we move on no one will care. So I read old magazines and loaf and talk and smoke, bathe in the surf or in the clear, running brooks, eat with wonderful appetite when "mess gear," as the sailors call it, blows, sleep with a soundness that defies description and wonder how it was possible for me to endure the life I led in New York for five weeks, let alone for years. There is no use disguising the fact, I have found what suits me, and that even though I realize that I have been exceptionally lucky in having a detail that allows me to wander without restraint where my own sweet fancy dictates.

DECEMBER 28

Banqui. Being worried about my enforced idleness spoke to Capt. Hunter about it. He said, "You stay right here." As that puts my remaining on his shoulders I was perfectly content, more than pleased, in fact, as I like the men in K Troop, like too the hill-surrounded, bay-bordered little town and its Arcadian population. When I take the pony to water along the smooth, shady street, watching the early sunlight streaming through the mountain passes, listening to the birds and playing cowboy with the lariat, I wonder at the foolishness that keeps otherwise intelligent men cooped up in large cities. More shots last night from the outposts and a man with a rifle captured. I don't know why it is, but when you are awakened from a sound sleep by firing there are a few seconds that your heart beats very quickly. I have inquired and find that it affects every one the same way. I imagine it is nervous expectancy. I have not felt it in a fight nor in a night attack after it has commenced. A splendid chance to write letters, was not paper scarce and envelopes without price. I had plenty, but alas, all my carefully considered equipment was left with the company when I left it for, as I thought, a few days on the 3d of last November. Went out with the troop for perhaps three miles north of Banqui, but there was nothing developed but a great number of rivers with rocky fords. Had the pony shod.

DECEMBER 30
Banqui. Nothing exciting yesterday or to-day.

DECEMBER 31
Banqui. Half rations again, owing to the *Wheeling* having an "empty ship." Three months ago this would have occasioned much real hardship. Our time during which we drew no rations was not without its lesson, and now it is indifferent to us, barring coffee and hardtack, whether we draw rations or not. For dinner to-day chicken soup, boiled sweet potatoes, boiled rice, coffee and hardtack, with bananas for dessert. The troop has discovered a "cache" and, learning from the bitterness of past experience the promptness with which the Government confiscates, the officers have not been informed. Poker, a dollar ante, is a common sight. Every one has money to burn. I estimate there must be several thousand dollars in the troop. It is of course possible that the sudden influx of wealth has been noticed, but the impossibility of detection—soldiers are like children at school when the question of informing comes up—may have stopped any investigation. Saw Lieut. W. H. C., Jr.'s record published in a Manila paper with an account of some entertainment he gave.[36] I think I am happier in the ranks than I will ever be anywhere else. Not for thousands would I give up the experiences of the last few months.

JANUARY 1, 1900
Banqui. *Wheeling* sailed this morning, taking the sailors and marines and leaving us alone again. A sort of "festa." Many strange people here, are dressed in their best. A pretty scene. One thing I have noticed recently which explains in a measure the difference between Regulars and Volunteers. Capt. Hunter, who is somewhat irascible, occasionally loses his temper at the troop and slangs them deadfully. They don't take it like Volunteers, but in grim silence,

explaining it afterward to such on-lookers as might happen to bear it and invariably ending by telling stories of his youngest boy, who is a great favorite with them. That, then, is the greatest difference. The Regulars know their officers, know their wives and children and who the wives were before they married. It gives them a personal interest and pride in the officer, since if they do not like him they are sure to like some member of his family. That is from the very nature of things lacking in even the best Volunteers. It never occurs to even a recruit in the Regulars to disobey. He would not find the sympathy which such doings gain in the Volunteers, where it seems to be considered smart and manly to show that they have no respect for an officer.

JANUARY 2

The rain commenced last evening and lasted all night. A tremendous surf on the beach. Two couriers came in yesterday (natives) with orders for K troop to proceed to Laog. Gen. Young takes Gen. Lawton's place on the "south line." I hear my company went there a month ago.[37] I am homeless now. My work is finished. I have made the map of Gen. Young's advance from San Fernando, Pampanga, to Banqui on the north coast, some 500 miles of road. What next? Quien sabe. But I go on with K Troop for want of orders. It is funny, but there is now no one on the "north line" to give them to me. I think I must make my way to Manila. Who would think that the death of Gen. Lawton made so much difference to a private soldier. The town seems lonely without the sailors and marines. Three outposts instead of the eight we had when they were here. Raining hard.

Manila

*T*HE EVENTS IN NORTHERN LUZON during the fall of 1899 proved to be the turning point of the war. With the near eradication of the Tinio Brigade at Vigan, Tangadan Mountain, and later Dingras, coupled with Aguinaldo's vagabond condition hiding in the central Luzon mountains, formal military resistance to the United States died early in 1900. Although sporadic, uncoordinated guerrilla activity flourished in some areas over the next two years (at times with shocking brutality on both sides), U.S. troops occupied all geographic areas of importance by the summer of 1900. Cultivating a cadre of Filipino politicians and businessmen, the Americans established in town after town and province after province an occupation called by some a progressive colonialism or a benevolent assimilation. To others it was simple imperialism. Whatever the title, Filipinos settled into the uneasy routine of American rule. The once fire-breathing U.S. soldier was now a security guard a long way from home.

The "hike" through northern Luzon was also the apex of Brown's military career. The destruction of Filipino forces ended his days as a trooper, and the turn of the new century brought him the sickness that would end his life. The typhoid he contracted on the march showed its first symptoms in Laoag. Brown, en route to Manila, arrived in Vigan and there was ordered to make a copy of his maps. After several weeks of being sick, often in a stupor, he seemingly recovered and threw himself into the work of finishing his maps. That done, he was sent to Manila for an extended rest. It was, however, the beginning of the end.

Now out of an Intramuros office in Manila, the headquarters of all U.S. military forces in the islands, Brown adjusted to the life of drafting and relaxation. After redrawing the maps, his steady work was rewarded with promotion to corporal. Brown seems content, responding well to the comforts of city life. Indeed, it is during his stay in Manila that the diarist reveals himself as a gentleman, or as he puts it, "a great swell."

Brown the adventurer, the man of action and martial spirit, was replaced by the Brown who enjoyed European cuisine, cocktails, Dickens and Kipling, and the promenade around the Luneta. It would have been easy for him to enjoy Manila. The city was an exhilarating place for a young American. The (presumed) end of the war brought an influx of many nationalities, contributing to the already cosmopolitan atmosphere of the three-hundred-thousand-person city. Social change and financial opportunity were in the air. Brown found his environment "fascinating." Adding to his enjoyment was his cousin Billy—William Clifford, a Marine Corps first lieutenant stationed at the naval base in nearby Cavite. They socialized together, regardless of the protocol between officer and enlisted man. These were his happiest moments in the Philippines.

Tempering his professional satisfaction and personal contentment are the occasional references to sickness and death, ideas that become increasingly more pronounced as the year progresses. Clearly, his experience with serious illness in January and the ensuing relapse the next month dilated his sense of mortality. He ponders a letter from a comrade sent home because of dysentery and considers the fate of a soldier dying of cancer. On his twenty-eighth birthday he notes that all the numbers add up to ten; thinking it superstitious, he attempts to convince himself that "I do not regret coming out here as I did."

From January through April Brown visited the three principal cities of Luzon: brief stays in Laoag and Vigan and an extended one in Manila. It is noteworthy that today one can still see the sights and landmarks on which Brown comments. Laoag, where the blocky bell tower still stands in the center square, remains the de facto capital of Ilocandia and reflects the serious, industrious nature of the region. Perhaps it is now more susceptible to Asian influences than American: one of Laoag's greatest resources are the Taiwanese who fly in to gamble in the resorts just outside of the city.

Vigan is today perhaps the most progressive city in the Philippines. More than anywhere else in the country it has preserved its architectural heritage. One can see virtually the identical sights Brown saw in center city Vigan, including the cobblestone streets pounded by the horses and *calesas,* the stucco houses, and the magnificent plaza shouldered by the Vigan cathedral. The city is dotted with grand nineteenth-century villas, many now operating as bed-and-breakfast establishments. Unfortunately, the seminary in which Brown was quartered burned down in the 1980s.

The American occupation of Vigan and the plaza is recalled on a memorial plaque at the front of the church.

Of all the locations that Brown visited during his Philippine experience, the city of Manila is the least recognizable today. A critical link during the Spanish galleon trade, the city, like its European master, degenerated into secondary importance during the nineteenth century. Then came the Americans. Manila was the ideal of exotic romanticism during the first part of the twentieth century, a city that conjured images of heat and sensuality, servants and white sharkskin suits—a Hollywood picture of colonialism. Then came the Japanese. Unlike Vigan, which survived the war unscathed, Manila had practically its entire architectural heritage reduced to rubble by Japanese bombers and American artillery. In 1945, the Battle of Manila, in which the Ermita and Malate areas absorbed the brunt of the fighting, claimed a half-million lives. Postwar Manila, a hastily rebuilt city without colonial influence, is a sprawling conglomeration of cities and communities known as Metro Manila. It houses over 10 million people, many of them impoverished migrants from the provinces. Despite the extensive changes, it still offers some of the sights that fascinated Brown. Malacanang Palace, where the miltary governors lived and which Brown certainly saw, became the presidential house in the 1930s. It was here that Pres. Ferdinand Marcos and his family beat a hasty retreat from the enraged masses in 1986. The Escolta is still there, although today it is a shadow of its boisterous self. The Luneta is basically in the same location, although its shape and dimensions are different. Some architecture did survive the war: Brown would recognize Intramuros and Fort Santiago (both are now being gentrified), and also the Malate Church (the convent has been replaced). Perhaps most interesting is Fort San Antonio Abad, what Brown called "Fort Malate." The old fort, once on the shore, is now several hundred yards inland, the result of a massive dredging and filling of Manila's harbor. Fort San Antonio Abad was restored during the Marcos years and is now situated next to a huge Stalinesque building that houses the national monetary administration, creating a visual contrast long remembered. Brown's sentimental vision of the moss-covered walls and the "haughty old Dons" has long since succumbed—like Manila's claim of being the "Pearl of the Orient"—to the choking smog, blaring horns, and vulgar poverty of a troubled Third World capital.

JANUARY 3
Left Banqui at 12:30 P.M., marching south to Nagpartian, which we reached at 4:30 P.M., ten miles.

JANUARY 4
Left Nagpartian at 6:40 A.M. Camped for coffee four miles north of Passaquin [Pasuquin] At 12:30. Left at 1:30 Passaquin at 2:30.

JANUARY 5
Left Passaquin 7:25 A.M. Arrived Baccara 9 A.M. Left 12:55. Arrived Laog 2 P.M.

JANUARY 6
I have purposely left the narrative of the last three days until now as they were practically the same. Our last act in Banqui was the institution of a civil government and the holding of an election.[1] This we did also in every town we passed through. I could not have believed that such a short time as has elapsed between our two trips of the same country could have made so much difference. Take Passaquin for example. When we went through there on our way to Banqui there was not a living soul in the place, not a chicken nor a dog. On our return there were thousands who hung on our every movement with a most intense curiosity, selling us bananas, eggs and chickens. They were also working on the roads and busy in the fields, and everywhere expressed much gratification at the collapse of the insurrection. It was so in every town. Here in Laog they, the military authorities, have even armed the natives and guard with captured rifles and they have numerous parades with a band. These natives are more like children than grown men.

JANUARY 7
Laog, province Illoco Norte. Last night the band came to celebrate something, I don't know what. It played however very prettily. For some reason I did not enjoy it as much as I did that night at Piddig. It was a good band, fifty pieces, elaborately uniformed. I think these

natives joined Aguinaldo merely as an excuse to wear a uniform. The bell tower is a most curious affair. It is about 75 feet square at its base and rises to a height of about 200 feet. It is built of brick and is very massive but not at all pleasing.[2] Laog is a large town on the bank of a river, about seven miles from the sea. Its streets are magnificent, with boulevards, and it has many houses of brick and stone. In its day it must have been full of people of wealth. Now most, at least half, of the fine buildings are in ruins and the rest sadly out of repair. This native civilization is a curious thing. It does not seem able to stand alone. With the Spanish it rose to a certain height, just high enough to want to go further, but it can't do it alone. With America back of the government it will reach a high standard, but I am convinced that at no time will they ever be capable of really governing themselves. Even the educated Filipinos are childish. It seems to be their nature. I do not think time will ever change it any more than it has the nature of British India. I do not think any one will say they are capable of self-government. Am pleased that the sentiment in the States seems so overwhelmingly in favor of keeping the islands.

JANUARY 8
Laog. Last night when the band played it seemed to harmonize with scenery and surroundings and to be perfect, though to my ear the music, though pretty and fascinating to listen to, seems as light and frivolous as is the Filipino character. I have just come down from an hour in the top of the old bell tower. The country is different from that I have seen elsewhere in these islands. In the first place the river, now very low, is responsible for perhaps a quarter of a mile of burning gravel on one side of the town. These shallow meres spread out tremendously when they rise. Low hills surround the town on all sides, in some places coming into it. All foliage is burnt and withered. The trees have lost many of their leaves. It is very hot in the sun. I do not understand the seasons, though I suppose this must be midwinter as the sun is further off now than it will be until next June.[3] One street in the town has substantial buildings, the rest of the town is the better class of nipa hats. Bought a pair of low canvas shoes yesterday of native make for which I paid one dollar. I went to a dance in a native family last night. We were

Bell tower in Laoag. Courtesy Joseph P. McCallus.

absolutely uninvited, wandering in because we heard music, but nothing could be nicer than the good manners with which we were made welcome and entertained.

JANUARY 9

Laog. After all there is little to write about here. I laze the day away, doing nothing, reading old New York papers, talking, eating better than any other enlisted man but the Top Sergeant and squadron Sergeant Major, who have taken me into their mess. I feel as if I would like to write many letters but have no paper nor can any be obtained in the province. I hear the blockade has been raised. If it has, and there is no reason why it should not be raised on the north of Manila any way, we will soon have everything, for this town is the capital of the province and the center of at least ten large cities. Last night, in the moonlight, the old bell tower looked decidedly picturesque, the first time I have ever thought it other than a monstrosity.

JANUARY 10
Laog. Had a chill last night and felt pretty bad all day.[4]

JANUARY 11
Felt pretty bad. Transport in. Took the chance to get to Manila.[5] It was a seven mile ride down to the beach and the pony turned a somersault which did not improve my feelings. A swell dinner on the boat through tipping the steward. Unfortunately was too sick to eat. Reached Vigan at about 9 P.M. No landing at night. Slept on the engine-room hatch.

JANUARY 12
Landed and walked five miles to Vigan and reported to Lieut. Smedberg, adjutant general. I am to stay here and make the General, Gen. Young, a copy of my map. Went to bed.

I do not know how many days I laid around headquarters, feeling as miserable as possible and able to eat nothing. Finally I was sent to the hospital where with care and attendance I rapidly recovered, being discharged on January 29 feeling a little week and very hungry. Had splendid care in the hospital, where, by great good fortune, the doctor in charge had been young Dr. Greenleaf's roommate on the *City of Para*. He knew all about me and gave me special care. Did a good day's work on the map.

JANUARY 30
Feeling first-rate, but hungry all the time. Worked all day on the map, getting it done as far as San Jacinto. I had acute gastritis. Must have eaten too much.

January 30, 1900.

Dear Mamma:
Don't worry about me as I am all right now. I would have written you when I was sick but felt too miserable. I knew any way it was nothing serious. You can hardly imagine what good care they took of me in the hospital or how comfortable I was there. I hear there are hundreds of letters

for me at Manila. I can get my map finished in a week and then I will be
sent down there. My Lieutenant telegraphs for me every once in a while, but
the General wants his map and of course his word is law.[6]

Hope you are well and also the rest of the family, to whom convey my best
respects, and say I will write if I ever get a minute. Am feeling fine now.

Your loving son,
Jack.

JANUARY 31
Vigan. Worked all day at the map. Walked down to the river, about
a mile, for a bath. Was surprised to find it tired me. I suppose if a
person does not eat for a couple of weeks he cannot get his strength
back in a day.

FEBRUARY 1
Vigan. Another long day on the map, varied only by a walk in the
evening. I have a room here in the headquarters building, and as I
have found an oil lamp the evenings can be very pleasantly spent.[7]

FEBRUARY 2
Vigan. All day on the map, I think I can finish it to-morrow. Quit
work at 3:30, I begin at 7 A.M., and took a walk through the city. It
was much changed from when I was here last December, a great
many stores open, you can buy anything you want. I notice the stores
are nine-tenths of them run by Chinos. The city watering department evidently consists of Filipinos who carry the water from the
river in tin cans holding about one gallon. They carry two cans on a
long pole balanced across their shoulders Chinese fashion. They
empty them on the street by means of cocoanut shells. Many hogs
here and bulls in the street, which gives the place an odd appearance. As I think I wrote last December all houses seem, on the
exterior, badly in need of repairs.[8] Feel better everyday. A fine dinner for a great change, roast beef with browned baked potatoes, or
are they roasted too?

FEBRUARY 3

Vigan, province Illocos [Ilocos] Sur. Another long day on the map, which I finished, to my great joy. Walked down to the river for a swim and found to my delight that the feeling of exhaustion I noticed a day or two ago was gone, so I guess I am on my feet again. I am, though, pretty thin, but have an enormous appetite. Spent the evening talking to Sheldon, one of the headquarter clerks. Like most of the smart men in the army, his life has been peculiar to say the least. When I left San Fernando, Pampanga, on the 10th of last October I had forty dollars. I have spent ten dollars for ponies and the remainder has gone for fruit and things I happened to want. I have now, of course having been away from my company I have not been paid, fifty cents American. So for many reasons I am anxious to get back to Manila and the company, though it will mean the end of a detail that has been wonderfully pleasant. Handed in the map to Lieut. Smedberg, Adjt. Gen. Prov. Cav. Brig., St. Div., 8th Army Corps. The name of the doctor who was so kind to me in the hospital was Van Dusen. Got a bunk yesterday and as I had already a mosquito netting I am as comfortable as I would be at home. No news and of course no mail. It is going on to the fifth month now since I have heard from home.

FEBRUARY 12

Vigan. I have really had nothing to write about for the last eight days. It has been lay round the office, eat and sleep and make an occasional addition, correction or change to the map. I did have one slight relapse that kept me on my back for a couple of days, but Dr. Van Dusan, who happened in every day, was very kind and got me round all right. I expect to go to Manila on the next transport, in about ten days. I miss the excitement of active service very much and shall try when I get to Manila to get some more, though with the insurrection crushed I do not see where I am to get it.

FEBRUARY 14

Vigan. Another succession of days of which I can find nothing to write. It must not be thought that these days are unpleasant. I read a great deal and in the evening after all the officers have left the buildings and the lamps are lighted we have some very interesting talks. I find I am acquiring much inside information as to the running of an army. The city itself is not so large in territory, ending abruptly in fields and marsh, but what there is of it is packed close together as in a city like New York. In the back of these buildings, not visible from the street, are some very pleasing gardens. The Doctor told me this morning I was pretty well saturated with malaria, but I think he is judging by my color, which is yellow but which is due I think to the fading tan, for I was burnt almost black when the campaign ended and of course since I have been at headquarters I have rarely been out in the sun.[9]

FEBRUARY 15

Vigan. Yesterday the *Romulus* came up from Manila with mail, and while of course mine was not sent up I managed to get hold of a comparatively recent *Harper's Weekly* and a January *Harper's*, which gave a delightful evening. Owens gets a transfer to the Signal Corps and goes to the lonely lighthouse we passed on our way to Nagpartian.[10]

FEBRUARY 16

Vigan. Some twelve or twenty prospectors appeared to-day, looking for permission to go into the mountains. I wonder if this is the first wave of American invasion.[11] Am perfectly well again.

FEBRUARY 17

Vigan. The scenery round Vigan does not impress one as being tropical. Occasionally there are patches of bananas, but the general landscape is hard, at this season of the year, to distinguish from a New England country scene. Of course I mean a view that does not include either native houses or the volcanic mountains. Mail from here is most irregular. About once in two weeks the U.S. transport *Romulus* wanders up the coast from Manila to Appari and then wanders back again, stopping at all the ports between. Of course after the letters get to Manila they have to wait for a steamer going to the States. This will show you why my letters are so far between just at present. I expect to go down on the *Romulus* when she comes back and will then find myself in Manila, where I shall find out what has been going on at home for the last six months. Also I will get six months' pay as I was last paid in September for July and August. Take long walks every evening. There is little of Vigan I have not seen. They opened an American hotel here day before yesterday. The American occupation seems to be progressing. Also the town is being cleaned, something I imagine has not happened for years. Gen. Young, through his adjutant general, very kindly gave me the privilege of going into the mountains of Alba [Abra] province to convalesce or to return to Manila.[12] I took the latter, feeling perfectly well.

FEBRUARY 18
Saw a December *Harper's Weekly* with pictures of our advance on San Isidro. The pictures looked very natural. I worked on every inch of that road and also in the cut shown at the ferry at Aryat.[13]

FEBRUARY 19
Vigan, province Illocos Sur. A slight shower of rain last night just after I had come in from my usual evening walk. There is a small-pox epidemic among the natives here and the yellow flags are flying everywhere. Considering the filth of their surroundings, it is not

A specimen of road between Arayat and Cabiao over which our troops marched in a pouring rain during the advance on San Isidro. Courtesy Harper's History of the War in the Philippines, 1900.

Dragging a gun from the ferry. Courtesy Harper's History of the War in the Philippines, 1900.

remarkable that they have it. I believe, though, they always have light cases. Occasionally a soldier catches it. Quite a number have died of it. Got sudden notice to go to Manila in the *Romulus*.[14] Now I had to draw rations and get to the beach, some four miles away, and I only had one hour and a quarter to do it in. Moreover, when I came to start I could not find a "caramattao" so I started on foot. It was very hot and I was in heavy marching order. Luckily I met a native driver driving a bull in a springless two-wheeled cart. Twenty cents, Mexican, and a hardtack and I was sitting on the bottom of the cart. The driver was riding the bull and we were galloping, to the beach, which I reached in time to catch the last boat to the *Romulus* but nearly shaken to pieces. I say the last boat, but just as we had tripped our anchor and started to sea a native boat, furiously rowed, brought the Captain of the Port alongside and it was ten hours before we got away. Much to my surprise I found seven of my old friends from K Troop of the 3d aboard, whose time was up. They were bound for the States. They welcomed me with open arms and took me into their mess to my great joy, as I did not have to cook.

FEBRUARY 20

At sea barring a short stop at San Fernando de Union. The ship being light and the sea heavy she rolled frightfully. You could neither sit nor stand. I luckily was not sick. The sea moderated towards evening and we had a fine supper, bacon, beans, fried canned corned beef and coffee.

FEBRUARY 21

Went inside Manila Bay about 7 A.M. and reached the city by 10 A.M. I cut on shore at once in a native boat, nearly capsizing in the "Nip" at the mouth of the Pasig River. Arrived at the barracks I was much astonished at the warmth of my reception. Every one crowded up to shake hands and say they were glad to see me back as they heard I was captured and killed a dozen times. It was very pleasant. Found a box three feet by four filled with letters and papers, nearly six months' accumulation. Am deep in them at present. Reported to the Lieutenant (Oakes) after a bath and a clean up. He was much pleased apparently to get me back, but seemed angry

Gen. Young had got a copy of the map. He could not blame me and did not. Also he "told me his troubles."[15]

FEBRUARY 22

Washington's Birthday. Not having had any money for some time was glad to find some waiting for me. Spent the day shopping and reading letters.

FEBRUARY 23

Manila. Was sent to the Palace in the walled city where the Chief of the Engineers has a drafting office.[16] My work of course is putting my map in shape. Worked all day. The Palace is four miles from our barracks at Malate and I, not being allowed commutation of rations, have to travel back and forward for my meals. I am furnished a pony. Took dinner at a restaurant in the Escolta the first civilized meal for months. It was very good but cost me three days' pay. City rapidly becoming Americanized. English signs everywhere, very few Spanish. An extraodinary number of saloons. Much impressed by the picturesqueness of the walled city.[17]

FEBRUARY 24

Manila. We are quartered in the old Spanish barracks at Malate.[18] They are very comfortable and conveniently arranged with plenty of shower baths and all conveniences. Well built and airy, they are not at all like the barracks I have always supposed Spain furnished her troops. They are large enough for a regiment, we have the space allotted to a company. Of course they are only one story high, a high stone wall, topped by an iron fence, surrounds them. Whether this was to keep the Spanish in or the Filipinos out I have not the faintest idea.

FEBRUARY 25

Manila. At work in the Palace. The map I am making is at one inch to one mile while my notes are at three inches to one mile. In Vigan, when I made my map for Gen. Young, I had to reduce it by tedious proportions, here I have a pantograph. Moreover I have a Filipino who traces my pencil work. Took dinner again on the Escolta. Ate a whole porterhouse steak to the astonishment of the waiter.

FEBRUARY 26

In the afternoon, while I was working, I was surprised to have some one throw his arms about me and dance around the room. It was Billy. My delight was fully equal to his. He insisted on my dining and spending the evening with him. He wore "mufti" on purpose. A delightful evening. I parted with him with much regret. The life out here is agreeing with him. He looks very well. He would not let me spend a cent.

FEBRUARY 27

Manila. Found an admirable place to take dinner in the walled city near the Palace. (In the army we dine in the middle of the day.) It is a Spanish restaurant where they serve an excellent table d'hote dinner for one dollar Mexican, which is fifty cents American. I was quite bewildered by the number of courses. Very clean and well served. Little fresh onions such as we have at home. The dinner includes a pint of claret.

FEBRUARY 28

Manila. Have been walking down to the Palace in the mornings and riding up, as the early mornings are delightfully cool. It is a fascinating walk. There are some beautiful places in Malate which are always so refreshing to watch. Then my walk carries me down the Lunetta [Luneta] past the two old Krupp guns which fired at Dewey and fell short, down by the old walls and the curious stone lunette and numerous outlying redans with moats.[19] All very perfect for the time they were built, a century or so ago. Then I cross the moat, filled with stagnant water, and I am right under the shrub-covered walls. Very picturesque from without but gloomy within. The old city is built close to the walls and the streets are narrow. The houses seem to all have iron-barred windows on the first story and at first the impression is not pleasant, then you glance in the open doorway (really a carriage entrance) and catch a glimpse of lovely courts, a bit of tropical garden perhaps, and you wonder you ever thought it unpleasant. It is true that as the wealth and fashion have deserted Manila Intra Muros [Intramuros] you sometimes catch quite other sights than those I have described, but the variety makes it pleasant. Then there are views and pleasant little parks and immense churches with dark, mysterious-looking interiors, so that altogether it is a most pleasant walk. Mail from the States. My letters of November 25 just received. The latest mail I received is January 20.

MARCH 1
Manila. I miss a good many faces in the company. I find they have been discharged as "time-expired men," some have "taken on" in other companies, some have gone back to the States. That is a new feature to me. In the Volunteers we are all sent out together. Here it is one or two each month. If I stay in my three years the company will be quite changed. My little Spanish restaurant is really very good. It is true that some dishes, which are very delicious, are curious in that I am absolutely unable to make even a guess as to what they are made of. That merely adds interest.

MARCH 2
Manila. As I walked down to the Palace this morning it happened to strike me how similar, and yet so different, my present mode of life is to that I led when I started working as a draughtsman in the old N. T. & T. Co. The long walk in the morning (I was just as interested in New York then as I am in Manila now), the hunt for a cheap restaurant in the noon hour and the whole day spent over a drawing table. I was at the bottom then, I am at the bottom now. I wonder if history repeats itself thus in the life of every individual?

MARCH 3
Manila. Billy came in about noon and asked we to come to Cavite and spend Sunday with him.[20] He said he had explained the case to his mess and all urged me to come. After some discussion I decided to go as it was an entirely different branch of the service. Consequently I got permission to "sleep out of quarters" and at 4:30 took the government ferry to Cavite. A delightful sail across the bay of about an hour's duration. Saw the remains of the Spanish fleet. As we had just passed the *Brooklyn* (the Runaway Girl she is called now in memory of Schley's disgraceful behavior at Santiago), looming big and terrible, the poor little sunken wrecks did not look very impressive.[21] It seemed hard, it was hard, to realize that the sinking of those little boats had changed the destiny of a great nation. Billy

met me at the wharf and was so unaffectedly glad to see me that he relieved all embarrassment. I will say now that all the officers treated me exactly as if I also had a commission, nor were there any embarrassing incidents, though all knew I was an enlisted man. Billy's mess is very comfortable, lodged in a building built on top of the walls of an old Spanish fort. We had a very good though of course plain dinner and his friends in the mess were a very jolly lot. We sat up till all hours talking. They have a "punkha" boy to work the fans over the table, the first time I have actually seen anything of the sort.

MARCH 4
Cavite. When I stepped out on the cool veranda this morning and saw the orderlies, the sentinels in the hot sun, and then saw the comfortable armchairs where I could loll at ease I felt for a moment out of place, but it wore off. While we were at tiffin both Billy and I had a horrible start when two army majors came to call on him. Luckily it proved to be Dr. Harris who was stationed at Portland so long. (Phip will remember him.) He was glad to see me and it seems had already taken the trouble to speak about me to the officers of my company. We all went to cock fight. Another long evening talk. I forgot to mention a most interesting walk. Billy took me all over the navy yard and old fortifications.

MARCH 5
Manila. Took the 9 o'clock A.M. ferry back to Manila. I am getting much interested in the map, which is much finer than the one I made for Gen. Young. I will try and get blue prints to send home.

MARCH 6
Manila. It is curious to watch the caramattas. In New York when you take a hansom you usually tell the driver you are in a hurry, hoping to induce him to get his horse out of a walk. Here, you get into a caramatta, even of the poorest, and the driver at once starts out to distance every other team that may happen to be going in the same direction. Never, until you get out, does he cease beating and exciting by every means in his power his diminutive pony. The marine officers at Cavite had a very funny topical song on the way. The chorus runs:

"Am I a man or am I a mouse,
Am I a governor general or a hobo,
But I'd like to know who is running this show,
Is it me or Emile Aguinaldo?"[22]

MARCH 7
Manila. Finished the map for the second time, but what a difference. I blush to think of the looks of the one I handed in at Vigan,
drawn with a common pen on wrapping paper! One of those little
things that exasperate so happened today. In presenting myself at
the paymaster's for my six months' pay he offered me some thirty
dollars too much, and on my foolishly objecting an error was discovered in the rolls which will delay the payment some time. I do
not remember ever having felt worse over a trifle. Why I don't know,
as I have money, not much, but enough for ordinary expenses. I
suppose it was seeing the crisp new bills, $140.00, handed out and
withdrawn.

MARCH 8
Manila. Was paid to-day, some hundred or more dollars, rather more
money than I ever expect to have again at once while I am an enlisted man. It was astonishing how many little things I wanted that
had not, heretofore, been considered indispensable. Ten dollars for
a tailormade uniform. We are great swells here. I returned to barracks quite loaded down. Met several of the colored officers of the
48th and 49th.[23] The regulations state that the salute is a matter of
courtesy only, also it is a court-martial offense not to give it. Nevertheless my innate courtesy was not sufficient to make me give the
salute. I am told they don't require it from white troops unless its
refusal is conspicuous or the nigger officers are heated with wine.
Some men have, however, got into trouble over it. Billy came in for
a few moments. The *Sunday Times*, Portland, comes regularly. I am
always glad to see it.

MARCH 9
Manila. Last night I had to carry my map to the Lieutenant to be
signed. Had quite a talk with him. I can see he is disgusted with
war. He had seen some men wounded and "then," he said, "I wanted

to go home" and "I don't see what men go into the army for any-way." Of course it strikes men in different ways. Some can overlook certain sides of it, some can't. It, the different mental effects, is very funny. Later he asked me to come up and see him in the evenings. It's all so queer. I am having so much better time and am so much happier than so many officers.

MARCH 10
Manila. Was made a Lance Corporal. "Lance Jack," we call it, du-ties and privileges of a corporal and pay of a private. Of course it's another step up and I am grateful, though in any other branch of the service I would have been—well after all I am the newest re-cruit in the company, which has men in it who have been first ser-geants and even sergeant majors in other branches for even ten and twelve years and they are still privates. I never will have to "walk post" again. I shall never "do fatigue," I am a boss. I work only when necessary for the encouragement of the men. I can never be "Or-derly." I won't be bossed except by officers. Non-coms. rarely "boss" each other even when rank permits it. It is a step on the ladder of promotion, and it's the first step that's the hardest to make. Yes, I am glad to get it. Incidentally I have done non-coms work ever since I have been in the company. The trip to the north was a sergeant's duty at least. The last not as an expression of dissatisfac-tion. The First Sergeant showed me some nice things the Lieuten-ant said of me in his official report, which he was holding for my maps.[24] Another thing I gain. I never will have to march in the rear rank, a discomfort that must be felt to be appreciated.

MARCH 11
Manila. We have guard mount in the evening and immediately after being "made" I was put in charge of quarters. As I sat on my bunk a few moments later, looking down the long barracks, they must be a hundred feet long, with their quadruple row of bunks and its some 150 men, I could not be a bit sorry that the old irresponsible days had passed. Heretofore no barracks happening need disturb me. The men might be noisy and drunk, might fight, might burn their little lights after taps. So long only as they did not bother me I was supremely indifferent. It was no concern of mine. Last night I was in charge.

None of those things must be allowed. It was very funny. I sent one old sergeant to bed who has some twenty-eight years' service and is old enough to be my father. Two nights ago it would have been unwarrantable impudence to have thought of saying anything to him. Last night it was simply, "All right, Corporal." I am convinced he was up merely to see if I dare speak to him. I dare! It was very droll. It's these amusing things that makes me so fascinated with the life. Rained hard most of the day, which was of a consequence cool and comfortable. This is the hottest month in the year. I saw a passage in Leila Herbert's "First American" in the December *Harper's Monthly* that I wish some one would investigate for me, would see if it is true or only one of those prophecies after the event. Hamilton was supposed to say after resigning from the cabinet of Washington something to the effect that the Constitution was a good thing as long as the country was small and inhabited by educated people, but that the country would outgrow it. A remarkable case of clear-headed realization of conditions, if it is only true. Is it?[25]

MARCH 12
Manila. Slight showers all day. Spent the day doing "bunk fatigue," which means lying on my bunk. I had a book that had been sent me from the States and got much interested. Showers all day. Although the thermometer must have been 80 and a slight exertion brought perspiration, some of the men complained it was too cold for a bath. We are getting used to the climate evidently. I think the East is getting into my bones. It is such a wonderful place, so full of apparently unappreciated possibilities, no wonder people want to come back. It is surely one's duty to see that our Government gets its share, its share not of China alone. It seems to make one dream big, this borderland of wonders.

MARCH 13
Manila. Showers all day. Read the last of my accumulation of papers and am now anxiously waiting for another mail. The company, with the exception of twenty-five men who are in the Camarine Provinces, is doing no duty but barrack guard so that my time, with the exception of reveille and retreat roll-call, the one at 6:30 A.M. and the other at 5:30 P.M., is all my own.[26]

MARCH 14

Manila. Mail from the States. Not many letters for me, but three from mamma and a most amusing letter from Billy Prescott, who wants a bolo or dagger with "lots of blood on it."[27] My correspondence arranges itself badly. The answers of all the letters I wrote at San Fernando, Pampanga, came while I was on the "north hike." The answers to these I am writing now will probably come just about the time we are sent out again. I saw in the *Sunday Times* of February 11 that I had been made a "non-com." Pretty entertaining as I was not made until March 10, almost exactly a month later.[28] Sent home a complete set of my maps. They show my journey from start to finish.

MARCH 15

Manila. My days are becoming systematized. Get up at 6:15 and have just time for a wash before reveille roll-call, then breakfast, after which I make up and sweep under and around my bunk. It is then time for "fatigue call," 7:30, when the barracks and yard are "policed" under the supervision of a non-com. It is funny how quick the morning goes, almost before I realize it. I read and write, it is 12 M. [noon] and we have dinner. Sometimes I go shopping instead of staying in quarters. After dinner it is very hot, a siesta perhaps. At 3:45 regularly I go for my shower bath, there are fine facilities. At 4:30 we have supper and at 5:30 retreat roll-call. We are free then till 10 P.M. "taps," after which no soldiers and civilians alike are not allowed on the streets. Usually I take a walk, sometimes on the Lunetta, which is perfectly fascinating and lovely with the band and the crowd and the sunset over the beautiful bay. It is a little too crowded with officers though to be comfortable for an enlisted man. So the evening goes quickly.

MARCH 16

Manila. Cleaned my rifle, a long job. A slight shower in the forenoon.

MARCH 17

Saturday inspection. I was ordered to take a detail of six men and be ready to go with the Lieutenant tomorrow morning. Where I do not know or for how long, so I mail these few pages, as I know by experience that short details sometimes stay out months. Spent some time in seeing that six men who go with me were properly equipped and had the hundred rounds of ammunition. We only take one day's rations, which may mean anything or nothing.

Dear Mamma:
I enclose the day's market report so that you may know the difficulties of housekeeping in Luzon at the present time.

Jack.

MARCH 18
Manila. One of the most delightful days since I have been over here. Marched my detail down to the Pasig River, some four or five miles, but it was in the cool of the morning. Then we met Lieut. Oakes and some two or three other engineer officers and took the government launch up the Pasig and some miles into Laguna de Bay to the Island of Palin [Talin]. The object of the expedition was to examine some stone quarries which the Spaniards used to work.[29] They want the stone for the projected docks commenced by the Spaniards. When they landed I used the detail as outposts. I have no idea what they thought of the stone. But the sail, it was the most wonderful I have ever taken. The Pasig is as crooked as the Songo [Congo?]. The banks are only a few inches above the stream which are of a consequence of a fresh and lovely green. Manila itself is a much larger city than I had supposed and stretches along the river banks for a considerable distance. At first there is much shipping packed along the stone banks two and even three deep, then ware-houses and finally fine residences with fascinating balconies over-hanging the river, iron gates at the head of landing steps or perhaps across some little tributary to the main stream. This feature, the beautiful places, the rich gardens inside fascinating stone-work, the picturesque churches some distance from the river, continues for some miles. it is a very populous district. Then come native villages, picturesque in the extreme seen from a distance which hides the filth of their surrounding, and always the stream is full of bancas, canoes hollowed with infinite patience from solid logs, and large, unwieldy cascos either drifting lazily down the stream or being poked

with much labor against the current. And so past San Mateo, where Lawton was killed, past Pasig and then out into the lake itself.[30] Seventy miles long, it looks like the sea, most curiously it comes to the land, which seems to seek to meet it, so that for perhaps half a mile the water gradually deepens from an inch to feet (of course outside the narrow channel), and fishing weirs seem to extend as far as eye can reach. Each pole has a gull or heron or kingfisher on it, so there are thousands of birds. Finally the lake is reached, surrounded by mountains and full of precipitous islands. It was fascinating, we were out all day, to study the different lights on river and lake, the difference, one could hardly recognize the same places, seen in the cool morning, in the glare of midday and in the soft light of the late afternoon. Then the march up the crowded Lunetta and one appreciated being back to cool shower baths and the certainty of a comfortable bunk at night.

MARCH 19

Manila. It is rather interesting to watch the different ways the men take to get rid of their money. The Government provides a sort of savings bank by allowing a man to make deposits with the paymaster on which four percent interest is paid. The money cannot be withdrawn until discharge or expiration of time of service. Some men deposit all they have and borrow what they use. A good deal of money is saved. Almost every one saves something. There is another class that runs to jewelry and expensive watches. One might not think that an enlisted man could indulge largely in such business, but it must be remembered that the troops are paid only every — months [?], in some cases not so often, so that out here an enlisted man may find himself in possession of some hundred dollars. Moreover as the Government provides everything he can spend every cent for luxury or dissipation. There is a class that does the latter, but it is a very small proportion. If a man's time expires while he is out here, and if he elects to re-enlist, the Government pays him a bounty, based on the water transportation back home. It varies with rank. One of our sergeants, who was discharged a few days ago and re-enlisted, received some $1500. As men are discharged every month and many re-enlist there is usually an air of joyous opulence around the barracks.

MARCH 20

Manila. This evening my walk led me to old Fort Malate, about half a mile above the barracks.[31] It was one of our usual evenings, evenings that never fail to excite surprise they are so delightful, so cool after the heat of the day. The fort is one of the outer line of defenses of the city. Built on the beach the waste swamps extend studying the old masonry, the deep embrasures, the highwalled parapet, the old well and the loop-holed citadel in one corner. It was very quiet, no noise at all except the sound of the sea on the beach and the cries of the marsh birds. Naturally one fell to dreaming. Dreamt of "A- Leigh" and the heroes of earlier times. It was a fitting place. And the awakening? As I went down the inclined way, leading to the parapet, there, in the black wall, was a patch of vivid color, the last colors of the sunset showing through an eight-inch hole, as clearly bored as if done with instruments of precision, and in the opposite corner was the wreck caused by the exploding shell. There men had died that the flag, which had floated so long above those moss-grown, shrub-covered walls, might be hauled down-with honor. Around the corner was an arc lamp, the outpost of Manila, a city which, behind the times as it is, is yet of a different age from the fort which tried to defend it. Poor old fort! And the men who built it? Do those haughty old Dons, who, in armor, doubt-less tramped its walls, do they care if a soldier of another nation, of a nation that was not born when those old walls were new, sits dream-ing on the wall, dreaming of the grandeur of his country and the degradation of Spain?

MARCH 21

Manila. To-night I was listening to one of the men tell of his expe-riences with people in the States. The story itself was not particu-larly amusing, but the exaggerated eloquence, the curious set phrases, seemed very familiar. At first I could not place it, but in a moment it flashed upon me. It was the tone, manner and expression of the comedian of the variety show and the continuous performance, a manner I had always thought hopelessly exaggerated and artificial. Now here was a man talking to me in just that way with no idea of the effect he was producing. It was difficult to keep one's face straight or to believe that I was really awake.

Fort San Antonio Abad. Courtesy Joseph P. McCallus.

MARCH 22

Manila. I got a letter from Walter Smith yesterday. He is in the hospital and as they cannot cure him, he has dysentery, they are going to send him back to the States. I saw quite a lot of him formerly, he was one of the volunteers from C Company, Engineers, but after I left Apalit we never seemed to get in the same details. He wanted a lot of shopping done for him. Now I hate shopping, but luckily I found a man to do it for me. Went up to say good-by. He looks like a skeleton and is of course very weak. The voyage will probably cure him. He is the third man, I think, from B Company sent home on account of sickness.

MARCH 23

Manila. There is a man in our company who I have always detested as he is a professional jester, a type very objectionable to me. To-night I was Corporal to the guard, for the first time in my military career; the young fellow I refer to was on with me and I got talking to him as one will when he has nothing to do. It seems he has an ulcer or cancer in his throat that is gradually eating it out. The doctors tell him he will surely die of it. His soft palate was eaten away only a short while ago. Yet he stays "for duty" and won't go on sick report. He keeps up his jests and his foolish songs. You cannot tell a great deal about men.

MARCH 24
Manila. On the guard all day. I got the "night in," which means I did not have to be waked in the middle of it to walk post. That was a distinct relief, but if we had been in the face of the enemy I am inclined to think I would have got even less sleep than my sentinels. I had invited Billy to come in and take dinner with me in the city to-morrow, but it seems he is slightly indisposed and can't come.

MARCH 25
Manila. After all there is a dreamy sort of attractiveness even about these hot days. Malate in the heat of the sunlight, with the population inside their close-drawn shutters taking the noonday siesta, reminds me somehow of Portland in August. Portland near home with the quiet streets and the air heavy with the scent from the gardens. Now it is funny doubtless to compare a tropical city with a New England one, but the association of ideas is there nevertheless. Perhaps I idealize Portland, for it is ten years or more since I have seen it in the heat of the summer. Spent some time with the Lieutenant learning his ideas for a pile bridge at Paranaque, the plans of which I commence work on tomorrow.

MARCH 26
Manila. Spent the day in commencing the working plans of the Paranaque bridge. It is a long time, five years or more, since I have made mechanical drawings but I have not forgotten, for if I did not actually make them I "bossed" those that did up to the time of the Spanish War. Everything was dirty and gummy from lack of care is the only reason it took me so long to begin. The drawings themselves are of the simplest. A plan, three sections and a few details will show everything. Old Tschappet, my "bunkie" on the *City of Para,* is up there too, tracing some Spanish maps. We work in A Company's office, one-half mile above our barracks.

MARCH 27

Manila. At work at A Company's quarters. Mail from the States was delivered to the company about 7 P.M. That is an event that always causes great excitement in the barracks and keeps every one in quarters. Even the band concert on the Lunetta will not draw the men from the mail. Of course being Regulars the men do not get many letters, hardly one apiece on the average, but some one always gets papers, which are always handed around and furnish topics for arguments that last until the next mail comes in. Personally I am lucky in being a subscriber to quite a number, though not nearly sufficient, of magazines.

MARCH 28

Manila. My 28th birthday. I just notice that each group of figures makes ten, a chance for the superstitious to argue much. Last year at this time I had just been mustered out of the 203d N.Y.V. and so have a pretty clear idea of the climate in New England at this time. Quite a contrast in every way now, but as I contrast mental states, and after all the mental condition is more important than the physical, I must admit that I do not regret coming out here as I did.

MARCH 29

They say the climate is bad for teeth. I myself have lost some filling, but I am inclined to think tough beef and hardtack have more to do with it than any influence of the climate. Out here, it seems, all ills are laid to the climate, most unjustly I think.

MARCH 30

My dinner for Billy came off to-night and as an event was a success, I think, for we both had much to talk about. The dinner itself was fair but nothing extra, owing to the limitations of hotels, even the best, to one of which we went, in Manila. For instance, the raw oysters were canned. Some simple things were however excellent. Some fried fish, a broiled chicken, were delicious. The wines were cheap and poor except the champagne, which was Heidsieck. Naturally it cost about half a month's pay, but I simply can't seem to get rid of my accumulated pay and was glad to get a chance to see Billy.

MARCH 31

The mangoes are just beginning to get ripe and appear for sale on the fruit stands. At present they cost five cents, gold, apiece, but as the season progresses I hope they will get cheaper. I thought those Sewell gave me last July in Honolulu delicious, but these are much finer. To my mind, or taste, they are the superlative of all fruits. Billy says at his mess they have them sliced, they are worse to eat than oranges, and iced for a breakfast fruit. They must be nice but probably like sliced oranges they lose a little of their flavor.

APRIL 1

At retreat to-night was published the sentence of the first man in the company to be tried by G.C.M. since I joined. Private Tobler forfeits ten dollars a month of his pay and is confined at hard labor for one year in Bilibid, the military prison here. As his time runs out while he is in confinement he also gets a dishonorable discharge. His crime was absenting himself when the detail for the Camarines was made up. I do not think any one had any sympathy for him. I am sure I did not as he was a professional shirk, a disagreeable thing in the army as it puts more work on whoever has the misfortune to be detailed with the shirker. Still a year in prison is pretty tough.

APRIL 2

Just now the evenings are the only part of the day I have to myself, the drafting taking up the day. Really it is a relief as otherwise there is nothing to do, also the drafting room is much cooler than the barracks. In the evening then I take my walks, usually up the beach to the old fort, about two miles. There are beautiful sunsets. To-night there was an angry red one and the wind blew hard up the bay. It blew so hard that a native casco could not get off the lee shore and her crew were working furiously at throwing overboard her deck load of palm leaves to save from being driven ashore. I find something new to interest me every time I take the walk.

APRIL 3

Once upon a time a man named Kipling, a man who knew more about soldiers than most soldiers themselves, wrote a story called "In the Matter of a Private."[32] It is a good story, but I mention it because it is a perfect picture of a soldier's life in barracks in the Tropics during the hot season. I do not think the officers realize what a picture of their barracks they can buy. If they do, it is criminal in them not to attempt to break the monotony. Still what can they do after all? With us, being new to the country, the tension has not snapped yet. Next year it will. But I should advise any one interested to read that story. Kipling writes better than I can. As for me, I have my work.

APRIL 4

A long talk with the "Top," as the first sergeant in the regiment is called, while we drank cooling drinks. It was evening of course or we would not have been drinking. He is an unusually clever fellow of only average education and his ideas being entirely deduced from experience and not from books are very interesting. After discussing everything from the internal management of a company down to mixing cocktails, we naturally wound up with religion. As he was raised a Roman Catholic his views were naturally very interesting.

APRIL 5

Finished the Paranaque Bridge drawings and commenced some detail drawings for some pontoon boats the Lieutenant wants to have built. I enclose the bill of fare for last week. It will be seen we are living very well, moreover the "Top" is managing so well that the company fund is not touched. It must be understood that there is abundance of soft bread at every meal and that whenever fruit is mentioned it is either stewed evaporated peaches or apples or prunes. There is no complaint possible about the food, which is always well cooked. It is possible that it is a little heavy for the hot weather.

SUNDAY.
Breakfast.   Bacon and Eggs, Coffee.
Dinner.   Boef a la Mode, Corn Starch Pudding, Mashed Potatoes.
Supper.   Doughnuts, Hot Cakes, Syrup Tea.
MONDAY.
Breakfast.   Fried Bacon, Potatoes, Coffee.

| Dinner. | Mutton Chops, Sweet Potatoes, Stewed Tomatoes, Soup, Coffee. |
| Supper. | Pork and Beans, Tea, Fruit. |

TUESDAY.

Breakfast.	Mutton Stew, Coffee.
Dinner.	Roast Beef, Mashed Potatoes, Fruit, Coffee.
Supper.	Beef Pot Pie, Stewed Prunes, Tea.

WEDNESDAY.

Breakfast.	Beefsteak, Onions, Coffee.
Dinner.	Boiled Beef, Potatoes, Apple Pie, Coffee.
Supper.	Hash, Stewed Fruit, Tea.

THURSDAY.

Breakfast.	Beef Stew, Coffee.
Dinner.	Pork and Beans, Stewed Prunes, Coffee.
Supper.	Coffee Cake, Hot Cakes and Honey, Tea.

FRIDAY.

Breakfast.	Fried Bacon, Potatoes, Coffee.
Dinner.	Beefsteak, Onions, Potatoes, Apples, Coffee.
Supper.	Hash, Stewed Fruit, Tea.

SATURDAY.

Breakfast.	Beef Stew, Coffee.
Dinner.	Sauerkraut, Pork, Coffee.
Supper.	Pot Pie, Stewed Fruit, Tea.

Respectfully submitted. Week ending March 31st, 1900.

APRIL 6

The Lieutenant interrupted the work on the pontoon boats to send me down town after a hundred and eighty-five dollars, Mexican, which I am to take out to San Mateo to-morrow to pay off some natives. While that is a relatively small sum it looks and feels big in a canvas bag. I felt quite conscious lugging it around the streets and finally hailed a caramatta and drove back in style. I took the opportunity while I was down town to get dinner at the English hotel and much enjoyed the coolness and the luxury of being waited on.

APRIL 7

Montabbon [Montalban?]. Got up at 5:30 so as to get my bath

before starting. Left at 6:30 with one private, a driver and a single mule wagon. Our road led by the water works, through Mariquini [Marikina], San Mateo and finally to Montabbon, in all about eighteen or twenty miles. It was a delightful journey like all in this curious land. Again I was surprised at the extent of Manila. Finally the town was left behind and we settled down to five or six miles of rolling country with rice paddies everywhere. But they were not the rice paddies I had known in the north when we tramped through and fought over them, waist deep in mud; they were no longer fresh and green and filled with water. No, their work for a season was done, and, baked hard as bricks in the ever-burning sun, they made the road like a burning furnace. And dust! I was glad we did not have to march. After we had crossed the river at the pumping station and as we rode up the Mariquini Valley it was not possible to longer complain about the heat. In the first place the road wound along the banks, river banks, through cocoanut and palm groves and the heat was at least less glaring, but then, there was the interest of it. This valley was fiercely fought over. It is immensely rich and populous and much desired by the insurgent army, therefore it was burned first by one side then by the other, as the Americans first advanced and then withdrew to fight elsewhere. Now what is happening? The population, driven no one knew where, is returned and is busy building new houses and taking care of the hastily-gathered rice. Everywhere was noise and business. I was at a loss whether to spend more time admiring the natural beauty of the valley or the ingenuity displayed in building the queer houses. It was a delightful morning and historically interesting too, for did we not go through San Mateo where Gen. Lawton was killed? All along the road were troops and guns tucked away in strategic and yet cool places, for while the insurgent armies are scattered, well—it is well to be safe and the troops are here. At Montabbon turned over the money and sought an Engineer Sergeant up there at work on some bridges and he gave me his tent, books and cigars to amuse myself with, for of course the mule could not make two such trips a day. Then in the afternoon reading in quiet, for the tent was in the shade and removed slightly from the hum of the camp, I imagined myself at Peekskill, at Chickamauga. It was not real, at first I did not see why, but I realized presently that it was the first time I had been under canvas on the island. In all sorts of quarters and in no quarters, but never before in a tent since I ceased wearing shoulder straps. But I did not sleep there, the Sergeant wanted his tent of course, so, as there were no vacant bunks, we slept in the church, I on a table that might have been anything. I noticed the altar was decorated with paper flowers stuck in beer bottles, empty, an incongruity that I should have thought would have affected even the natives.

APRIL 8
Manila. We had decided to start at daybreak to get rid of as much as possible of the journey in the cool of the morning. Up therefore before sunrise and started as soon as it was light enough to see. If the valley had been beautiful in the glare of noon one can imagine how much more so it was in the half-hour or so before the sun got above the mountains. It is Palm Sunday and all the natives were dressed in their best and going to church carrying palms. Also the village streets were full of strange, gaily-decorated platforms, the use of which I cannot guess. Many natives were kneeling before gaily-decked shrines in their own houses, plainly visible through the windows. Not until we reached the pumping station did we get coffee. There a good-natured cook of F Company of the 27th Volunteers gave us, besides the coffee we asked for, fish-balls, bread and apple sauce, a welcome addition to the cold bread and bacon hurriedly eaten at Montabbon. Thanks to our early start we were in the barracks by 10 A.M., when, after the old rifle was cleaned, a bath was most refreshing. Coming back we drove through a part of New Manila, as the city outside the walls is called, that I had never seen, the part of the city occupied by the foreign consuls and the wealthier class. It contains fine, palace-like structures, set in gardens of gorgeous palms. A fascinating place in which to live.

APRIL 9
Manila. For weeks Tschappet has been growling because he got no time to himself. To-day he had a day off. It was hard to imagine how he spent it. He took the entire day in lettering name plates for rifles and boxes for men he liked in the company. Instead of working for the Government he was working for his friends. That was his holiday.

APRIL 10

Manila. For the last day or two the Lieutenant being either too busy or something else to look over my work, I have had nothing to do but read in the delightfully cool quarters of A Company. A Company has a good library and I have been amusing myself with Dickens. A few letters and papers from Hong Kong to-night. I got one from Blue, February 26, that was missent to Phillips, Me., instead of to the Philippines.

APRIL 11

One of the men in the company did a rather remarkable trick that I had read of but never seen done. He lay flat on his back and allowed another man to jump on his stomach from a five-foot elevation. The man who did the jumping weighed 175 pounds. It is a development of muscles that enables him to stand it, but it was a very striking sight.

APRIL 12

It seems the three days before Easter are a great holiday or fast here. Under Spanish rule it was a complete holiday, even the caramattas being kept off the streets. There are none on the streets to-day. If you go anywhere you must walk. I am not sure whether it is done voluntarily or with the idea that the law still holds. I am told, on somewhat doubtful authority, that, formerly, if one appeared on the street without being dressed in black at any time during Lent, he or she would be arrested.

APRIL 13

Had hot cross buns for breakfast today in honor of its being Good Friday, also had no meat at all all day. I think I have remarked on the fact that the majority of the men are Catholics, though, in the army at least, I fear the religion is only a form to be observed occasionally. The 8th Army Corps is no more. I am now in the 2d Division of the Department of the Philippines. It was in the 8th Corps that I did my marching and fighting. I am sorry, for purely sentimental reasons, to have it go out of existence without a word.[33]

APRIL 14

Woke up this morning with my left eye as badly swollen as if some one had "pasted" it, I presume some insect stung it while I was asleep. The Lieutenant insisted on my going to the doctor, who, finding I had a little fever, saw in it symptoms of the most alarming nature and ordered me to bed.[34] Needless to say I did not go, though, as he sent his steward down every two hours to take my temperature, he did not find any after the first time. I had to stay in quarters. A good deal of excitement over a little bite, and it shows the inconvenience which may arise from having your officers interested in you.

APRIL 15

Easter Sunday. The day was rendered noteworthy by a wonderful dinner. The company had been talking about it for a week. Oyster stew, roast chickens, each man got half of one, mashed potatoes with a gravy full of kidneys and liver, corn, canned of course, a rich plum duff with real brandy in the sauce, and chocolate to drink. It really was a wonderful dinner and very nice. I went to the trouble of finding out how much it cost, for of course all additions to the ration are paid out of the company fund. Imagine my surprise to find that it only cost $20.00. It was a dinner for about seventy-five men. For some reason or other the Top Sergeant has taken me up recently and to-day he devoted to entertaining me. He had a carriage at the barracks at 2:30 and took me to the races at the Manila Country Club, where we staid till sunset. The track is not so different from those in America. Of course it is surrounded by bamboos with an occasional banana tree or palm, and the space inside the track is laid out in rice paddies, but the rest is strangely American. There is the betting ring, and of course the bar, like any track, and you get the same drinks, only you pay from three to four times as much for them. The races themselves were quite interesting, but I did not bet, not having any spare money, and a horse race where you do not bet is not much excitement. After the races we drove round the Lunetta and listened to the band and then went to dinner in the walled city. It was a nice hotel with the dining tables round the interior court, so one could sit comfortably eating and watch the towers of the old churches rising over the walls. The hotel is for officers only I believe, but we dined en famille with the proprietor and his wife. Perhaps it was that which caused the dinner to be so good. It was the best I have eaten since I left Honolulu. Also the wines were good. The proprietor, a French-man, sang some songs after dinner, among them the Fenicule Fenicula (if that is the way you spell it), which I first heard in Venice and do not remember having heard since, and I would have re-membered it as I always was fascinated by it.[35] It was after taps when I got to bed. The proprietor's wife had been in Australia for four years and reminded me of the Molly we, Phip, Jim and I, met on the coach to Versailles.[36]

APRIL 16
We certainly have a most excellent Top Sergeant. I do not write this because of the "blow" he gave me yesterday, but simply to record certain ideas of what a Top should be. In the first place he is fond of the service and proud of his position. Then he has been in the service long enough (ten years) to know about it and not so long as to become an old fogy. He is a little higher class than the majority of the company, though, through running away from home, his education is only average. He is always working for the company, as is shown by anything requiring the action of the company com-mander, he is between the company and its officers, acting as a buffer for the wrath on both sides. Discipline is kept up to the mark and it is solely through his efforts, for to such an extent is be trusted by the C.O. that the company never sees the shoulder straps except on Saturday morning inspections. The result is that the com-pany, which was growling and kicking and losing in discipline when Meade was Top, is now cheerful and uncomplaining and gaining discipline every day.

APRIL 17
Mail from the States last night. I received some money which came in handy, as I had succeded in getting away with all I had and was wondering if I should have to do my own washing again. Old Tschappet got a letter and documents showing he had fallen heir to some $5000 through the death of his brother-in-law. I hope it will do him some good.

APRIL 18

The early mornings here are certainly delightful. It is cool. There is never any breeze. The bay lies before you, an unruffled sheet of water, so smooth that it melts into the morning mist and one cannot tell where the sea ends. In the foreground there will always be a lot of natives sunning their ponies, it is all the cleaning the ponies ever get, and that is all the movement on the bay.

APRIL 19

Malate, where we are stationed, is a suburb of Manila, about as far from the walls as Glen Cove is from the city. The road leading to it from the Lunetta along the shore is well built up, so one does not notice how far it really is. Tonight I walked at right angles to the coast and was in the country in a few hundred yards. Rice fields everywhere with strange and beautiful palms against the sunset; across substantial stone bridges built over sluggish streams of muddy water where the caribous wallowed after their day's work; past collections of native buts with their chattering swarm of inmates, some of them lighted up with the flickering light of the cooking fires, some lighted with the small native candles, but all making cheerful centers of life and light against the moonless night; everywhere were native police, proud and important, and everywhere too the patrols of the military guard.

April 19, 1900.

Dear Mamma:

Much obliged for the birthday remembrance, which reached me safely and came in very nicely, as I had recklessly spent all my money and was beginning to feel the need of little things. You know though that I do not want you to send me money as I have all I need. I appreciate the remembrance very much.

Everything going on very nicely. I am sorry you all thought my commission so much nearer than it really is, but I suppose you have found out by this time. Do you still like the journal?

Your loving son,
Jack.

APRIL 20

This evening it was the 4th Cavalry Band that played on the Lunetta, and as it is the best of all the military bands there were many people to listen, a seemingly endless procession of carriages driving slowly round the oval which was packed with people lazily reclining in easy wicker chairs (you can hire one for the evening for four cents, American). I, too, sat there and alternately listened to the band and to the Corporal with me, who told me stories of Wounded Knee and the Fight at the Mission.

APRIL 21

Saturday seems to be as much a church day as Sunday and the churches are surrounded with swarms of the little carriages that bring the congregation. There seems to be quite a little trafficking also. The natives want fruit and also candles, the latter I suppose to burn at the altar. The candles are sold by women and it is curious to see them pick out a carriage, sometimes half a mile from the church, and if the occupant shows signs of making a trade they, the sellers of the candles, follow the carriage with a curious kind of a long, swinging trot, the basket still balanced on their head, way to the church. Billy came in and we dined together.

APRIL 22

Sunday. About the only noteworthy thing is the fact that I had my head shaved, which makes me rather of a sight and remarkably conscious.

APRIL 23

Near A Company's quarters, where I am working now, there is a gang of natives building a sewer. It is very curious how little work they manage to do. They laugh and chatter and throw the dirt at chickens who wander about, but they hardly do as much work in a day as a laborer in the States would do in an hour. They only get about thirty cents, gold, a day, so I don't imagine it matters.

APRIL 24

Now that the sun is getting farther north I have imagined that it is not quite so hot. March is the hottest month in the year I am told.

It may be I am more used to the heat, it was much cooler in the north, but at any rate I do not notice it (the heat) as much as I did. Finished the drawing of the pontoon ferry this morning. I wonder what next. The crew of the British ships were playing football, the Rugby game, on the Lunnetta this evening. I do not think I ever saw it played before. The men did not look different, barring the uniforms, from our crews.

APRIL 25

Of course the population of Manila is distinctly military even now, but there is a great increase of civilians the last four or five months. Now when the band plays on the Lunetta there is a distinctly European, as distinguished from native, crowd. Good-looking traps with big horses are not uncommon where formerly there were only the shabby caramattas drawn by the half-starved native ponies. There are a lot of curious turnouts also. There is one distinguished looking old man who drives in an open Victoria with a gorgeous Chinaman for a footman, a truly magnificent creature dressed in the lightest of blue silks with a black skull-cap and long pigtail. He is quite conscious of his splendor and sits very straight and is altogether very impressing.

APRIL 26

It is rather odd that the first thing one learns of a language are the "cuss words." I myself can swear in the purest Castilian, in Tagalo, in Illoco and other Malay dialects, but what struck me was that in the course of my walk last night I came across a band of native children, whooping and playing in the streets, the oldest was not over ten, and cheerfully swearing at each other in good American.

APRIL 27

While the Manila Dagupan Railway was in the hands of the Government a number of the men of our company were detailed to work on it, some as station agents, some as locomotive engineers, some as conductors.[37] It was a perfect gold mine to them. I do not know how much money they contrived to get, but it must have been considerable as they charged the planters two and even three times the established rate for trains and freight cars. With the people so used to giving bribes and paying tribute it will take some time to get honest government employees.

APRIL 28

Yesterday A Company moved out of the quarters they have occupied for so long, nearly two years, and moved to Dagupan. We are to have their barracks. Much more comfortable they are than ours, with a mess hall where we can eat in comfort, not sitting on the ground with one's food plentifully seasoned with the dust of the barracks yard. Among other improvements we are to have a canteen and a laundry paid for by its (the canteen's) profits so that washing will be free. But how A Company hates us and how cordially we return the hatred! A Company has been here longer than we.[38] That was the first grievance, there are a dozen others. Our taking their quarters is the last and worst. The men would not speak the last few days they were here.

APRIL 29

Down by the Pasig there is a regular impasse, a street with a wooden gate at the end which separates it from a few hundred feet of rice fields and the river. It is the native quarter, a region of nipa huts which range in size from the small squares containing only one room to the more pretentious "casas" of two or three. Here the population is swarming, the houses close together. Old women sit by the roadside crouching over the pots and pans that hold the various unsavory and disgusting messes that serve for food. These women are always clothed in dirty, torn rags, a marked contrast to the senoritas, who are laughing and chatting near them and who are dressed in clean cottons of the brightest colors, and to the young men in the most immaculate of white clothes. Running everywhere are the children, mostly with no clothes at all and never with more than a little shirt. The rice fields are fresh and green, there are palms and bamboo at intervals, and the life and color in the evening light makes a fascinating picture. One must not look too closely. All the huts are raised some four feet from the ground and, remarkable as it seems, that is the solitary sanitary device. You see the clean-looking girls, with their freshly-starched clothes. You look at the houses and you wonder how they do it. In fact, the only thing in these islands that

I do not wonder at is the mortality among the children, which, in the absence of any statistics, is vaguely stated as enormous.

APRIL 30
San Mateo. Was ordered late yesterday afternoon to report to the Chief Engineer, who would give me money, $65.00 Mexican, to be conveyed to San Mateo in the Mariquini Valley. As the banks do not open until 9 A.M. I expected a hot ride. It was easy to get the check cashed, but while waiting I noticed with considerable inter- est the comfortable-looking Chinese merchants who came, each with an escort of nearly-naked coolies, who carried stout bags to carry off their masters' money, so cumbersome is a depreciated sil- ver currency. The ride out was not so bad as I had expected, the sun being overcast. It was interesting, as our teamster had been in the Colorado Regiment when the insurrection broke out and was able to point out the lines held by our regiments on different days, where the officers were killed, the bridge where the first shot was fired.[39] Beyond Mariquini we were stopped by a guard, a new experience to me, who as an Engineer soldier in the north had had the freedom of all lines and precautionary orders. It seems that a Volunteer had wandered beyond the lines, had insulted some women and got boloed for his pains. I enclose the pass which was instantly given when I saw the C.O. of Mariquini. It was raining hard then, which ac- counts for the blurs. At San Mateo I reported in due form, but the impressiveness of my military manner was ruined by one of the officers getting up with, "Why, halloo Brown; what the devil!" it was Capt. Sturgis, late Battalion Adjutant of the 203d N.Y.V. It seems there were lots of my old friends in the regiment, the 27th infantry U.S.V., Taylor of the 8th N.Y., who was my chum at Chickamauga, Judson of the 12th and Sturgis and Hannah of the 203d. I was perfectly willing, even anxious, to keep on my own side of the line, but they, being Volunteers, would not have it, so I passed the afternoon drinking Scotch and talking over old times. Dined with them, and a very good dinner it was. They insisted on having a bed made up for me, but that was too absurd, so I left and rolled up in my blanket with the men, separated only by a wall from the fellows who, a little over a year ago, were copying my uniforms and my manners.

Manila. The water supply of Manila is taken from the Mariquini River, pumped through iron pipes into a tunnel through the hills that border the river valley and then through pipes into the city mains.[40] There are no reservoirs, but the tunnel holds about two days' supply for the city. Coming in from San Mateo to-day we stopped and went down into the tunnel, which has steps, absolutely unguided, leading into it about every mile. I took no measurements, but should judge it to be about five miles long, 100 feet deep at the pumping station, on the surface where it ends, and to have an oval cross section about 12 by 6 feet. When we reached Malate the company had moved into the barracks formerly occupied by A Company.

CHAPTER 5

Paranaque

*I*T IS IRONIC that Brown, who was ecstatic at being able to leave his profession as an engineer in New York for the adventure of a frontline soldier, found himself a bridge inspector outside of Manila. Such is the peril of victory. As the expedition in Pampanga taught the Americans all too severely, the country needed an infrastructure, and road and bridge construction became one of the highest priorities of the early U.S. regime. Company B, commanded by Lieutenant Oakes, began the work of repairing bridges, roads, and ferries at Bacoor, Naic, Batangas, and other locations within the recently formed Department of Southern Luzon.

In May, Brown was sent to the town of Paranaque, a few miles south of Manila, to begin erecting a bridge across the Paranaque River. It was a detail of mixed blessings. Brown helped design the bridge, which piqued his professional pride. He initially seemed to enjoy the challenge of the assignment, but it is clear that the job soon grated on his nerves. He now worked with American civilian contractors and Filipino laborers, neither of whom impressed him. Housed in the battle-scarred convent, the poor companionship and frustrating days of work crowded him into a psychological corner. His mental discomfort in Paranaque stands in marked contrast to the dramatic ebullience he expressed in northern Luzon and Manila's cultured serenity. Moreover, it becomes increasingly apparent that he is sick.

The theme of sickness is woven around the building of the Paranaque bridge. He suffers at least one relapse of the "low fevers" characteristic of the continuing typhoid condition, which keeps him from writing for eight days. Others around him are taken ill and some are sent home to die. "I don't believe this can be a very healthy place," he remarks. His illness undoubtedly prompted the variety of enigmatic statements and strange departures from his normal observations that crop up in these last months. Most notable is the retelling of the sailor's cannibalism story. Its inclusion is bizarre: with all the tales he must have heard while in the service, why record only this one? Does its macabre content mirror his own mind? His maudlin reverie on May 16 and the baffling statements he made on July 13 about a "purely metaphysical discussion" are so out of character that it suggests he is writing to someone other than himself or his mother. It also suggests he is quite troubled.

The journal ends abruptly. Although Brown makes no confession of sickness at the end of August, the fact that he was shipped home in November after weeks in the hospital suggests that a severe typhoid relapse or a complication from typhoid must have occurred around the time of his last entry. There is no record of him writing anything more after August 23.

Brown would probably not recognize much of present-day Paranaque. In 1900 it was a city separated from Manila by grasslands and nipa huts; today it is a physical part of the megalopolis. Brown's bridge at Paranaque was eaten through by sea worms months after its completion, but its replacement, the Don Galo Bridge, stands at the same location as Brown's: approximately nine kilometers south of central Manila. Despite being at the same point on the river, the surrounding environment has changed remarkably. Now incredibly polluted, the Paranaque still empties into the bay. Like Manila, Paranaque's shoreline was completely redrawn at several points during the twentieth century. Both the town and the bridge were nearly on the beach in 1900; today the shore is several hundred yards away.

Native carts and horses being taken across the Paranaque River in bancas.
Courtesy Harper's History of the War in the Philippines, 1900.

Nevertheless, there are at least a few landmarks he would recognize. The old Spanish road running from Malate through Paranaque and farther south, although paved today, is essentially the same route. Saint Paul's, the splendid church with its magnificent baroque alter, still guards the bridge's southern approach, although a two-story McDonald's restaurant across the street now ably assists it. Moreover, when one looks down at the river, *bancas*, large and small, still ply their trade—a sight Brown would surely recognize, regardless of the massive amounts of garbage in the water.

MAY 2
Am ordered to Paranaque to superintend the construction of the bridge I drew. By the way, there is a picture in one of the last *Harper's Weekly* I received showing natives ferrying people across where the bridge is to be.[1]

MAY 3
Paranaque. After all it was not until nearly 9 A.M. that we started. Goodness, how hot it was! Passed the line of the insurgent trenches built when the army only held Manila and not all of that. Passed the site of Camp Dewey and finally, after a ride of about eight miles, came to Paranaque River and our station.[2] I have one private with

me, for the next two or three months. There is a ferry to be moved first and then I am to run the lines and levels for the bridge, inspect material and act as general supervisor over the contractors. The bridge will be 233 feet long, to which must be added 150 feet for approaches. Do you wonder where I learned to run a transit and level? To tell the truth I never had either in my hands until to-day, but last August, when we were stationed at San Fernando, I read with considerable interest a treatise on surveying. Found no diffi-culty. The adjustments are as nothing when compared to a sensitive piece of electrical apparatus.

MAY 4
Paranaque. Spent most of the day working out some examples of similar triangles. Would have given much for a glance at a trigo-nometry or the use of a table of logarithms. A battalion of the 49th, colored, holds the ferry, but we are comfortably quartered in a large room with the signal operator and wagon master, both white. This is the way I measured the width of the river. It is slow and takes more labor. I have to use right triangles, as with no books or tables they [*drawing that originally appeared here is no longer extant*] are all I can solve, which gave me the distance between the bridge abut-ments, 233 feet.

MAY 5
Paranaque. Now that one gets a chance to look about a little it seems that this will be a very pleasant detail. The town itself is on both sides of the river, running back on the high road perhaps a mile or over, the south bank and for at least half that distance towards Ma-nila. Of course it is only a collection of native huts and nipa huts at that, but the town has a large stone church and two other smaller ones.[3] They all show the marks of Dewey's shells, for this was a famous insurgent stronghold, and the shore is lined with rifle pits and breastworks for two or three miles.

MAY 6
Paranaque. There is a great deal of travel across the ferry, the coun-try caramattas carrying fruits, vegetables and nipa thatch into Manila, peddlers carrying cotton cloths and a thousand other things

into the country. There is hardly a moment during the day that people are not crossing. Towards evening when everybody wishes to cross at once it is a very lively scene, the chattering natives in the bright-colored clothes, the canoes hastily paddled across, some holding four or five native ponies, some so crowded with women and children that should the slightest breeze ruffle the river which lies so placid in the twilight they would surely fill and sink. I watched the ferry for fully two hours last night, hoping, I must admit, to see some such catastrophe, but though, as the sun sank, they, in their hurry, crowded the canoes so deeply that the passage became a succession of feminine cries, nothing happened.

MAY 7
Paranaque. While the contractor is having his own troubles with the native workmen, just at present they won't work because he paid the most deserving some few cents more than the others, I try to keep myself amused. Not that it is difficult. The ferry is an ever-changing panorama, or one can watch the native fishermen, or the poor devils diving for oysters.

MAY 8
Paranaque. It was broiling hot. The "hombres" were lazily seeing how little work they could do. I was sitting on the end of the crib work lazily flicking chips into the water and thinking, well, not thinking of the army. A chip grounded in an eddy and attracted my notice to a pile of submerged masonry, the relic of the old stone bridge blown up by the insurgents.[4] I reflected. "Look here, Hunter (the contractor's foreman), if you want to move your abutment a few feet to the right you can save a couple of days' work removing that stone. I don't object in the least." "All right. By the way, I was speaking to J—, the contractor, about you yesterday. The job is worth about $50 gold to you I guess. There may be some other little things later, nothing that will hurt the bridge, nothing to compromise you, you know." I looked at him and felt myself flushing as I did so. I felt my fist close, then, well then I laughed. What did it matter. How could he know that I was anything but a Corporal of Engineers. I am no fool. I know how often it is done. Does not any extra ability in the army show that a man "has done something"? "Of course,"

I said, and I laughed again. " But I'll have to see J— about that."
A little later my assistant said, "Suppose a pile won't go down
quite eight feet. We ought to make a little something, don't you
...think?" Now that troubled me. He is an old soldier and a good
one as I know well. Moreover he has been working on the railroad (I think I wrote about the railroad). I don't want to stand
between him and a little extra money. I guess I will have to give
him a few dollars myself and encourage him to think I got many
moneys from J—. It is not his fault he is detailed with a gentleman in disguise.

MAY 10
Paranaque. The work goes on very slowly. After supper we all have
a swim in the river, which is very warm as to temperature and rather
dirty into the bargain. A pipe on the cribhead and a half-hour or so
of talk. It is funny how much we have to talk about. Hunter is a
discharged soldier from A Company and came here in the first expedition, saw the taking of Manila and the outbreak of the insurrection. His assistant is a deserter from one of our ships, who saw
the trouble in Rio and other things. I myself have now a few anec-
dotes at command, and my assistant or rod man was on the railroad
bridge at Angeles and Bayambang and was station master at Bautista.
A glass of bottled beer from the States in one of the native saloons
and then bed, usually about 8:30.[5]

MAY 11
Paranaque. Every once in a while some one in the company does
me some kindness that makes me think there are better men in the
army than I used to know in civil life. When I was detailed out here
it was a few days before pay day and I had no money. Not exactly, I
had eight cents, Mexican. Of course all my friends in the company
knew it, everybody knows everybody's business in barracks. To-day
I received an envelope simply marked "From Wey," containing ten
dollars, Mexican. "The Corporal said he knew you was broke," said
the teamster who brought it, "and thought it might come in handy."
I'll admit I was much touched by the thoughtfulness and evidence
of good-fellowship.

MAY 12

The Lieutenant Colonel of this Volunteer regiment, now in command of this battalion is a captain in the 24th Regulars. He was Adjutant on the *City of Para* until we reached Honolulu. I mention this because I want to remember it.[6] It is amusing to watch the native workmen. The pile-driver in use on the bridge works by hand. The hammer has to be lifted by a winch. The Filipino is not as strong as a white man and he is twice as lazy. The consequence is that towards midday the weight fairly crawls up. There is much shouting to be sure but very little work. They seem unused to hard work. If they are hauling on a rope it is difficult to get them to pull together. My opinion of them falls with every day's work I see them do.

MAY 13

Paranaque. This is one of the tales the sailor told as we sat on the bridgehead in the tropic moonlight, told with much profanity and wealth of detail that I must omit, told, too, without any apparent feeling, with no change in voice, with no animation save an occasional low chuckle as some new detail occurred to him. It seems to me it is worth saving. Seven days and a half without water is quite a bit of endurance. There was not any introduction. No one was talking and he suddenly commenced from his corner in the shadow of the pile-driver. "Yes, by God, that was a tough experience, the toughest I ever had. Sometimes I think I saw the ship around a point before I dropped off, but I'm not sure. None of the others remembered anything. It was towards daylight that I woke up thinking I was in my bunk and that some one was throwing water on me. It was water that woke me up all right, but I wasn't in my bunk. No, you bet I wasn't. I was in the bottom of the long boat and she was half full of water. I could not at first remember how I got there, but it came back to me after a while. I remembered that we had brought four bottles of rum and three of wine, no, it was five bottles of rum and two bottles of wine, with us and I made for those. God, but I was thirsty. Every bottle was broken, every bloody one. I never did find out how it happened. We carried a two-gallon jug of water in the boat, one of those wicker-covered things, a demijohn. I went to that. The cork was out and the water was slushing round the bottom of the boat. We used to anchor with an old piece of a windlass tied out the end of a lead line. I saw this line running over the bow and thought we were anchored all right. I never thought of looking to see where we were. The two other men were rolling round in the water in the bottom of the boat. The Captain was coiled up in the stern sheets. If I could not drink I could sleep and I was going to bunk with the Captain. We'd been drunk together. He could not kick if we shared the same bunk. There was plenty of room, you know, he on one side and I on the other. Well, anyway, the noise I made crawling aft woke him up.

"'Where are we?' he asked, sitting up and rubbing his eyes. 'Oh, go to sleep, we're anchored.' 'Anchored be damned.' Then the other men woke up and we pulled in the line. There was only about eight feet of it, no, not more than six. They must have anchored too late. Anyway the line had chafed off under our bows. 'Do you know where we are, boys?' Yes, we knew where we were well enough. We were in the boat. The old man did not mean that though. 'You're in the Gulf of, Gulf of—(I never can get that name straight. It's between the north coast of Trinidad and Venezuela. It commences with C or H. Well, the name don't matter). The current has been carrying us eight miles an hour since we went to sleep.' We knew the Gulf well enough, only three days before a French smack had come in where we were anchored after trying for three days to get out of it. It was no good doing anything till we could see. We were all more or less drunk yet anyway, so we laid down again.

"At daylight we started pulling, but it turned out afterward that we did not pull for Trinidad but for the Venezuelan coast. The men growled and cursed a good deal at first and wished they were lucky enough to be in jail like the other man. By and by they got tired of that. I remembered there was a bottle of lime juice in the locker aft. Would you believe it? That was empty too.

"About dinner time on the second day we sighted land. You know how it is. It might be a day before we reached it. The Captain said, 'God, boys, I feel thirsty. I'd give everything in the world, if I owned it, for a drink.' Nobody felt much like talking then, but we wondered how he thought we felt if he felt that bad. A little later he said, 'I feel damned bad, boys, I guess I'll take a nap.' Towards evening we could feel the bottom with our oars. It was a low shore with rushes growing out. We had to work our way in. The Swede said, 'We can feel the bottom with our oars now, Captain,' but he did not answer. Then he went up to him to wake him for we wanted to know what to do. He had a red handkerchief over his face and his head was resting on a sort of a valise. He had had a hard hat, but had lost it the first night. The Swede pulled the handkerchief off his face and there were his eyes staring straight up and sort of glassy. He was dead. We left him where he was for we expected to get assistance soon and we wanted to bury him. He was a good man, though he got us into trouble by giving us too much booze.

"Finally we got ashore. It was the damnedest shore you ever saw. Mangroves. You could not see twenty feet, no, not so far as that. The trunks were not more than nine feet apart and went straight up. There was a broad-ax in the boat and with that we dug a hole in the sand. It filled with the cleanest water, but God! it was salt. We went further in and dug again and again. We must have dug fifty holes, with the ax, mind you, but they were all the same. We did not dare go very far in for fear we would get lost and came back to the boat to sleep.

"All the next day we paddled along the coast against the current. It did not seem so strong inshore, so we kept so close in that the in-shore oars touched bottom at every stroke. We landed occasionally to dig holes, but they were all the same. Towards evening we found a cocoanut grove, but the trees were too young to bear. The fourth day was just the same. No, the Norwegian and Swede walked up the coast about two miles to see if they could not find something, leaving me in the boat with the dead Captain. There was a small strap for a boom in the boat and we used this for an anchor, pushing it down in the mud to make it stick. When they came back they brought three cocoanuts. There might have been a tablespoonful of milk in each one, meat and all there was not more than a glassful. We divided it. It did about as much good as a box of matches in hell, yes, just about.

"That night the Swede said he would take the first watch, that he was not sleepy. About eleven I was waked up by something clammy being on my face. I took it off, thinking it might be a scorpion. It was moonlight, like it is now, and I saw what it was well enough. It was a piece of human flesh. The Swede was sitting on the stern eating as fast as he could and crying, 'Eat it, eat it, it's good,' He must have been drinking salt water. No man would have gone crazy so soon if he hadn't. Don't you think so? Well, by and by he laid down and went to sleep at once. 'What do you think of that?' said the Norwegian. 'He's mad,' I said, 'but mad or sober the Captain goes overboard at once.' First we tied the Swede with what was left of the lead line. There had not been any sharks before, but now they came by hundreds. Some one must have sent them a telegram. The Captain was lifted high in the air as they played with him. You see we did not have any weights to sink the body.

"In the morning the Swede seemed all right, so after we had hid the broad-ax we untied him. When it got hot the fit came on him again and he jumped overboard. We got him out and tied him down again, but not till the Norwegian got a black eye and my face was pretty well banged up. After that we did not untie him nor give him anything. There was not anything to give, for that matter.

"Nothing much happened the next two days. We went ashore occasionally, but found nothing. I knew that certain parts of snakes are good to eat if you can cut their heads off before they bite themselves. We could not catch any. One bit me once, but the Norwegian sucked the poison out.

"In the morning of the eighth day we were still pulling slowly up the coast. Suddenly the Norwegian turned round and looking over the starboard bow said, 'I see a sail.' 'Go on,' I said, never looking around, 'it's your imagination. It's a white rock you see.' 'Yes, I guess you're right. I think I am getting blind anyway.' In about an hour he looked round again. 'It is a sail.' Then I looked around. By God, it was a sail after all. (This was the only time his voice rose.) It was a small schooner coming down wing and wing. When I looked I saw the shake of a sail that jibed. We let go our sails that were brailed up and rowed straight into the wind so as to make them shiver. They said afterwards they saw us as soon as we did that. She came straight towards us, but we had a good ways to pull yet for the water was so shallow she could not get in close. Finally we got aboard, then without untying the Swede we made a rush for the water cask. I made to lift it and drink, but Lord, it weighed 200 pounds. They bloody soon stopped that and gave us about a teaspoonful each and then in about an hour a little more. It wasn't till the next day I got all I wanted."

"You didn't tell on the Swede, of course."

"No, we told him about it on the voyage home. He felt bad about it too. But he was crazy when he did it. He did not come right for four or five weeks."

MAY 14
Paranaque. Beautiful moonlight nights these. The river is really beautiful; the shore fringed with bamboo through which shine the lights of the native huts, the ungainly boats moored a little way from the bank, all making a picture that makes the most unromantic of us think ourselves capable of writing volumes of descriptive poetry.

MAY 15
Paranaque. Work on the bridge goes forward very slowly. No piles, no lumber, no anything but profanity. A long, hard day's work for twelve men and the result only two piles driven.

MAY 16
Paranaque. A phonograph is one of the last things I expected here, but it seems this Volunteer outfit, the 49th, has one. Last night I sat on the balustrade of our balcony and listened to it sing for some hours. It seemed very odd to hear the old songs one used to hear at Weber & Field's or at Koster & Bial's. It brought up curious memories, inconsistent memories, or so at least they seemed when one looked down on the shell-torn church, the walls patched with coarse stone and interlaced with barbed wire, the natives and the ever-

present soldiers. A curious change of scene. But the songs were the same old songs. I suppose you have forgotten them by this time. They were new when we left.[7] Had a rather narrower escape of losing a hand than I really fancy. Was measuring the depth the pile had been driven when the weight broke and the hammer came down a bit suddenly. I just pulled my hand away in time. As it was the hammer caught the very edge of one finger, just the smallest conceivable bit of skin, which of course tore loose. No damage more serious than a slight scratch.

MAY 17
Paranaque. The Quartermaster of the battalion (49th) was building a pier. He took the trouble to ask my opinion as to how it should be done. He did not build it the way I suggested and I was somewhat amused some three hours later to see the whole pier slide into the river. I dare say my way would have been equally disastrous, but as he did not try it he imagines, or so I suppose by his manner of treating me, that I am a second Capt. Eads.[8]

MAY 18
Paranaque. Every once in a while one meets something so home-like as to be a sort of a shock. To-day it was a device the women use for stretching their embroidery work. It did seem strange to see such a thing in this little collection of fishermen houses. This is the hottest weather I have experienced since I have been here. Every one is wishing for the rains to commence.

MAY 19
Received telegraphic orders to go to Manila (Malate), if I could leave the work; I could and did, getting in about 4:30 P.M. Found the Lieutenant wanted me to take the preliminary examination for an appointment as 2d Lieutenant. Told him I had not completed my two years' service. He urged me to try anyway, so I put in the application.[9] It was good to get back to the company even temporarily. While I had been away the Camarine detail had come in, so there were twenty-five men whom I had not seen since I started out north. They were all glad to see me and showed it. Then to sit down to a nice supper and be waited on (it is astonishing how much better

Regulars live than Volunteers), to see about you men you knew and trusted. Well, a commission is not the only thing in the world. I can understand perhaps why so many good soldiers refuse to accept commissions, why they prefer to stay in the ranks.

MAY 20
Sunday. There were many things to talk about and the day passed quickly enough. Our quarters at Malate are very attractive with a little shrub-covered square and cool fountain in front of them. A pleasant place to sit in the evening after the band has stopped playing on the Lunetta.

MAY 21
Manila. Drew my pay for March and April. Alas, it did not do me much good as after I paid back the money I had borrowed, paid the money I owed for cool bottles of beer obtained on credit after my money was spent last month, I found myself the proud possessor of $5.00, gold, from which you can readily see I am becoming an "old soldier." Tried to buy some books to cram a little for the exams if I am allowed to take them. I could only find a Spanish geometry and trigonometry. I will be badly prepared indeed unless my record helps me.

MAY 22
Left Manila on horseback and had a delightful ride to Paranaque in the cool of the morning. Took a private out with me to bring back the horse. Found the contractor had taken advantage of my absence to drive some piles remarkably under the specification. Made him pull them out, a hard job, and drive new ones.

MAY 23
Paranaque. Now that I look around it appears as if the luck that has stood by us so well has flunked me out in the end. I am shy some three weeks on the time, which makes me wait, I am afraid, another year for my exam. If I do not have to wait I go up badly prepared. I have been on active service continually with no chance to prepare. Now at the last minute my only books are a trigonometry and a geometry, both written in Spanish, for the rest I must trust to

memory. It was ten years ago or more I studied them. Lieut. Rees, 3d Infantry, formerly a Corporal in B Company (he got a commission last October), rode out to see me bringing me copies of the exam he took. I could pass that, but God knows what will happen to me.

MAY 24
Paranaque. A bright, starlight night, no moon. The little village is as quiet as can be, an occasional burst of song. Suddenly comes the old muttering, the distant rumble of the guns. How it makes the pulse beat. Not for months have I heard it. Suddenly there is great excitement, this regiment has never been under fire. How the telegraph wires click. What ideas these Volunteer officers have. Men who have never heard a shot fired can tell you the caliber of the guns firing. What nonsense! There was a slight shock of earthquake at 4:15 P.M.

MAY 25
Paranaque. All sorts of curious things come down our little river. Sometimes it is some ungainly old casco loaded with salt which is pushed along, by naked, perspiring natives, bent so low over their pushing poles that their foreheads swept the bamboo out-riggers. To-day it was a little flotilla of large canoes filled with dancing, gesticulating, singing natives. One of the canoes had a band and the music added, if any addition was necessary, to the completeness of the scene. It was a wedding party. The bride was most curious. I can't begin to describe her costume, which was bright in color and shining with ornaments. On her head was a curious half-crown, half-hat, with plumes and silver beads. Where they went I don't know. Straight out to sea they went and soon were out of sight, a mere blot in the scorching, dazzling sunshine. The firing yesterday was night target practice at San Pedro Maccati [Makati].

MAY 26
Application for examination disapproved.

JUNE 4
Paranaque. Well, I have been under the weather again. Not a real sickness, like the last, but a disagreeable kind of low fevers that

made it difficult to work and were not of sufficient importance to stop me. The result was that last week was a rather miserable one in spite of a splendid big home mail which cheered me up a good deal. Made a foolish mistake in my record I sent home. My service begins on the 2d of May, 1898, not the 12th, as I wrote. I am afraid the chance for the commission this fall is slim.

JUNE 5
I am, so the Doctor tells me, going through that agreeable state call convalescing. He is a nigger and I have not much confidence in him even if he did cure me.[10] His theory seems to me to give medicine by shovelfuls, which is not, I believe, in accordance with the latest practice. It continues as hot as previously. I am sure I shall be very glad to see the rains commence. This constant heat gets irritating. It is not bad if you can keep out of the sun, but that is difficult to do when one is working.

JUNE 6
D Troop of the 4th went through here to-day. This is the troop I was in Carraglan with last November. They seemed glad to see me and I was quite glad to hear from them again. There are not many changes, a few secrets I did not know, that was all. My spirits are getting better every day, which must mean I am all right again. Rained hard all last night and is threatening to-day. I guess we have not much longer to wait. The bridge is coming on very slowly.

JUNE 7
Paranaque. Somewhat to my surprise the Lieutenant rode out this morning to see the bridge. He did not say anything, so I imagine he found it satisfactory. Said he was sorry that my application had been refused and advised me strongly to write home and get influence used if possible. If not, I will have to wait another year. Weather not so hot now, days more inclined to be overcast.

JUNE 8
Paranaque. Really, things haven't been as bad as one would think from reading this installment of the journal. I was homesick I guess more than anything else. I was tempted to tear this up, but I send it

to show that one has different moods, disagreeable as well as pleasant.[11] Your letter, dear mamma, telling how the planks were taken up and the birds were coming home again, made me see just how things looked and I was anxious to be there.[12] Well, I am cheerful again now, so the incident can be regarded as closed.

JUNE 9

Paranaque. Rather a cool day. The contractor had his whole force, some twenty men, trying to bail out the trench for north abutments, a hopeless sort of a job without apparent ending, but it's got to done some way. The contractor's boss is down sick, throwing all his work on the sailor. My assistant is sick too. I don't believe this can be a very healthy place.

JUNE 10

Sunday. America need never fear the competition of the cheap labor from the Philippines. The labor is cheap. The masons, carpenters and laborers on the bridge get from forty cents to sixty cents, gold, a day, but they won't work steady. It seems a week's wages, even at that low figure, will keep them in food and give them money enough to gamble with for an indefinite period. While their money lasts they won't work any more, and so every Monday morning we commence work with practically a new gang of men. Sometimes a man will lose all he made during the week on the Sunday cock-fight, but that rarely happens. And their work even at the best is pretty poor. They are not a strong race physically. Two laboring men in the States can do as much in a day as five of them. Another curious thing, the sun seems to affect them more than it does Americans, also they can't stand the cold of a shower. If you insist on their working in the rain they stand still, helplessly shivering.

JUNE 11

Paranaque. After all, a person can get a good deal of satisfaction out of this world in the pure joy of being alive. I could not help feeling so this morning at sunrise as I stepped out of the old convent to go down to the river.[13] It is not a wonderful view we get here, but it is very satisfying; the blue of the distant mountains over the green of the bamboos that fringe the river. It makes one contented, as I have written, just to be able to see and to appreciate these things. All the morning on one pile. Now it is raining gently.

JUNE 12
Paranaque. The days are almost always overcast now, a welcome relief from the sun. It is curious, a curious sort of picture, to see us at work. There are four of us white men, only one of whom does any work. The rest of us sit round in the shade, under a native house perhaps with its hogs, children and perhaps a horse, and watch. The foreman has a native sweetheart who is usually squatting at his feet or following his movements with a dog-like devotion. They are mostly animal, these natives. It was only a couple of days ago that the President (a native) of Bacon, a town some ten miles from here, was caught alone and unarmed and cruelly butchered with bolos.[14]

JUNE 13
Paranaque. Work on the bridge suspended temporarily for want of material. A lazy day in consequence. It was one of those overcast days, cool, with an ever-present threat of rain. As for me, I read the *Century* for some months back, very interesting articles on China, which seem to gather fresh force with the news of the landing of our sailors and marines near Peking. It would be interesting to fight in China against the Russians. Will it come to pass?

JUNE 14
Another lazy day. No work on bridge as there was no lumber or stone. Read all day and blessed the luck that gave me so many back numbers of *Century*.

JUNE 15
Paranaque. A little work putting up false work for bridge.

JUNE 16
Discovered false work was wrongly placed and would throw the piles out of place. Raining hard and telegraph wire not working, so started on foot for Malate to see what the Lieutenant thought. Meanwhile stopped all work. Lieutenant thought with me that piles must be in proper place. A regular typhoon now, blowing hard and

Modern bridge at Paranaque. Courtesy Joseph P. McCallus.

raining. I only walked about half-way in before a caramatta overtook me and I got a ride. Very pleasant to see the company again
and get some of their good food. It was like going into Delmonico's
after this miserable Volunteer outfit. The contractor came in to plead
with the Lieutenant, but the latter was firm.

JUNE 17
Staid in at Malate all night, the men furnishing me with what was
needed. A regular typhoon. Fine breakfast and dinner, some plum
duff that seemed to melt in your mouth. It's a shame the way the
Volunteers live. A large mail from the States. It seems hard to realize that they are all at Glen Cove again.[15] Rode out to Paranaque
between showers. Hawbe took the horse back.

JUNE 18
Rain all day. No work on the bridge, owing to lack of material. A
long day, with magazines as a God-send. Hot argument about silly
subjects in which I was in no way interested. After supper walked
all over the town on this side of the river, during the rain, in an

endeavor to get a little much-needed exercise. It is not in any way different from twenty other small towns, having the same smells, the same over-abundance of children and the same dirt. It is always a marvel to me how the natives contrive to wear such clean clothes when they live surrounded by filth. The market was not particularly interesting nor was it on so large a scale as I expected. They say the population is about 10,000.[16] The industries are fishing and making salt by evaporating sea water. The latter can only be pursued in the dry season.

JUNE 19
Paranaque. Rain. Drove two piles and had to stop as had no more. I have come to the conclusion that nine-tenths of the Signal Corps telegraph operators are a bit crazy. We sleep in the telegraph office and have to see considerable of the operators. Of course it is a monstrous unhealthy sort of life and none of them take any exercise. Five of them have gone into the hospital, sick, since I have been out here.

JUNE 20
Paranaque. Rain. Last evening I walked up the beach for perhaps a mile, a very picturesque walk, with the trembling surf and the distant fleet at Cavite. Our own shore was odd too, the trenches of the insurgents hardly visible in the dense, low shrubbery, the little native huts showing through an occasional opening.[17] I was more surprised however at the number of boats along the beach. I must have passed three or four hundred of them, of all shapes and sizes from the little ones, five or six feet long, up to the big fishing canoes, fifty or sixty feet in length. Considering that they all, with the exception of the very largest, are hollowed out of single logs, the labor represented was immense. Some have lasted for generations. To-day I complete one year's service in the ranks. A year ago to-morrow I enlisted at Washington barracks. A short, exciting year.

JUNE 21
Paranaque is situated on three sides of a river, that is the river forks in the town itself, one branch running northeast, the other southeast. The third side of the town is uncleared land. Situated not two

hundred yards from the quarters, it seems to be absolutely unvis-
ited. For that reason my assistant and I, no work being done on
the bridge, took our revolvers and went on an exploring trip. On
the north side of the river a shaky bamboo bridge leads to the terra
incognita. Across this bridge I rubbed my eyes in amazement. It
was a new country. No windswept barrens. Behind the fringe of
bamboo lay an ideal little native village. Rice fields, every kind of
tropical fruit that you can imagine, huts half buried in luxuriant
foliage. It was like a dream and the contrast between it and the
poor little fishing village across the narrow stream made it the
more remarkable. The news comes that three regiments are ordered to China. I have volunteered by letter. I wish I might be
allowed to go.

JUNE 22

Word came over the wire yesterday that the troops were surely going to China. No work was being done on the bridge and I re-
solved to go in and see the Lieutenant and apply for China. So I
walked in, some eight miles. Imagine my disappointment at finding
the detail already made out. I begged to be included. I offered to be
reduced, to go as a second-class private, anything if they would
only let me go. It was no go. The Lieutenant who is going is
Fergusson, not Oakes.[18] The latter, who I have always been with,
told me plainly be wanted me with him and would not let me go.
What could I do? It is a great disappointment. Lieut. Oakes said
he was scheming to take the whole company; that if he went I
should certainly go. With that I was obliged to be content. The
men are all anxious to go. Of course the way we have been jacked
about the enthusiasm that formerly made the men eager for fights
has passed. We have so many that no one is disappointed if he
misses one. But China. It is a sluggish imagination that is not stirred
at the thought of service there. Had a talk in the evening with men
of the various regiments under orders to go. All are glad of the
chance, those men who have no imagination welcoming the change.
Men in my company are offering ten and twenty dollars to the men
on the detail to effect an exchange. Walked back this morning, luckily getting a ride to Marikebon, about half-way. Still no material
for the bridge.

JUNE 23

Paranaque. There is one curious thing. The Doctor of this battalion is of course a negro, a rather intelligent negro and of course educated. I am rather amused sometimes at the somewhat patronizing way he talks to me. If he uses a large word he immediately explains it. As usual they have all kinds of stories about me, and so last night this young fellow said he would like to talk to me, said he had heard about me, that we would have drinks and cigars. Naturally I did not go. Of course he has a commission and I am an enlisted man, but I retain the privilege of my prejudices and I won't be patronized by any one, least of all a nigger.

JUNE 24

Paranaque. No material, no work on bridge. It is rather hard to kill these no-work days.

JUNE 25

Paranaque. For the past week I have been trying to compare the negro with the Filipino. Now it may be objected, after the *City of Para* and my experience here, that I am prejudiced against the negro. Well, possibly I am, but it is also certain that I waste no love on the Filipino, however much I admire his courtesy. Here I get a good chance to compare them. To the best of my belief if the Filipino had had the opportunity that the negro has had since the Civil War he would be a superior race mentally to our American negro. The negro is of course by long odds his superior physically. Now the two races are about on a par. I really cannot choose between them but I think the Filipino gives more promise for the future. It's a difficult question.

JUNE 26

Paranaque. It is a very disagreeable job, this being inspector. I used to hate it as cable expert in the old N.T. & T. Co. Here, where there are only a few people to talk to, it is particularly hard to have to row with any of them. I think I have a peaceful disposition. It is so much easier to be pleasant. Here it is continual rows about lumber, stone, piles, cement, goodness knows in what they don't try to cheat. It makes one feel like a spy, like anything but a gentleman. I am beginning to believe in Capt. Carter's innocence, to believe at least that he made no money out of his fraudulent contractors.[19] What a lying, disagreeable set they are to deal with.

JUNE 27
Paranaque. Cavite looks deserted to-day. The fleet has gone to China. I wonder if Billy has gone with it? If he has it will not make me any more contented to stay here. Still the rains hold off. Since our typhoon which lasted three or four days we have had no rain. Work on the bridge almost suspended. No piles. A little work by stone masons on the piers, but that is all. I wish I could see the end of it. Quite a change since I wrote at noon. Now it is raining hard with every prospect of its being another storm.

JUNE 28
Paranaque. Did I ever describe our quarters? Last night, as I lay on my cot listening to the rain, it happened to strike me they were odd enough to deserve a description. It's a barn of a room, rather larger than our dining-room, with a ceiling perhaps half again as high. On one side is the curious balconies all the houses of the well-to-do have, with its sliding shutters, with shell window-panes, opaque, but yet allowing light to penetrate. In our room the shutters are mostly gone, so that that side of the room is uninhabitable in a storm. Also there is a hole made by an exploding shell in the roof and ceiling, so that a heavy rain drives us to a narrow strip of dry flooring against the wall. There is not any furniture but the three bunks, the telegraph table and a few boxes for seats. At night we each light our candle and attend pretty strictly to our own business, for we are pretty well talked out after two months of being together, we never talk to the niggers, and a conversation between ourselves is apt to end in elaborately courteous phrases or else in silent rage. What do we do? I write or read, my partner plays solitaire for hours, as he has invented or been taught a game that can only be done about once in five hundred times. It is interesting to hear him curse his luck and the cards. The operator sits over his instrument, reading all messages, and moans about his hard lot and grumbles about everything from his Captain through the President and Senate to the Supreme Court, at which he is especially

bitter, being a firm Bryan man.[20] Then either Minkles or I get pro-
voked and argue or laugh him into such a passion of rage that one
not knowing us would expect murder as the only outcome. Presently we are friends again. Eight o'clock usually finds us in bed and
nine asleep. If we have a visitor, some white soldier caught by the
night on his solitary way as messenger, lineman or some man on
pass rejoining his regiment, some man favored by an invitation to
join its from a passing escort or squadron changing station, then
we are apt to unite forces long enough to find out by adroit ques-
tioning what his views are of the army, the war, religion, anything.
There is sure to be something we can disagree with and overwhelm
him with our well-known and often-used arguments or bits of well-
polished sarcasm. The next night we are amicable for a while as we
tell each other how foolish he was, but finally we are bound to
disagree about something and then more rage, more or less openly
expressed. I have often thought how much our guests must enjoy
our chatty evenings, particularly when we make fun of his most
cherished ideals. I am afraid I haven't described our room as fully
as I had intended.

JUNE 29
Paranaque. A letter from Billy written a few days ago saying he
sailed for China the next morning.[21] He was much pleased at the
chance to go and was openly exultant. I am sure I envy him, but
comfort myself with the hope that I may go a little later.

JUNE 30
A day or so ago one of the natives' large canoes loaded with the
most delicious pineapples. There must have been thousands of them.
As a result we have been able to get them very cheap, three for five
cents, gold. They make a most agreeable addition to the ration. A
severe thunder storm this afternoon. The Adjutant here is also trying for a Regular commission and lent me a book on international
law. It being Sunday I spent the day reading it.

JULY 1
Paranaque. Light showers. When we first came here (Paranaque)
the trees, of which there are a number in a walled enclosure in

front of the church, had only a few straggling red blossoms. In my ignorance, I supposed the trees dead and so described them in many letters. A month later they were covered with beautiful flowers with a rich, heavy scent. Now the leaves have come and the combination is beautiful.

JULY 2

This corresponds to the spring of the year as nearly as I can make out. Now they are preparing the ground for planting. Some young birds fell out of the nest in the rafters to-day.

JULY 3

How the anniversaries are coming round. A year ago to-night was the last time I was in New York. On the 5th we left Willett's Point. I never knew a year to pass so quickly. And I have been lucky too. Nothing unfortunate but the failure to get permission to pass the exam for a commission. My health is as good as when I landed, a fact which I congratulate myself not a little.[22] A feast in the company tomorrow. Though telegraphed an invitation by our First Sergeant I feel I must stay here as the contractor works to-morrow.

JULY 4

No sign of any celebration here till towards evening, when every one appeared to become drunk. Now, about 8 P.M., there are several quartettes wandering about singing for drinks. Really they sing very well, and very effective it sounds from this little distance. One wonders what you are all doing at Glen Cove. One's memory goes even farther back, way beyond any personal experience, and one cannot but think what the signers of the Declaration of Independence would think could they see what has become of their experiment. Not a brilliant thought? No, I suppose millions are thinking the same thing. It is fascinating though and curious.

JULY 5

Heavy rain. There are two or three ways one can look at the natives here. One is the enlisted man's standpoint. The soldier starts in with a fine contempt for the insurgent, who would not stand up for a square fight but who always wanted to fight from ambush and who playfully boloed the stragglers. This feeling is intensified by the fact that the soldier knows that he has to pay twice as much as any one else for whatever he may buy from a native. Then, in addition, the soldier meets the rough-scuff of the Filipinos, the hangers-on at the native canteens. The native has some reason for cheating the soldier, who, on their part, go on the principle that "marching orders cancel all debts." So the enlisted man has a poor opinion of the native and undoubtedly writes home to that effect. An officer, on the contrary, is better able to judge the capabilities of the race. He can form an accurate opinion if he remembers that he sees the most intelligent class and sees them only when they are on their good behavior. Under the protection of a strong and liberal government like our own they may become a race which amounts to something, but it will take time. There are of course brilliant natives, a remarkable fact when one considers how they were kept down by the Spanish officials and the priests. To my mind the most unpromising lookout for the future welfare of the Malay is the fact that they have allowed the Chinese to monopolize the business of the island. The Chinaman here is the Jew of America, only here his business supremacy and his ability is much more in advance of his competitor. The native is too lazy to compete with a good business man.

JULY 6
Paranaque. A detail of six men under Corporal Burke came out from the company to build the approaches to the bridge.[23] Most glad to see them as it gives us some one to talk to and a decent mess, which we have longed for for two months. Mail from the States, which was much appreciated. Heavy showers.

JULY 7
No work on the bridge. No piles. Ran the levels for a drain the Colonel (Col. Ducat, 49th Infantry) wants built. Was much interested in the work as it was the first I had ever done and as having no text-books I was obliged to work out my own methods. I suppose I was clumsy at it, but got it done correctly and to my satisfaction. Corporal Burke served fifteen years in the 7th Cavalry and is interesting.

JULY 8

It is really wonderful how much difference there is between the Regulars and Volunteers. For two months here we have been living as bad as possible. Now this detachment of Engineers has been here only two days and yet, with the same source of supply to draw from, we are living over a hundred per cent better. I never saw the difference between knowing how and not knowing how so plainly marked. Great news every day from China makes every soldier long to get there. Saw a very striking and yet quite true article of Senator Beveridge's about the curious feeling the officers and men out here have for the flag.[24]

JULY 9

There is in the detail now here one young fellow of some degree of intelligence but of overweening confidence in the importance of his own personality. This evening I amused myself for some hours in expressing, for his benefit, the most extreme views on the absolute unimportance of the individual blended with pronounced idealism. It was a horribly inconsistent mixture and I was tempted to gross absurdities which luckily were undetected. But it was very amusing. Bossed the construction of the drain I ran the levels for. I am now anxious for a rain to test it.

JULY 10

It seems a curious subject to write about, but the native funerals here are very curious. They range in all grades from the pathetic spectacle of the corpse rudely wrapped in a bamboo mat, followed by a single mourner, to the elaborate ceremonies of the rich, which necessitates a long procession headed by the priest and altar boys in fall regalia, a brass band (sometimes playing the "koochee koochee" dance or, still more incongruous, "A Hot Time in the Old Town To-night"), and with the corpse, carried by many pall-bearers, on an elaborately decorated float which is surmounted by a canopy. Over half of the deaths are of babies.

JULY 11

Paranaque. Education does not remove the animal instincts from the negro. There are some highly educated negroes here with this battalion, but even those do not seem to think like white men. All of them are intensely superstitious, from the one who, having taken a splinter out of my finger, begged me to chew it (the splinter) lest erysipelas set in, to the Doctor, who is seriously put out if he has to be present at a death-bed where there is no priest or at least prayer. I am rapidly acquiring a very poor opinion of the race and should heartily support any attempt to disfranchise them, or to limit their suffrage.

JULY 12
I think the rainy season, like everything else that is disagreeable out here, is immensely exaggerated. It is supposed to begin in June, but you can clearly see that if it does it is not very bad for I have faithfully recorded every shower save those that occur in the night. We have been here eleven months to-morrow and I can honestly say that I have not found the climate as trying as that of New York. I do not say it is as pleasant, but I do say it is not as trying. Personally I like the rainy season best, it is cooler and the country is more beautiful.

JULY 13
Now I was about to start off in a discussion, on a purely metaphysical discussion on some subject that happened to interest me. But would you like it? No, of course you would not, and that makes me think that it must bore you all now anyway. Shall I stop it? I will begin it again as soon as anything happens. Of course you have got to stand it for three months until I get your answer, but you need not show it to any one if you think it unsuitable. Out here on the bridge there is not much of incident.

JULY 14
Simply to show the opinion the Regular holds of the Volunteer officer, I will tell you a rather good thing Corporal Burke told me. It's typical of the distrust. It seems he was detailed as photographer under a Volunteer officer and eventually they had words. Now Burke is an Irishman and his tongue is not always as well disciplined as its supposed master. "Captain," says Burke in a white rage, "I am a professional soldier and an amateur photographer,

but you're a professional photographer and an amateur soldier." The Captain, being a Volunteer, did not "take it up."

JULY 15

Paranaque. A beautiful Sunday morning. I was thinking how beautiful it all was, the blue river, the fresh green of the bamboos, the crowd of people in bright costumes going to church, when the human note introduced its usual discord. Of course it was about the bridge, small piles this time, and when it was over all work was stopped for a parley among the powers that be. It really looks as if I should put in the balance of my enlistment right here watching this everlasting bridge.

JULY 16

Gambling seems to be the native's greatest vice. It was rather strikingly shown last night when Hunter paid off his men for the week. One of them I have often noticed as one of the best men in the gang. He has a wife and children. About two hours after they had been paid he came to Hunter to borrow a few cents to buy his supper. He had lost all his pay gambling. Inquiry showed that over half of the men had done the same thing. They are perfectly contented to live on a few cents' worth of rice and fish, sleep in a leaky hut with no furniture and work hard for seven days, for the few moments' excitement the game gives them. It will take some years to eradicate that trait, if indeed it can be eradicated. I wonder what their wives say to them?

JULY 17

Paranaque. Capt. Biddle (Chief Engineer of the Department of the Philippines) came out early this morning and interrogated me quite closely about the points in dispute in the bridge and contract.[25] I imagine from what he said that neither Jones nor Hunter had painted me in a very amiable light. Luckily my experience in the N.Y.T. Co. has stood me in good stead and I had notes and dates on every part of the bridge and on every stick of timber. It seems that there may be a court of inquiry about the whole wretched business. Not about me, but about the contractor and his methods. I can guarantee the bridge. It's all right, but it has been hard to get it so and has cost the contractor all his profits. He is kicking now. Heavy showers in the afternoon.

JULY 18
Paranaque. Measured the piles the contractor has on hand and rejected all of them as not up to size. It will be a long time before he can replace them. Much talk with the foreman and measured the depth of the river again. No use, the piles won't do. Light showers.

JULY 19
Quite often, recently, I have gone to the bridge-head in the evening and selecting some soft piece of lumber watched the river and the stars and dreamt long dreams while Corporal Burke talked. Many interesting tales he knows, adventures in the Indian country and most everywhere else, but he has a tiresome manner of telling them and I have had him talk to me for hours there on the bridge-head with no very clear idea of what he was saying.

JULY 20
Sent for by the Lieutenant. I had to go in to Malate. It is very pleasant to do that, to see the company again. It's a change and then too every one seems glad to see you and has a pleasant word, so that it is really a little homecoming. Missed Walter Camp by about three minutes. He had just been in to see me. Took the First Sergeant down town to dinner and got a very fair meal, but not such a one as he gave me a few months ago. The company is changing now. Men's time is expiring every month, and while some "take on" again quite a number go back to the States and re-enlist there, thus getting a trip and a chance to say "hello" to their friends.

JULY 21
Back to Paranaque. The contractor is going to take a month or so to get new piles and meanwhile, after a few odds and ends are finished, work will stop. Mail from the States up to June 9th also a picture of you, mamma, in the newspaper. Phip sent me one copy and Aunt Emily another. I wish you good luck on your trip and regret I cannot hear the speech. Why not send me a copy of it ?[26]

JULY 22

Paranaque. If one asks any one what a native Filipino eats one is apt to get for a reply, "Oh! rice and fish chiefly and a little fruit and meat when they can get it." Like most general answers that is all right as far as it goes, but it does not begin to describe the little mixtures they make from them. Take two groups I saw eating last night for an example. The woman who was cooking was squatted in the middle of the road and her hands were filthy. Never mind, she did all the mixing with them. By her side were two baskets and an oven. One basket was full of slender roots, each perhaps two or three inches long and with just a fringe of the green part showing. The other was full of boiled shrimps, each medium in size between our prawn and minnow. The oven was full of something that looked like the soup part of a bisque of lobster, but it was oily and smelt strongly of garlic. Over one of the native cooking dishes was an iron pan half full of cocoanut oil frying away cheerfully. The woman had a small ladle in her hand, made out of a cocoanut shell and about as big as the bottom of a teacup. This she would half fill with the roots, patting them till they were well interlaced. In the top of the little nest just made she would place two of the boiled shrimps and pour into the ladle a little of the pink mixture. A little of the hot grease was added to the mess and ladle and all was put into the frying-pan. In a moment it was firm enough to stand alone and was dumped out of the ladle into the pan from which it was shortly afterwards taken to be eaten with avidity. Some before eating them dipped them in a sort of sauce which from looks and smell was merely some green fruit rotted in water. The cake when done was the color of a brick. They were sold for one centavos (five-eighths of a cent). I was much tempted to taste one, but the filth and dirt made it impossible. It must be remembered that these are the poorest of the Filipinos, outside of the beggars and outcasts of the cities.

JULY 23

In the last mail I received some of my old text-books. They are a great resource here and help to pass the time in a most agreeable way. The last day or two I have spent chiefly in studying them.

JULY 24

While sitting on the bridge-head talking to Burke who should come down but the Colonel (Lieut. Col. Ducat, 49th,) and without much ado he too commenced to talk. I was much interested in what he said, for while I do not think him very intellectual nor at all a profound thinker, yet of course his position has given him a better opportunity to judge the Filipino than my own. He thinks much better of them than any ideas I have written and thinks the Philippine Islands will become a powerful State. I rather agree with him there, but he thinks that it will be through the efforts of the natives themselves, a fact that I am rather skeptical about. He wound up, as is customary and right, with a fierce denunciation of the Friars. The approach of an officer broke up the discussion, as it is of course infra dig. for a colonel to discuss anything with a corporal.

JULY 26

Work on the bridge practically suspended. No material of any kind. I could, under my orders, report back to Manila, but am now so comfortable here as to want to stay as long as possible.

JULY 27

Paranaque. These nigger regiments have to be handled differently than the white troops. In this battalion the one source of power seems to be the Colonel, the only white officer here if one excepts his adjutant, who is only an overgrown boy, the colored officer lacking both force and authority. The men are a rough set of scamps picked up anywhere and everywhere. This pay day they all decided that they would not pay their debts, or "jaw bone" as it is called out here. Now of course that produces an unpleasant feeling in the mind of the native who is cheated out of his money, just the feeling the authorities are trying to do away with. Unfortunately there is no law or army regulation that can be evoked to make a soldier pay his debts if he don't want to. Curious, but a fact. The Colonel has had refuge for his feelings in bulletins. I give one of them:

If you want the remark 'service honest and faithful' put on your discharges you had better brace up and pay your debts to these poor people who were foolish enough to trust men who do not pay. Shame be to any man who will beat a woman. Just as sure as there is a God I will bring you to your knees if you do not remove this disgrace from my battalion.

(Signed)

There was another more violent one in which he compared them to thieves and cut-throats and told them politely that if they lived till he got through with them they would all be hanged, but it was too long to memorize even temporarily and I do not care to be seen copying it.

JULY 28
The last two or three days I have been busy brushing up my mathematics and reading a little history. Not that I think that there is much chance of my having to use it, but I should hate to get the chance to take the examination and fail for the lack of a little preparation. The examination is very simple.

JULY 29
Sunday. We did get a heavy shower this evening. It is pouring now, the wind is blowing the rain in through our shutterless, paneless windows in solid sheets, more comes through our shell-torn roof, so we have scattered to our bunks, which through experience we have already placed in dry corners. One is safe enough from the wet on one's bunk, and comfortable save that once in a while an unusually heavy gust will blow out one's candle and leave one to grope for matches in the darkness. It is a bit different from last year when "our barracks were the great outdoors."

JULY 30
Paranaque. Today the Colonel wanted some advice about photography. It seems an Engineer soldier is popularly supposed to know everything, and we had quite a chat over it. It may be curious but I declined with polite thanks the permission to amuse myself making prints of his negatives. Nevertheless he is a gallant old fellow

who was badly hit and left for dead at the taking of San Juan Hill, Cuba. I took the photograph which he gave me of himself with some pleasure and will, if I think of it, send it along when I send this. He is a fine-looking man but very conscious of it. He has a way of taking one, apparently, into his confidence at the first few words you say. I do not see enough of him to know if he really does.

JULY 31
Even in the Philippines the course of true love does not always run smooth. It seems that the meztiso or half-breeds consider themselves above the mere native, so that when a young Filipino asked to marry the daughter of the half Spanish druggist he was indignantly refused. He wanted that girl pretty badly so one night he stole her. It was not an elopement. They don't do things that way over here. He just stole her. They caught them the next day after much excitement and demands for military force which was not given. The girl was locked up in the President's house and the fellow locked in the military jail. That was a month ago. I don't know what arguments were used, but finally the fellow was liberated, and last Sunday the two were married and celebrated the wedding in a grand festa in which half the village took part.

AUGUST I
Paranaque. Was made full Corporal from Lance today, vice Burke promoted Sergeant, vice Hernan discharged. This change brings me about $4.00 more a month and gives me a warrant, otherwise there is no change. I should have been horribly disappointed if I had not been made. This is the first vacancy since I was made Lance.

AUGUST 2
Received a telegram to report to Malate, all possible work having been done on bridge until piles arrive. Will go in to-morrow. Read a story of Captain King's called "Ray's Recruit," a story of a gentleman ranker, which succeeds in giving a good description of things that do not happen to a person of the class he describes when they try soldiering.[27]

AUGUST 3

Malate. And so to-day, just exactly three months from my arrival, I left Paranaque. I hope I shall never have to go back there, but I fear that as soon as the piles come I shall have to. A great relief to get into comfortable quarters again, with shower baths and particularly with a set table, waiters and people to wash dishes. It is much nicer than squatting down anywhere in the dirt and then having to wash your own plates. Took the First Sergeant down to the English hotel and had a really fine dinner about 6 P.M. The service and cuisine is much improved since I last took dinner with Billy.

AUGUST 4

Malate. It seems that the natives, or Spanish, pick the young mangoes when they are only about three inches long and pickle them. I never saw any till to-day, when I got a chance to taste some. They have a flavor something like the pickled limes that the children eat at school at home. I do not think them nearly as good as olives, but am told that people here are very fond of them. They are called "pajos," a name which is evidently local as I fail to find it in the Spanish-English dictionaries. "In charge of quarters," the first company duty I have done for months. Feel quite proud of my new chevrons.

AUGUST 5

Malate Convent.[28] A small mail from the States, bringing us up to June 25. It is an interesting sight to see the mail distributed to the company. Usually it arrives in the evening. The mail orderly dumps the big sacks on the floor and by the aid of one or two flickering candles and a few volunteer clerks proceeds to distribute it. All around him is a close-packed ring of men in various degrees of unclothedness. The barracks are close these summer nights and the crowd does not add to the ventilation. All of them do not expect mail, some never get any, but all wait patiently and silently. Every one has a good-natured word at the size of my collection of letters and papers, which come with unceasing regularity. The distribution does not take long, but new subjects to talk about keeps every one good humored until it is time to speculate on the non-arrival of the next mail.

AUGUST 6

Malate Convent. We were fighting the war over again in the canteen this evening, and one of the Sergeants in speaking of my trip
and the occasional reports they heard of me from other organizations reminded me of a fact I have always considered curious and
yet do not remember to have ever mentioned. I never was with an
organization long that it did not turn out that they were guessing
about my nationality. It is a curious fact that I was never suspected
of being an American. I have been called German, Swedish and
English, but have always had great difficulty in persuading any one
that I was a pureblooded Yankee. I don't understand it either.

AUGUST 7

Malate Convent. The band concerts on the Lunetta are still as attractive as ever. There is really nowhere else to go in the evening
and so every one who has leisure is sure to be there. It is very pleasant to sit on the edge of the Bay, watch the crowd of carriages and
listen to the music. Very pretty, too, to see every one rise and un-
cover when, at the end, the band plays "The Star Spangled Banner."

Malate Church and Convent, nineteenth century. Courtesy Malate Church.

AUGUST 8

One of the old men from A Company was down here today, discharged after thirty years' faithful service. I studied him with great care as I was much interested. He is fifty-two years old, but looks hale and hearty enough to serve ten years longer at least. As he has been out here over two years, one sees the climate cannot be as deadly as some people would make it out. For thirty years' service the Government retires an old soldier on three-quarters pay and allowances. As Lush was retired an Engineer Sergeant he will have for the remainder of his life nearly forty dollars a month, enough to make him, in his circle of friends, well to do.

AUGUST 9

Still the rainy season fails to materialize in any marked degree. Showers once or twice a week we do have, but the steady downpours of last year have not yet materialized. A year ago tomorrow we dropped anchor in Manila Bay.

AUGUST 10

Malate Convent. Corporal of the guard again, an uneventful tour of duty. Wondered a little as I lay down on a guard-room cot with all my clothes and belt of ammunition, and prepared to sleep comfortably, at the change which the year has made. Time was when the like condition would have kept me awake. Now I call sleep comfortably as long as I can get a chance to even sit down, nor does the passage of men or even the usual bugle calls awaken me. But let the sentry at the guard house stop walking his beat or let there be any unusual noise and I am awake in a minute.

AUGUST 11

A small mail from the States, bringing me up to July 2, also a letter from Billy at Tientsin, China. I quite envy him; at present it seems as if we had little chance, as if the additional Engineers needed would be sent from the States. I have given up all idea of getting a commission until next June at the earliest, at which time I have a right to ask for an examination, a right which is a matter of law and for which I shall be indebted to nothing save my own record and ability to pass the examinations. I do not have the slightest dread of passing another year in the ranks, though it would be idle to pretend that I had not rather be in a wider field. My two years' service is completed in September, but the army regulations only provide for one examination of candidates each year.

AUGUST 13
Malate Convent. The last two or three days have been rainy. A person in the States can hardly realize how wet it is out here when it rains. Everything leaks, but even did it not the houses would still be damp to an extent never realized at home. The houses have such an airy, open construction that it is impossible to shut the damp out nor would it be possible without suffocation. Then the lower story, on which no one ever lives, usually has a river running through it from the interior court. You can imagine the conditions. If a book is left alone for a couple of days it becomes covered with green mould. A year ago to-day, after having lain three days in the harbor, we first landed in Luzon and marched about 6 P.M. to the nipa barracks about a quarter of a mile below our present quarters. How odd the old city appeared then, how natural it is now.

AUGUST 14
The second day of continuous rain. It is a little confining to be in barracks all day long, but there is really nothing else to do during one of these down-pours. How it does rain! It is hard to realize that last year we lived in it.

AUGUST 15
Malate Convent. What a curious thing a big republic is. Only yesterday I read in the paper what Bryan says he will do if he is only elected. How he will give them autonomy under the protection of the United States, just what the commission now here tells them they cannot have.[29] Who can blame the natives if they are distrustful and show an inclination to fight some more. Such statements should be punished as high treason. As Gen. Lawton is supposed to have said, "If I am shot the gun will be loaded by our friends in the States." It hardly seems possible that a man like Bryan would be permitted to speak in public, much less run for President.

AUGUST 16

The rain continues almost incessantly. If it were not for my books I should be lost. As it is I am gaining the most connected view of the world's history that I have ever had. Of course one dreams of things inaccessible once in a while but not often enough to destroy my peace of mind nor my cheerfulness. We have rumors that the States are going to raise a very large army for China and there is much talk of commissions by those who consider themselves eligible.

AUGUST 17

Malate Convent. The typhoon is still blowing. There is really nothing stirring. The boats in the bay are inaccessible and no business is possible.

AUGUST 18

At last the storm seems inclined to break though the typhoon still blows. We hear that the rain has taken out some bridges. Some one will have to go from here. I should not be sorry to stay here a little while longer. With the men now out there are scarcely thirty men in the quarters for duty. Our sick is very large, twenty-five per cent of our total strength, chiefly stomach troubles and dysentery. Five men are invalided home. Two are dead.

AUGUST 19

The storm is still raging. It is curious that this great city in the middle of this fairy land is almost out of food because it is so rough that they cannot communicate with the ships in the bay. It is a striking commentary on the Spanish regime that this, a land where anything and everything will grow, which offers the finest opportunities for raising cattle imaginable, cannot supply enough food stuffs for its own consumption. As I write, beef is $1.00, gold, a pound.

AUGUST 20

Malate Convent. The typhoon is breaking, giving us a welcome chance to dry blankets, etc. To-day also they succeeded in reaching the *Grant* and bringing off some of her mail. It was nearly a month old though, as she has been discharging troops and cargo at Taku.[30] (How our geography grows. How familiar become names never heard of before. Where are we going to stop?)

AUGUST 21

The Grant brought out some young Engineer officers, just from West Point. One of our Lieutenants brought them in here, the draughting room, to show them a truss bridge he was designing. "Why," asked one of these schoolboys with charming youthfulness, "how in the world do you get books way out here?" I think he really believed that every one was helpless without books. The storm completely broken but sea still quite rough.

AUGUST 22

Every one is wondering what is going to happen to the army at the hands of the next Congress. They have been promising the Volunteers that they would be sent home this fall, but all the troops destined to relieve them have been stopped at China. I do not doubt that the withdrawal of our troops from the interior, a necessary thing if the Volunteers go back, will cause the insurrection to break out again, as the natives will take it for weakness. They will be right, too. I do not see why our politicians will not meet the issue squarely and give us the increase to the Regular service that is indispensable. Nor do I see what the labor unions have to fear from an army 10,000 miles away. I do not see either how the decent people in the States allowed that disgraceful affair at St. Louis, so I suppose I am not modern.[31]

AUGUST 23

Showers. A small mail. All I received was an invitation to Old Home Week at Portland. I would have liked to have been able to be there. There is really nothing to break the daily routine. I have my books and continue to keep busy. A large portion of the company is sick, from pure inaction I am inclined to think.

CHAPTER 6

California

Helen Clifford Brown Holt

*J*OHN CLIFFORD BROWN left no information as to what happened after the final entry of August 23, but it is fairly easy to piece together his last four and one-half months. Two sources of information, Helen Clifford Brown Holt's "Recollections" and Brown's MIT alumni entry, both correspond, stating that he was hospitalized in Manila—probably at the military hospital in Malate—until being shipped home in November. The two accounts correlate with U.S. Army records, which state that Brown left Manila November 2, 1900, aboard the transport ship *Thomas*. He must have landed in San Francisco in late November, and then was quartered at the U.S. Army General Hospital at the Presidio. Army records also show that Brown was paid up through August 31 and afterward had pay due until his death. This indicates that Brown became seriously ill again soon after August 23 and remained so until his departure for the United States. Mrs. Holt's account says he had a relapse aboard the transport ship and suffered others until the end in January, 1901. The army reported that his remains were shipped to Maine at private expense.

His sister Helen documented his final weeks in California. Her description of the last days of both her mother and brother offers a study in pathos. Mrs. Holt, then twenty-four, single, and, by her own admission, sheltered from the responsibilities of independence, traveled across the country with her mother to visit her dying brother. Two women making such a journey unaccompanied at that time was no trivial undertaking. Yet they made the trip and reached Brown, who had been furloughed at his brother Nathan's request, at the Occidental Hotel in San Francisco.

The family gathered at Brown's bedside, hoping to provide succor to the desperately ill young man. Tragically, the cold that his mother caught while on the train developed into pneumonia, leaving the family to cope with two dying loved ones. The weeks before Christmas could only be described as dolorous for all concerned. Mrs. Brown died on December

20 in the room next to her son. Thus, the woman to whom much of the journal is written, who had left home so obviously concerned about her son's health, ironically died at his deathbed.

As his mother passed on, Brown continued to decline. Despite the seeming recoveries and progress he made, the complications from typhoid were causing his body to degenerate rapidly. He was emaciated. As the MIT reverie noted: "When Mrs. Brown reached California, she would have never recognized her son. He weighed less than ninety pounds, and was so wasted as to remind his mother of the Indian famine sufferers." Nathan Brown had John Clifford moved again, this time to the Van Nuys Hotel in Los Angeles, where it was assumed the warmer climate would improve his condition. It did not. Another relapse occurred and he died five minutes after midnight on January 16. His brother Nathan was probably there when the end came; it was he who arranged for the body to be sent back to Portland.

According to Brown's obituary, his remains, shipped home by train, arrived in Boston the night before the funeral. Services were held at 11 o'clock on a Saturday morning and are described as "brief and simple." Scriptures were read and a choir sang. The army barracks at nearby Fort Preble provided pallbearers and a corporal's salute was fired at the family plot in Evergreen Cemetery. He was interred in the Brown mausoleum with his parents and grandparents (his grandmother died two days after his death, further adding to the family's misery). His brothers and sisters later joined him.

It is somewhat surprising that one is more likely to find artifacts of Brown's journey in the Philippines than in the United States. Brown came back on the *Thomas,* the transport ship that shortly took hundreds of American teachers to the Philippines, resulting in their being known as "Thomasites." It has long since been scrapped. The Presidio of San Francisco, the army installation where Brown was initially hospitalized, is now a federal park. The last two stops on Brown's journey are the two California hotels: the Occidental in San Francisco and the Van Nuys in Los Angeles. Neither exists today. The Brown family vault stands as it has for more than a century in Portland's Evergreen Cemetery.

The following is taken from Helen Clifford Brown Holt's "Recollections of an Old Lady." This portion of the work was subtitled "California Trip" and positioned within the first chapter of the unpublished 1951 manuscript.

Helen and Jack Brown. Courtesy Helen Holt Emerson.

My brother Jack was a member of many fashionable clubs in New York, as after his graduation from Tech., he had a fine job as an electrical engineer in New York. The Calumet and the Racquet are the only names I remember. But his chief interest in that line was the 7th Regiment, always looked upon by me and most of the family as a sort of rich man's amusement, a Richard Harding Davis variety of playing at war.[1] However, when the Spanish War happened, almost every man in that regiment took a commission and joined the fight. Jack, however, wanted to go as a private, and did so, enlisting in the Engineer Corps, and being sent almost at once to the Philippine campaign. He was advised not to do this, and it nearly broke my mother's heart. But nothing would move him. As a matter of fact, the tragedies that followed proved that the advice of his older friends in New York was good. His journal, written in the form of letters he wrote home, gives a wonderful account of his hardships and courageous attempts to make the maps, plan the bridges, and so on, that his company was sent to do, with no commissary, no supplies of any kind provided. So they ate what they could find, drank water when they were lucky enough to find any, usually foul, of course, slept in the open, rain or shine, and died by the wayside in consequence. Jack, however, survived and got back to Manila, where he succumbed to enteric fever.[2] It was by an extraordinary piece of luck that he was found there by his cousin Billy Clifford, then in command of marines on a warship in the harbor.[3] He had Jack removed to a transport which was sailing for America (as soon as Jack was recovered sufficiently) and before the ship sailed, had him placed in a hospital. Jack was very strong and was soon recovered. But he had the insane appetite which those fevers leave with their victims and, on the third day out at sea, he and a group of other boys starving on the hospital food, broke into the commissary on the transport and had a royal feast one midnight. The consequences were terrific. Two of the boys died in the relapse that followed and Jack also had a severe relapse. He was met, by Billy Clifford's arrangement, by a doctor when the boat arrived at San Francisco, and Jack was placed in the military hospital at the Presidio, with a special nurse. His condition was so grave that my brother Cliff, staying with his wife in nearby Los Angeles, was notified by the doctor. When Cliff and Susanne arrived in San Francisco, they realized that my mother should be sent for, so they telegraphed at once to her to go.[4]

My mother was a very timid traveler. Since my father's death she had made only short trips to Boston, or to the mountains in summer, and always with reluctance. She had been so safeguarded in the old traveling days that the responsibility of ticket buying and such things loomed large. I, of course, had never traveled alone. But there was no one to go with her but me, and so the family made plans for a hasty departure. Mr. Boothby, our friend, General Passenger, Agent of the Maine Central, made the complicated arrangements for a trip to California. He asked a friend of his to meet us in Chicago, got us a drawing room in both trains (for we had to change in Chicago) and smoothed it for us as well as he could. But we were two miserable worried, unhappy people who took the train for New York after hastily packing. I was to have been bridesmaid for Nettie Leighton, (Dr. Leighton's older sister) to whom Walter Fogg had been very devoted, in a few days. But she understood, of course, that I had to go back on her. Phip went on to New York with us and put us on the train, but a telegram which arrived before we left Portland made us feel we might not arrive in time to see Jack living. The whole trip is so much like an evil dream to me; it is hard to make anyone understand what it was like. Day after day on those trains which were much slower than they are now, not knowing whether we would arrive in time, sleeping little, eating little, and my mother seeming less and less well as we went along. It was really amusing to look back upon when the man met us at Chicago, for Mr. Boothby had not told us that he had arranged this help for us, and my mother was convinced that he was a confidence man, and would have nothing to do with him until he produced a letter, which he had fortunately kept, from Mr. Boothby. It was a natural mistake, for he was a dapper, rather overdressed young man, too subservient and oily. As we got out of the Pullman my mother fell, which shook her up a good deal. She had taken cold, too, on the train, as the drawing room was very hot, and very drafty when we tried to cool it off, and I began to worry about her health, she looked so ill.

However a telegram was waiting for us at the hotel where we went to rest for a few hours, as planned ahead, before going on which said that Jack's condition had improved. Cliff had him transferred with his nurse, to the Occidental Hotel, which was then the best hotel in San Francisco (burned down in the earthquake) and that the news that we were on the way had cheered him up a lot. Cliff and Susanne had rooms in the same hotel and would remain with us as long as we needed them. So we were in better spirits for the last part of the trip but my mother's cold did not improve. She seemed worse and almost dazed with weariness. The sight of Susanne and Cliff waiting for us at Oakland, where we got off the train and took a ferry across the bay, was a relief so great to my own worry and weariness that it was hard not to weep on their shoulders.

Rooms had been engaged for us adjoining Jack's: a sitting room, bath, and bedroom. Fireplaces with coal fires made the dense fog that greeted us seem less dreary. It was touching to see what my mother's arrival meant to the gaunt almost unrecognizable boy in the bed next door. His nurse we liked at once, (she was an army nurse), a perfect darling. It had been hard for Cliff to get her away from the Army Hospital to come with Jack to the hotel, as naturally she was stationed there. But he managed it somehow, and she remained with Jack through his entire illness, even after we went home, and she went with Cliff to Los Angeles for the warmer climate (More of her anon).

We unpacked and settled down and Cliff and Susanne planned to go back from the cold foggy city to their lovely Los Angeles, where they could be out all day long. But my mother's cold grew worse and finally, when we found she had fever, we sent for a doctor. We knew no one to ask except the hotel as to whom the best men were, until I remembered that there were two sisters named Smith, who lived in San Francisco, whom I had met and liked and entertained when they were visiting Molly Brown, one summer.[5] I got in touch with them, and they gave us the name of their own man, who came promptly. He said the house physician was a good man whom we could depend on, but that he would be in consultation and would come whenever we needed him. We had him stop in to see Jack, whose doctors were army men. He approved of what was being done for him, but was not optimistic. A relapse after severe enteric is bad, and others are apt to follow, he said.

My mother was a strong woman, seldom ill, but the conditions preceding the cold had made her unable to resist the germ, and we were soon told that she had double bronchial pneumonia. In those days, before the wonder drugs, that was practically a death sentence. So we notified the family at home, sent telegrams to them twice a day, got two nurses, and tried to keep from Jack how bad the conditions were.

Finally when the doctors ordered oxygen tanks brought in to the corridor outside our rooms, we notified the family that there was little chance for recovery. To our dismay we heard that they were leaving at once to come to us. I say with dismay, because we felt it was too late for them to try to arrive in time to see my mother. But they started, Nan and Phip picking up Tot in Boston, with Phip as courier. If Phip had come on alone, it would have been wiser, but Nan and Tot would not listen to advice, and Frank could not keep Nan at home when she heard Tot was going, although she was pregnant and far from well at the time. We met them with news everywhere we could, but we could give them no encouragement. My mother fought bravely, but to no avail.

At the last we used tank after tank of oxygen or she could not breathe at all. There were no tents, and the tube was inserted into her mouth, and whenever it was removed to change tanks, or to attend to her in any way, she begged for it. Finally, one very, gloomy morning, I went into the bathroom at seven to dress and, as I did so, the night nurse said, "Your mother has passed the crisis, the lungs are clearing, and she is much better this morning." I had felt there was improvement from the sound of her breathing and the stopping of the oxygen, but I didn't dare ask. I could hardly believe it, but my mother slept peacefully, already looking relieved of that struggle for breath. But before I left the bathroom, the nurse cried out: "Come quick," and as I ran toward her she said: "Her heart. She's going." And so it was. Before we could get Cliff or the house doctor, she was gone.[6]

Phip and Tot arrived the next morning. We were faced with the decision as to what to do about Jack. He had had a slight retrogression in strength, and his nurse wanted us to wait. So we did, but only for a few hours, because with Tot and Phip arriving we knew we musn't keep it from him for long. He stood the news better than we feared.

We had, of course, to start home as soon as possible and it was hard to leave Jack, even though Cliff and Susanne were to stay with him and take him, as I said, to a better climate than San Francisco when he has able to travel, which he was before we left. We saw them off on the train, Jack looking so emaciated now that he was dressed, but able to walk a little, and hungry again!

Then the three of us started home on the long journey with my mother's body. . . .

There followed for me a very difficult, unhappy period; one of difficult adjustments; a sort of pause, an interlude between two phases of my life. An aching loneliness, a helpless feeling of being incompetent, due to grief and fatigue, for the accumulated fatigue of the experience was not easily shaken owing to my mental condition. It was hard to go back to Portland and think of our house without my mother. Neither Phip nor I could even imagine how we would be able to get on.

There was another blow that retarded our family from recovering from our first one. This came in February [*sic*]. Jack had gone to Los Angeles, as I have told you, and was improving well, sitting out in the sun, and hoping to go home as soon as the Maine weather would permit.[7] His faithful nurse, Miss Anderson, was making plans to go back to the hospital, when suddenly, another relapse. Under the conditions, it could not be expected that he could survive it. One night, just as I was going to bed, Phip knocked at my door. Nelly had heard the doorbell's insistent ringing, and brought him a telegram telling us of Jack's death. I remember leaning against the edge of the door, saying over and over, "No, no, no." Miss Anderson wanted very much to come east with him, but the hospital wouldn't increase her leave. They had been so unusually lenient, allowing her to stay away so long with Jack, that we were not surprised. The funeral of a soldier is, to an unaccustomed family, beautiful, but heartrending. For years, even now after so many years, the sound of taps brings back to me the picture at the tomb. The soldier escort about the flag-draped casket, the guns fired over it, and last of all, the bugle. Twice when visiting—at the army posts, and even later at Fort Williams, I have been unable to keep back the tears at the sound of taps. I was so young, so impressionable, I suppose. We always feel sad at the sound of taps but to me for years, it was hard to bear with well-bred composure.

Afterword

*I*N EARLY FEBRUARY, 2000, I went to Portland to speak with Helen Holt Emerson and her sister, Julia Holt Bradford, the daughters of Brown's sister Helen and the closest descendants of John Clifford Brown. On my first morning there I went to Evergreen Cemetery, purportedly the second largest burial ground in New England. Located on the outskirts of the city, the cemetery is rolling and tree covered, and I was told that wolves occasionally come out of the nearby Maine forests to visit the dead. A substantial snowfall followed by an ice storm had hit Portland a few days before and the ground sparkled a hard white. Despite a bright 9 A.M. sun, it was very cold.

I first saw John Clifford Brown's resting place from below. The hilltop family tomb is a massive granite structure: gray, squat, and unadorned. Its simple style made it conspicuous among the surrounding Victorian crypts and statues. I cautiously walked up the hill from the road below, the ice-topped snow crunching underfoot. At the top I stood at the door to the vault, which clearly had not been opened in a long time. According to the chart the caretakers had given me, inside were interned John Clifford Brown, his parents and grandparents, his brother Phip, several Brown wives, and children who had died during infancy or shortly after. The last person to be placed there was Nathan Clifford Brown in 1941.

Standing in front of the mausoleum, I considered the panorama from Brown's eternal perspective: on that day it was a frozen, glittering place, dotted by pines and headstones half-buried in the snow. Statues of soldiers and angels angled up from their bases, comically covered in white. The road below was impassable to all but a four-wheel-drive vehicle. The world was absolutely quiet and still. Looking at this scene, my breath instantly condensing in the air, I could not help but think that it was a long way from the noise in Manila. Such a long way from the sunsets over the China Sea and the Paranaque River. Lifetimes away from a long-forgotten war.

The life of John Clifford Brown—at least the life portrayed in his letters and journal—was a complex one, filled with the conflicting or oddly juxtaposed elements of the upper class and the enlisted man, of a sound education and an unabated martial spirit, of artistic sensibility and nineteenth-century imperialism. That he was in the Philippines as an engineer and that his journal records the march of Brig. Gen. Samuel Young's flying column make his work more useful than scholars have noticed. While other primary works have recorded events of the wartime experience, few have done so with Brown's meticulousness. He could never have guessed as he carefully jotted down those lines a century ago that his notes would contribute to a better understanding of his country and culture.

In a very tangible way, Brown's service in the Philippines was a small step in America's march from the Civil War into the twentieth century. Brown's role in the defeat of the Filipino soldiers in the mountains, followed by his building of the bridge outside of Manila, was the manifestation of American political and cultural ideology, a potent mix of violence, racism, and social construction. The ideas of vigorous masculinity and dedication to the strenuous life—which can be traced from Oliver Wendell Holmes through Brooke Adams, Henry Cabot Lodge, and, most emphatically, Theodore Roosevelt—are present in Brown. For while he does not mention Roosevelt or the others, Brown clearly epitomizes the concepts they espoused: America's rightful place in the world order, the moral benefits of the military code, and the idea of sacrifice wrapped in global adventure. Such ideas may seem eccentric to many of today's readers, but careful inspection shows they have been and still are a force within America's political culture.

Brown's observations are equally valuable and entertaining for scholars or casual visitors to the Philippines. His odyssey is filled with superb details of the land as it was at the turn of the century, and it documents the beginning of American influence in Asia. A tour of Manila or La Union or many other places will show just what an impact Americans have had on their former colony. For both Filipinos and Americans, such observations can be awkward—and sometimes amazing. I distinctly remember standing by the side of the highway in Pampanga, gazing at dominating Mount Arayat and the lush green fields below it, and thinking that Brown had seen the same thing a century ago. During that moment of reflection, several Filipino children walked by offering me the ubiquitous and apparently obligatory "Hey, Joe!"—a moniker first introduced by GIs during World War II. In an instant, the worlds of Brown, of Bataan, and of the present collided there on MacArthur Highway. The children could have been direct descendants of the patriots who fought Brown for their country's independence. They could just as easily have been descendants of those who fought alongside Americans against the Japanese. In any event, their smiles were bright and they did not seem to care if the highway they were walking on was named after a U.S. general who both lost and saved the country, and whose father had directed U.S. forces in the Philippines a half-century before.

Given the odd moral juxtapositions inherent in Roosevelt-era ideology, and given Brown's opinion of Filipinos, it is both interesting and ironic that the most important product of his sacrifice was the Philippine nation. Forty years after Brown's death, the Philippines remained under the control of Americans, who were known as benevolent colonizers—surely one of history's most fascinating oxymorons. English was taught in schools where the children saluted Old Glory, but in truth the United States had little interest in maintaining anything more in the Philippines than a few military installations. The idea of independence was first raised seriously shortly after Aguinaldo's fall. Finally, after several decades of political bickering, it was at last scheduled for 1946. The Japanese thought otherwise. World War II linked Filipinos and Americans in a common struggle, and a sentimental residue of friendship remains to this day—at least among older Filipinos. The effect of the war on the Philippines was ghastly. With much of Manila in ruins, the national infrastructure in shambles, and with a tremendous number of Filipinos recently buried, the United States declared the Philippines independent and left in 1946. During the 1950s and for half of the following decade, the U.S.-Philippine relationship was strong, and the country seemed well on its way to substantial development. Then came Ferdinand Marcos. Amplified by the abuses of the U.S.-supported dictator, there was a sharp rise in nationalism with young Filipinos during the late 1960s and anti-American sentiment ran high in the country. Most of this has subsided and in its wake a strong American cultural influence remains. Nevertheless, the economy has never really recovered from the crimes and blunders of the Marcos regime. Blame for this has sometimes been attributed to the century of U.S. involvement and influence.

The Philippines, quite understandably, has never been at ease with its American period or, for that matter, with America today. While the number of Filipinos with family members in places like Stockton, California, and Jersey City, New Jersey, is astonishing, and while many Filipinos think of America as a literal extension of family and self, there remains a notable sense of anxiety, perhaps distrust, toward their former imperial master. Colonialism simply does not fit well into the national psyche. The Philippine-American War seems particularly disconcerting. For example, during the 1998 Philippine centennial celebrations, the large parade in Manila honored the heroes and martyrs who defeated the Spanish, as well as the World War II guerrillas who fought against the Japanese. The Philippine-American War and the period of American governance that followed were conspicuously absent, curiously not mentioned, as though they had never happened. This caused journalists to wonder aloud and nationalists to demonstrate in the streets. Brown's legacy, it seems, also includes feelings of historical discomfort.

Ultimately, what Brown has left is a sad story of an idealistic and weathered young man. It is a travelogue of exhilaration, ugliness, and mortality. While Brown's prose is essentially emotionless, the reader cannot help but feel his initial ebullience, the excitement of campaigning, and finally the dread of sickness. One can easily detect the physical and mental changes in Brown during his stifling stay in Paranaque. The hotel room in San Francisco, where his weight was down to ninety pounds, must have been morbid. The fact that his mother died at his bedside is especially grim. The end of his journey came shortly thereafter, and with it sadness and resignation. John Clifford Brown passed away single and childless, with no markers, memorials, or tributes to remember him— save, of course, his writing. His memory survives only in the words he wrote as a U.S. soldier in the Philippines, serving as a gentleman in disguise.

Notes

Introduction

1. The background on John Bundy Brown was drawn from the following: Kay Lazar, "Medal's creator rose from humble roots," *Portland (Maine) Press Herald,* Sept. 1, 1995, 16; Herbert Adams, "John Brown's legacy," *Portland (Maine) Press Herald,* Nov. 10, 1989, 10–11.

2. Helen Holt Emerson recalls this version of John Bundy Brown's death:

   > They had a wooden walk built up to Bramhall in the winter. He was coming home from a party or something and slipped on the edge [of the walk] and hit his head.
   >
   > He was in bed, and he said get his lawyers that there was something he wanted to do. He had a hard time talking—this was the way I heard it—he could hardly get it across to whomever was there. He wanted to get his lawyers because he was going to add [a new element] to his will taking care of his sons' wives and his daughters' husbands. There was nothing in his will at that point to acknowledge their existence.
   >
   > So mother remembered hearing these hoof beats of the horses pounding on Bowdoin Street to Bramhall in the middle of the night. She remembered that clearly. When the lawyers got to his bedside they said, "We have the will here; you can sign it." And he couldn't because he was too far gone. They said it would be okay if [he] just made a cross witnessed by all of them.

   Despite the cross signature, the will would be in legal limbo for over ten years (Helen Holt Emerson, interview by Joseph P. McCallus, Feb. 5, 2000, Cape Elizabeth, Maine).

3. The information on Philip Henry Brown was drawn from *Representative Men of Maine: A Collection of Portraits with Biographical Sketches of Residents of the State Who Have Achieved Success and are Prominent in Commercial, Industrial, Professional and Political Life, To Which Is Added the Portraits and Sketches of all the Governors Since the Formation Of the State,* 245.

4. Helen Clifford Brown Holt, "Recollections of an Old Lady," 1, provided by the family, copy in editor's collection.

5. Ibid., 5–6.

6. Ibid., pp, 6–7.

7. Philip Greely Brown, obituary, *Portland (Maine) Herald,* Dec. 19, 1934.

8. Emerson interview.

9. *Sunday Telegram* (Portland, Me.), Dec. 23, 1934.

10. William H. Clifford, obituary, *Washington Post,* Jan. 26, 1962; personal papers supplied by his grandson, William Clifford.

11. Emerson interview.

12. Holt, "Recollections," 1, 2, 3–5.

13. John Clifford Brown, obituary, *Portland (Maine) Evening Express,* Jan. 17, 1901.

14. All of Brown's military records were obtained from the National Archives.

15. Karl Irving Faust reported in 1898: "Fevers of various types are prevalent, especially typhoid" (*Campaigning in the Philippines,* 130). Jason H. Bass, recalling the condition of U.S. troops in March, 1899, said that "malaria and dysentery seemed to be the prevailing ailments although there was a well filled typhoid ward" ("Early Days in Manila," *The American Oldtimer,* Aug., 1939, 26). According to one historian: "army surgeons . . . made the mistake, all too common in medical practices at the time, of diagnosing many of the first typhoid cases as malaria or other mild fevers. Investigators later concluded that almost every regiment brought to camp a few men infected with typhoid. Many had the disease in its incubatory stage, when none of its symptoms were evident" (Graham A. Cosmas, *An Army for Empire: The United States Army in the Spanish-American War,* 272). In a related situation, Dr. Nicholas Senn reported that "Typhoid fever, which prevailed in all of our large camps before our army sailed for Cuba, soon gained a firm foothold at the seat of war and did its share in increasing the mortality and shattering the efficiency of the service" (quoted in Frank Freidel, *The Splendid Little War,* 295). For more on typhoid and the U.S. soldier in the Philippines, see Ken De Bevoise, *Agents of Apocalypse: Epidemic Disease in the Colonial Philippines,* 42. Some of the medical principles of the time can be found in Charles E. Woodruff's historical curiosity *The Effects of Tropical Light on White Men.* In it, the author argues—with statistics to prove it—that blond-type U.S. soldiers in the Philippines (men who had blue eyes, light brown hair, and a ruddy or fair complexion) were more prone to sickness and death than the brunette type (212–16). According to this remarkable notion, Brown would have been at a distinct disadvantage.

16. Holt, "Recollections," unnumbered introductory page.

17. Emerson interview.

18. Brown's relationship with Florence McMullen presumably was a strong one. It is through this never-mentioned relationship that we get a glimpse of both Brown's passionate side and his lasting effect on his family. Helen Holt Emerson recalls hearing about the two young people from her mother:

> In those days the term girlfriend had not been invented. But evidently Jack and Florence McMullen were fond of each other.

When he went to war—I guess he didn't say anything but it was understood [that they would someday marry].

[On his deathbed] Jack knew them [his brothers and sister Helen]. In the midst of everything he said to them: "I think Florence would have married me. I would like her to have my ring." He had his hand on the covers of the bed. They didn't tell him the ring wasn't there. They thought either because he was so emaciated the ring fell off or somebody stole it. They didn't tell, and they would do it—what he asked. When they got home the rest of the children and mother chipped in and bought a diamond to give her from Jack. It was a nice little solitaire diamond.

She, of course, burst into tears and said, "Yes, I would have married him." But she said, "I don't think I should keep the ring."

They said we want you to have it to remember him and so forth. So she finally decided she would accept it on the condition that if she married somebody else she would return it [to his sister Helen, then unmarried]. And if she ever married she would give it to her daughter on her eighteenth birthday.

Mother got married. I was the oldest child. On my birthday I got it. My oldest daughter, Julie, when she was eighteen we gave it to her. And Julie gave it to her daughter. And that's where it is now.

[All of my daughters know the story of the ring]. Definitely. In fact, Mrs. Gulick, that's who Miss McMullen turned out to be, was still living. She was in special care in Mercy Hospital. We told Julie, our oldest daughter, to call Mrs. Gulick and tell her the ring was still being treated the way she wanted it to be done, and that she [Julie] had it now. She finally did it. They said Mrs. Gulick's voice lifted right up and sounded really happy, and really understood that the ring was following this cycle.

19. Massachusetts Institute of Technology, *Report of the Thirtieth Anniversary of the Class of Eighteen Ninety-Three*, 86–88.

20. Holt, "Recollections," 9.

21. Ibid., 40–42.

22. "Engineers Bound for Manila," *New York Sun*, June 6, 1899.

23. For more on the cult of the "strenuous life" and its impact on American culture and politics, see Clifford Putney, *Muscular Christianity: Manhood and Sports in Protestant America, 1880–1920*, and Kristin Lee Hoganson, "The 'Manly' Ideal of Politics and the Imperialist Impulse: Gender, U.S. Political Culture, and the Spanish-American and Philippine-American Wars" (Ph.D. diss., Yale University, 1995).

24. At first, U.S. forces saw themselves as the Filipinos' allies. A superb example of such a transition can be found in Bradley A. Fiske's *War Time in Manila*. Fiske,

the navigator aboard the USS *Petrel* and later the USS *Monadnock*, two ships in Commodore Dewey's fleet, describes the split in attitude commonly held by U.S. troops in 1898 toward Aguinaldo's army:

> The afternoon after the American troops landed at Cavite, Hall and I and some others of the Petrel got into conversation with an Army Lieutenant, a very handsome man whose name I cannot recall; and in the course of our talk he spoke of the Filipinos as "niggers." I cannot tell you how unpleasantly this word sounded to us, especially because the accent of the voice and the context showed that it was used as a term of dislike. After an embarrassed pause, one of us said—
>
> "You know we fellows in the Navy here have become very friendly with the Filipinos, and we like them very much. We've seen a good deal of them, too, and seen them fight, and seen them wounded and dead in the hospitals. They're really an entirely different kind of people from niggers; and besides, they're fighting on our side, and we think we ought to treat them well":—and then we all went on to tell him what we knew about the Filipinos.
>
> The Army Lieutenant seemed much astonished at our ideas, and although he listened to what we had to say, it was plain that we did not make much impression on him. So we changed the subject, and in a few minutes we parted; quite cordially, but with that vague feeling of hostility, that a strong difference of opinion usually carries with it (*War Time in Manila*, 89).

25. For Roosevelt's remarks, see Howard K. Beale, *Roosevelt and the Rise of America to World Power*, 72. For an extended discussion of the relationship between the frontier wars and the Philippines, see Anne Paulet, "The Only Good Indian is a Dead Indian: The Use of United States Indian Policy as a Guide for the Conquest and Occupation of the Philippines, 1898–1905" (Ph.D. diss., Rutgers University, 1995).

26. For a discussion of race relations in the military at that time, see Willard B. Gatewood Jr., *"Smoked Yankees" and the Struggle for Empire: Letters From Negro Soldiers, 1898–1902*, and *Black Americans and the White Man's Burden, 1898–1903*; Richard E. Miller, "Black Troops in the Philippines," *Bulletin of the American Historical Collection* 8, no. 4 (Oct.-Dec., 1980) 75–88; and Richard E. Welch Jr., *Response to Imperialism: The United States and the Philippine-American War, 1899–1902*, 101–16.

27. In discussing the Philippine-American War this work has consulted the following studies not previously cited: Teodoro A. Agoncillo, *History of the Philippine People*, 8th ed.; James H. Blount, *The American Occupation of the Philippines, 1898–1912*; H. W. Brands, *Bound to Empire: The United States and the Philippines*; John Morgan Gates, *Schoolbooks and Krags: The United States Army in the Philippines, 1898–1902*; James A. Le Roy, *The Americans in the Philippines*; Brian

McAllister Linn, *The U.S. Army and Counterinsurgency in the Philippine War, 1899–1902*, and *The Philippine War, 1899–1902*; Glenn Anthony May, *Battle for Batangas: A Philippine Province at War*, and "Why the United States Won the Philippine-American War, 1899–1902," *Bulletin of the American Historical Collection* 13, no. 1 (Jan.–Mar., 1985), 67–90; Stuart Creighton Miller, *"Benevolent Assimilation": The Conquest of the Philippines, 1899–1903*; Orlino Ochosa, *The Tinio Brigade*; Russell Roth, *Muddy Glory: America's 'Indian Wars' in the Philippines, 1899–1935*; William Henry Scott, *Ilocano Responses to American Aggression, 1900–1901*; William Thaddeus Sexton, *Soldiers in the Sun: An Adventure in Imperialism*; Leon Wolff, *Little Brown Brother: How the United States Purchased and Pacified the Philippine Islands at the Turn of the Century*; and Dean C. Worchester, *The Philippines: Past and Present.*

28. Smith S. Leach, "Historical Sketch of the First Battalion of Engineers During Its Tour Abroad," Occasional Paper no. 7, U.S. Army Engineer School, 1903, 17. Leach almost surely used Lt. John Oakes's 1900 report. See chapter 4, note 23.

29. Thirteen public repositories and three private/commercial collections are known to have copies of *Diary of a Soldier in the Philippines.*

30. *Annual Reports, Acts of the Philippine Commission Ended June 30, 1905*, vol. 14, 204.

Chapter 1: The New West

1. Brown entered the army at one of its major points of transition. Responding to the need to replace the temporary personnel in the regular and state volunteer forces, as well as to the sting of congressional commissions investigating the administrative blunders of the war with Spain, the army made large-scale, positive changes in late 1898 and early 1899. It mustered out most of the 1898 volunteers and a large number of regulars who had joined only for the Spanish campaign. This was followed by an enlistment drive during the first half of 1899 that brought the regular army's units to full strength.

Although there is no evidence to support it, Brown must have been affected in some way by the enlistment drive. According to his records, he enlisted for a term of three years on June 21, 1899, at Washington Barracks, Washington, D.C., and was assigned to Company B of the Engineers. Little information is available about enlisted engineers of the time, but it is known that they were mostly specialists (as Brown seems to understand judging from his comments of June 25, 1899). It is interesting to speculate on what Brown's position within them was like. At the beginning of the war with Spain, the Engineer Battalion was employed along the East Coast constructing submarine mine defenses in important harbors. Two of the four companies that made up the battalion served in Cuba. Brown was stationed at Willets Point, New York (now Fort Totten), home of the U.S. Engineer School, an institution dedicated to the practical aspects of military engineering. The school, which accepted both officers and enlisted men, focused on such topics as electrical issues, astronomy, photography, and, of particular importance, submarine mining (see note 6 below). The school trained officers in need of fleshing out the theoretical knowledge gained at West Point and rankers who had at least some experience in or the aptitude to learn civil engineering, reconnaissance, cartography, and explosives. It can be assumed that Brown was serving with enlisted men who had more experience in technological matters and a higher level of education than he would have in an infantry unit. However, it is doubtful many enlisted engineers had the education and background Brown did. For more on the army's reorganization and the engineers of the period, see Cosmas, *Army for Empire*, 297–306; U.S. Army Corps of Engineers, *The History of the U.S. Army Corps of Engineers*, 72–32; U.S. Army Engineer School, *History and Traditions of the Corps of Engineers*, 39–43; Henry L. Abbot, "Early Days of the Engineer School of Application," Occasional Paper no. 14; and David M. Dunne, "The Engineer School—Past and Present," *Military Engineer* 41, no. 284 (Nov.–Dec., 1949): 411–16.

2. He is apparently referring to *Tom Brown's Schoolday* by Thomas Hughes (1857). It is interesting that Brown would be reading such a novel: it was a book for adolescents, featuring a common-born English boy and his experiences at the influential Rugby. The themes of class identity, institutional tradition, and morality achieved through physical strength are intertwined throughout the work. The novel is one of the earliest proponents of English "muscular Christianity," a movement that later made the trans-Atlantic voyage to America's East Coast. There it flowered during Theodore Roosevelt's era. Putney remarks that the president "viewed *Tom Brown's Schooldays* as one of the two books that every boy should read" (*Muscular Christianity*, 20).

3. The *City of Para* was a civilian transport contracted by the military. It made a number of trips to the Philippines in 1898 and 1899. For a description of the military transport system, see Faust, *Campaigning in the Philippines*, 61–70.

4. John Brown was born in Torrington, Connecticut, in 1800. After living in a number of locations, he and his sons settled in Osawatomie, Kansas, in 1855. Here Brown began his militant free state volunteer group. It is unknown if John Clifford Brown identified with or romanticized his namesake.

5. Angel Island is the largest island in San Francisco Bay. After the Philippine-American War it was an immigration station, and it is now a state park. For a photograph of the barracks at Angel Island, as well as a number of photos of troop transport ships in Manila and San Francisco harbors, see photographs in *Different Views, Customs, and Traditions in the Philippines*. Brown did indeed sail that afternoon. *Harper's History of the War in the Philippines* records that on July 13, 1899: "Transport *City of Para* sailed for Manila with troops D and H, Fourth U.S. Cavalry, headquarters, and Company A, F, H, and K, Twenty-Fourth U.S. Infantry, and Company B, Engineer Battalion, under command of Brig.-Gen. Theodore Schwan, U.S.V." (209).

6. The July 6, 1899, *New York Sun* article appears under the title, "Engineers Bound for Manila," and the subtitle, "Company B, a Notable Organization, Leaves Willets Point."

Whitestone Landing, July 5.—Company B of the engineers, 150 strong, officered by Capt. William Siebert and Lieuts. Oakes and Ferguson, left Willets Point at 7 o'clock this morning for Manila. A large crowd of relatives, friends and sweethearts stood on the dock and saw the boys off on their long journey.

The company formed in front of its barracks in heavy marching order and marched, headed by the post band, to the steamer *General Canby*, which took them as far as Jersey City. There they got aboard a train which started at 11:15 A.M. for San Francisco, going over the Pennsylvania and Southern Pacific railroads. Four men failed to show up when the company left and their places were immediately filled by volunteers from D Company. Two of the missing privates showed up later and they were assigned to D Company.

This is the largest and strongest organization that ever left the post. It contains a number of men whose services were thought indispensable here, prominent among them being Sergt. Edward Carroll, commonly known as the "torpedo Sergeant," who is the submarine mining expert of the army. He taught the engineers who mined the harbors on the Atlantic and Pacific coasts during the Spanish-American war. Lieut. John C. Brown of the volunteers, who served throughout the Santiago campaign, went along as a private.

While Brown was a member of volunteer regiments during the Spanish-American War he never served overseas.

7. Arthur Sewall (1835–1900) was the father of Harold Marsh Sewall (1860–1924), U.S. minister to Hawaii during the annexation in 1898. Although he does not mention it, Brown knew or at least knew of the younger Sewall as he was once engaged to Brown's sister Ann ("Nan"). According to Helen Clifford Brown Holt, her sister Nan had six suitors, all of whose last names began with the letter S:

But she finally accepted one of the six, Harold Sewall, who was slightly older than she was, but very charming. He was bald, tall, slender and rather lordly, as he came from the Bath family well known as the founders of the famous ship building business, multimillionaires. The head of the family also owned most of the Boston and Maine railroad. His beautiful great place can still be seen in Bath, surrounded by a brick wall. I think it is either a funeral home or a private hospital. But it has changed hands several times. Harold was consul general in Hawaii, and at the time of Jack's enlistment, Jack visited him there on his way to the Philipines.

Note to Page 68   265

I was never told any details about the end of this affair. Harold was evidently a gay dog, and there was some scandal about another woman which made Nan feel that if he were unfaithful to her before marriage, there was little hope for the future (Holt, "Recollections," 39).

8. He is presumably referring to Princess Kaiulani, who died on March 6, 1899. She was the last heir to the Hawaiian throne. For a spirited description of Kaiulani, which mentions Minister Sewall, see Alden March, *The History and Conquest of the Philippines and Our Other Island Possessions*, 274–76. See also, William S. Bryan, ed., *Our Islands and Their People*, 424.

9. Lieutenant H. L. Greenleaf, assistant surgeon, examined Brown at Washington Barracks.

10. He is referring to a member of the 24th Infantry (Colored) (see note 14 below). The 24th and the 25th Infantry Regiments were at that time the only two African-American units involved in the war. In early 1900 they were joined by the 48th and 49th Volunteer Infantry Regiments. By the summer of 1900 the number of black soldiers in the Philippines was about twenty-one hundred. Many of these soldiers, especially noncommissioned officers, were veterans of the Spanish war and thus far more experienced than Brown and his engineers. See Gatewood, *Black Americans*, 263. Frederick T. Arnold also recorded the incident:

One of the darkies who contracted lock-jaw two days ago, died this morning and was buried at sea this afternoon. The ceremony was brief—only lasting about half an hour during which time the boat was stopped. After the three volleys were fired and "taps" played, the band struck up a quick-step, the engines started, and we resumed our journey, much as if nothing happened. Of course, if we look at it from a "war standpoint," it was a small thing, but it seemed so much more sad to be left in mid-ocean, all alone, than to be placed in a churchyard where, one has so much company—though in a churchyard it is apt to be very much like in a large city—one is not likely to know his neighbors. This man, no doubt, was very thankful to be relieved from his awful agony, by any means and be left anywhere. It was the first case of the kind and I don't care to see another. And when one thinks that ninety per cent of the cases are fatal, it is surely a disease to be dreaded (Spanish-American War Survey, 4th Cavalry Box, U.S. Army Military History Institute, Carlisle Barracks, Pa. [hereafter USAMHI], 6).

11. It was strictly a rumor: Aguinaldo had no gunboats.

12. The reference to "Scamp" is uncertain. Brown's surviving relatives did not recognize it as the nickname of anyone they knew. It might possibly have been a family pet.

13. The USS *Oregon,* built in 1893, was one of the *Indiana*-class battleships; the *Massachusetts* and the *Indiana* being the others. It served in the Spanish-American War, the Philippine Insurrection, and World War I. The ship was reduced to scrap in 1946 despite Oregon citizens' attempt to preserve it.

14. *Harper's History* confirms that the *City of Para* arrived in Manila on August 10 (210). According to J. A. Bunch: "I had my first glimpse of Manila from the deck of the palatial CITY OF PARAR [sic] which dropped its mudhook in the Bay on August 9, 1899 with the 24th Infantry aboard. We disembarked the next day where the Manila Hotel now stands today. We had to wade ashore knee-deep and in places hip-high in the mud, racing for dear life to beat the breakers to the beach. It was a wet and muddy lot of soldiers who assembled on that beach to the old Malate Barracks, a bamboo structure which formerly housed Filipino soldiers" ("Recollections of the Twenty-Fourth Infantry," *The American Oldtimer,* July, 1940, 34).

  For more on the 24th Infantry's trip to Manila, especially with regard to race relations, see Jack D. Foner, *Blacks and the Military in American History: A New Perspective,* 90–91.

15. The "old fortifications" he mentions are Fort Santiago, a large Spanish installation that was used extensively by the Japanese during World War II. The Luneta, now Rizal Park, was and still is a popular place for relaxation and entertainment in the center of Manila. It is unclear where Brown's barracks was actually located. The engineers did have a workshop just south of Intramuros, which today would be in Ermita. The infantry was sometimes billeted in the Cuartel de Malate (see chapter 4, note 18).

16. The Mexican peso was the currency in the Philippines at the time.

17. His immediate commanding officer was Lt. John C. Oakes.

18. Malate was then considered to be on Manila's southern outskirts.

19. This may be the Walter Smith mentioned in the March 22 entry.

Chapter 2: Pampanga

1. The reference to "the fight at the church" is uncertain. Malolos, the first capital of Aguinaldo's government and where the Philippine Republic's constitution was drafted at the Malolos church, was captured in March, 1899. The town, however, was deserted and burned by the Army of Liberation. No true battles were actually fought within the city.

2. Brown is referring to Col. Frederick Funston's leadership at Calumpit on April 26, 1899. Funston, accompanied by the 20th Kansas Volunteers, crossed the Rio Grande on a raft and with just forty-five men threw hundreds of Gen. Antonio Luna's soldiers from their trenches. See Marion Wilcox, ed., *Harper's History,* 194–98; Linn, *Philippine War,* 108; and Sexton, *Soldiers in the Sun,* 144.

3. It is unknown how Brown received this information.

4. There is some confusion about the date and time here. Sexton reports that the town of Angeles was taken the previous day, August 16, by the 12th Infantry

(*Soldiers in the Sun*, 170). The U.S. forces were counterattacked by Filipino troops at 5 A.M. the following day but were able to drive them off.

5. This is 2d Lt. Harley B. Ferguson.

6. The area around the town of Calumpit formed a natural defense that comple mented the intricate system of trenches installed by General Luna. The Rio Grande is eighty feet wide and deep at this point. Filipino troops under Luna were routed here in April, 1899. See Linn, *Philippine War*, 104–109. The unidentified Englishman with the interest in the railroad is probably Horace L. Higgins, who was general manager of the Manila and Dagupan Railway Company. See his description in Albert Sonnichsen's *Ten Months a Captive Among Filipinos*, 98–99. General Luna was one of the leading Filipino commanders. Fond of European tactics and harsh discipline, and possessing a wild temper, he was assassinated in 1899—presumably by Aguinaldo supporters.

7. The map Brown was working on may have been incorporated into the larger and more detailed map 4 reproduced in *Annual Reports, 1900*, pt. 2. Titled "Map of Central Luzon showing a portion of the Field of Operations of the 8th Army Corps, compiled by Wm L. Sibert, Capt. Corps of Engers, U.S.A., November 1899," it depicts the routes taken by Lawton's, Wheaton's, and MacArthur's columns.

8. Brigadier General Arthur MacArthur (1845–1912) was then fifty-four years old.

9. He is probably referring to Lieutenant Ferguson.

10. It can be assumed the book belonged to Capt. William L. Sibert.

11. A "bino jag" refers to drunkenness on bino or vino, a cheap, extraordinarily intoxicating wine made from palm. Drunkenness was a serious problem among the U.S. troops. See Miller, *"Benevolent Assimilation,"* 191–92, and Roth, *Muddy Glory*, 40–41.

12. The State Volunteers were just that: volunteer citizens recruited in each state to fight in the Spanish-American War. Nearly half of VIII Corps was composed of such volunteers in the summer of 1899. Technically, their obligation ended when the treaty with Spain was signed in April of that year, but Otis was so shorthanded that he kept them on for months. Regular army and U.S. Volunteers eventually replaced them. The latter was a federally organized body of soldiers recruited solely for Philippine service. Otis describes the arrival of the U.S. Volunteers in *Annual Reports, 1900*, pt. 2, 210–11. It is interesting to note Brown's strong, constant disdain for the abilities of the volunteers, both state and national. This was probably the result of the natural rivalry between the two branches. It is also possible that Brown may have had a difficult time as an officer in the volunteers. In any event, his critical view of the volunteers contrasts with many other eyewitness accounts and historical scholarship. In fact, Linn considers the national volunteers to have been "outstanding soldiers," while noting that all three elements—regular army and State and U.S. Volunteers—were "probably as good or better than any in this nation's history" (*Philippine War*, 326).

13. The position of the Chinese within Philippine society has always been tenuous. The Chinese were victims of Spain's restrictive economic and immigration policies during the early nineteenth century. By Brown's time, with an approximate

population of ten thousand, they had somewhat recovered their roles as merchants and artisans. This rebound, as well as the importation of Chinese laborers, made many Spaniards and Filipinos uneasy. Indeed, an anti-Chinese sentiment was common throughout the islands. In many respects it still is prevalent. See Gates, *Schoolbooks and Krags*, 8–12.

14. Brig. Gen. Lloyd Wheaton, then sixty-two, was a Civil War veteran and popular with both his men and correspondents. See Linn, *Philippine War*, 93.

15. The maltreatment of prisoners on both sides is one of the unsettling legacies of the war. While the misconduct of U.S. troops is well documented, it should be pointed out that the Filipino forces were also guilty. See Agoncillo, *History of the Philippine People*, 230; Linn, *Philippine War*, 124–25; Miller, *"Benevolent Assimilation,"* 188; and Roth, *Muddy Glory*, 48, 54, 56–57.

16. Brown is correct about the rainy season in Luzon, which lasts from roughly mid-June through mid-September.

17. "Engineers Bound for Manila."

18. "Blue" was his sister Helen's nickname.

19. The *Morgan City* was a transport ship that sailed for Manila on August 10, 1899. It wrecked on the coast of Japan on September 4. For the ship's records through June 1, 1899, see Faust, *Campaigning in the Philippines*, 61–70.

20. Sexton, *Soldiers in the Sun*, 171.

21. The *New York Times*, in an article headlined "MacArthur Takes Porac," reported the following on September 28, 1899:

> Gen. MacArthur entered Porac after half an hour's fighting. The American loss was slight, and the insurgent's loss is not known. The enemy fled northward. When the Americans entered the town they found it entirely deserted.
>
> The attacking party moved on Porac in two columns. The Ninth Infantry, with two guns, from Santa Rita, was commanded by Gen. Wheeler, and the Thirty-sixth Infantry, under Col. Bell, with one gun, accompanied Gen. MacArthur from San Antonio.
>
> Both columns struck the town at 9 o'clock and opened a brisk fire, which was replied to by the enemy for half an hour. Then the insurgents fled, and the Americans marched over their trenches and took possession of the place.
>
> Just before the fight Smith's command, at Angeles, made a demonstration by firing artillery up the railroad track.
>
> Liscum reported one casualty and Bell reported four men of his regiment wounded. The artillery did not have any men injured.
>
> Today's movement was a strategical success and resulted, besides the possession of Porac, in the clearing of several miles of county thereabout.
>
> The two columns from Santa Rita and San Antonio united before Porac, according to programme, stretching around the place for some miles.

The insurgents are estimated to have numbered 600 men. Ten dead Filipinos were found, and the Captain and Commissary of Mascarno's command were taken prisoners.

While the American loss is five wounded. There were many prostrations from the heat.

The movement against Porac began at daybreak this morning and was conducted personally by Gen. MacArthur, Gen. Wheeler, with the Ninth Regiment and a battery advanced by two roads while Gen. Wheaton, commanding the Twelfth and Seventeen Regiments, moved to block the insurgents from retreating to the north. The Thirty-sixth Regiment accompanied Gen. MacArthur.

Two Filipino majors came to the American lines last night with messages regarding the American prisoners, who were to arrive this morning. They also requested permission from Gen. Alejandro, one Colonel, and two Lieutenant Colonels to visit Gen. Otis. They were refused entrance to the American lines until noon Friday on account of to-days fight, and Gen. Alejandro alone will be allowed to visit Gen. Otis.

The next day, the *Times* revised its casualty figures to nine Americans wounded, two "probably fatally," and fifty Filipinos killed or wounded. For commanders' reports of the operations at Porac, see *Annual Reports, 1900*, pt. 6, 280–82. These substantiate Brown's observations. Another contemporary account can be found in Marshall Everett, *Exciting Experiences in Our Wars with Spain and the Filipinos*, 508.

22. Brown here is in close contact with two of the war's most interesting officers, Brig. Gen. Joseph "Fighting Joe" Wheeler and Col. Franklin Bell. Wheeler, then sixty-three years of age, was a former Confederate cavalry officer and an Alabama congressman. In an attempt to bring former Confederate officers and southern voters back into the fold, he was made a general by President McKinley and served in Cuba. There and in the Philippines he was known for his energy, bravery, recklessness, and disorganization. For an account of Wheeler in Cuba, including several interesting photographs, see Freidel, *Splendid Little War*. See also Wolff, *Little Brown Brother*, 277–79. For more on the role of Col. Franklin Bell and the 36th Regiment at Porac, see "History of the 36th Regiment United States Volunteers," *The American Oldtimer*, June, 1941, 12–18.

23. This is Holy Rosary Church.

24. He is essentially correct about the objectives of the attack on Porac. Sexton, however, reports that there were only six hundred defenders (*Soldiers in the Sun*, 171).

25. According to Lieutenant Oakes: "The San Fernando detachment and company headquarters were attached to the First Division, Eighth Army Corps, and proceeded to Mexico on October 10. This day 50 Macabebes were turned over to my command for laborers, and Sergeant Casey placed in charge of them" (*Annual Reports, 1900*, pt. 5, 162).

26. As events will show, Brown is quite right about going to the northern end of the island after defeating Aguinaldo's troops.

27. Oakes recorded the following: "October 11. In pursuance to Special Orders, No. 1, Mexico, P.I., dated October 19, 1899, the detachment left Mexico and proceeded to Santa Ana. Roads were made passable to this town and part of the way to Arayat, when the detachment returned to Santa Ana for camp" (*Annual Reports, 1900*, pt. 5, 162).

28. According to Oakes: "October 12. Detachment and Macabebes started at daylight from Santa Ana and worked all day corduroying roads between that place and Arayat, which was reached at 5:50 P.M." (ibid.). The *Laguna de Bay* was a converted Spanish gunboat. For a discussion of its service, see Faust, *Campaigning in the Philippines*, 253–57.

29. Mount Arayat is 1,026 meters high.

30. On October 13 Oakes wrote: "Noncommissioned officers made a sketch of the town" (*Annual Reports, 1900*, pt. 5, 162).

31. The attack Brown heard may have been the one on the U.S. garrison at Angeles during the early morning hours of October 16. According to Lieutenant Oakes: "October 15. Ferry begun, the entire detachment working all day on ferry and approaches" (ibid.). For a photo of the ferry at Arayat taken by Corporal Bourke (also spelled Burke), whom Brown later met at Paranaque, see *A History of the 22nd Infantry*, 104.

32. William Dinwiddie, reporting for *Harper's*, wrote:

> General Lawton lost no time in starting the forward move after his arrival. A small engineer corps under Lieutenant Oakes was busily cutting a great roadway down through the twenty-foot-high embankment to the river's edge, where the new ferry-boat was to travel on a rope from shore to shore, carrying a hundred men at a time. It took them two days to complete this work, but by the evening of the 17th, under final supervision of General Lawton, who seemed to be everywhere at once, instilling force and energy into his entire command, Major Ballance's battalion of the Twenty-second was crossing, preparatory to a night advance on the town of Libertad, four miles up the river (Wilcox, ed., *Harper's History*, 300).

33. For a complementary account of the march from Arayat through Cabanatuan and finally to San Fabian, see Krebs's journal entries in A. B. Feuer, *Combat Diary: Episodes from the History of the Twenty-Second Regiment, 1866–1905*, 132–34. On October 18 the Macabebes executed a mostly successful attack at Malibutad, where they captured "about 70 prisoners," according to Ballance (*Annual Reports, 1900*, pt. 4, 297).

34. Oakes reported that the bridge was repaired on October 20 (*Annual Reports, 1900*, pt. 5, 163).

35. For a description of this inscription, see Sonnichsen, *Ten Months a Captive*, 184.

36. Oakes seems here to make a reference to Brown: "October 24. One man on map of town. Aprons of ferryboat reinforced, rope stretched, and ferry made ready for operating. Rise in river caught rope and broke it. Boat secured on other side" (*Annual Reports, 1900*, pt. 5, 163).

37. Brown's mileage compares favorably to the tally made by headquarters. See *Annual Reports, 1900*, pt. 4, 346.

38. The house he mentions is probably the Florentino Pamintuan mansion; today it is a bank. See Ramon Ma. Zaragosa, *Lost Era*, 133.

39. The quartermaster he is referring to is Col. Guy Howard, who was en route to Manila to secure shallow-bottomed boats for fording rivers. See Wilcox, ed., *Harper's History*, 301; and Sexton, *Soldiers in the Sun*, 178.

40. Oakes reported: "October 27. Sent 3 noncommissioned officers and 23 privates and Macabebes on forward with movement on Santa Rosa" (*Annual Reports, 1900*, pt. 5, 163). For an account of the battle, see Lawton's communiqué in ibid., pt. 2, 222; Young's in ibid., 268–69; Ballance's in ibid., pt. 4, 301–302; Wilcox, ed., *Harper's History*, 301; Feuer, *Combat Diary*, 134–35; and Sexton, *Soldiers in the Sun*, 179.

41. The Macabebes were from a small ethnic group recruited from around the town of Macabebe, just north of Malolos in Bulacan. Many of them had seen service with the Spanish during the Philippine Revolution. Perhaps more importantly, they were traditional enemies of the Tagalogs and consequently against the "insurgency." The Macabebe Scouts eventually evolved into the Philippine Scouts, renowned for their discipline and bravery in World War II. See Leo Fischer, "The Macabebes," *The American Oldtimer*, Apr. 1936, 31–33. Lowe's scouts, commanded by Lt. J. C. Castner, were part of Ballance's provisional brigade. See "Lowe's Scouts," *The American Oldtimer*, June, 1940, 20–24.

42. Captain John G. Ballance was one of the most noteworthy personalities of the war. General Young called Ballance and his battalion "the finest and most efficient one I have ever seen in the American Army" (*Annual Reports, 1900*, pt. 4, 267). An extended account of Ballance's activities can be found in several chapters of *A History of the 22nd Infantry*.

43. The Macabebe Scouts were formed by Lt. Matthew Batson—then thirty-three years old—in September, 1899. See Edward M. Coffman, "Batson of the Philippine Scouts," *Parameters* 7, no. 3 (1977): 68–72; Matias M. Lobo "How the First Scouts Were Organized," *The American Oldtimer*, Sept., 1940, 27–33; and J. N. Munro, "The Philippine Native Scouts," *Journal of the United States Infantry Association* 2, no 1 (July, 1905): 178–80. For an interesting account of Batson's alleged metamorphosis from humanist to racist anti-Filipino, see Miller, *"Benevolent Assimilation,"* 182–83. See also Batson's "Report of Organization and Operations of the Macabebe Scouts, September 1–November 19, 1899," Mar. 29, 1900, *Annual Reports, 1900*, pt. 5: 123–37.

44. The impressment and physical abuse of guides was a standard practice for U.S. troops and was in compliance with army regulations of the time. See Linn, *Philippine War*, 221.

45. Brown is probably referring to Lt. J. R. R. Hannay, Company K, 22d Infantry,

who worked closely with Company B in Cabanatuan. See also Oakes's statements in *Annual Reports, 1900*, pt. 4, 397.

46. Lawton's report, dated October 31, states: "Batson rode ahead [to Cabanatuan] and captured telegraph operator with all dispatches and instruments" (ibid., pt. 2, 225).

47. It seems remarkable that Private Brown would be invited to sit and smoke cigars with Lieutenant Oakes, his commanding officer. This illuminates the strange personal-professional paradox facing the diarist.

48. He is referring to Lt. Col. Edward M. Hayes. For more on the amount and type of captured munitions, the sick and wounded Filipino soldiers, and other aspects of the operations around Talavera, see ibid., pt. 4, 271, 307–11; and ibid., pt. 2, 228.

49. A report by Lawton dated November 7 substantiates Brown's observations:

> I have to report that our outposts and camp were attacked by a strong force of the enemy, said to number 300. . . . Attack was made at 4 o'clock A.M. . . . They undoubtedly expected to surprise us, but my outposts were on the alert and my command formed line promptly and moved out in support of the outposts. The enemy made three successive charges to trumpet signal sounded by the trumpeters of their column. During the last charge one of the enemy was killed within less than 50 yards of our lines. Captured one very severely wounded, with Mauser rifle and ammunition. From bloodstains must have been several more casualties. We were fortunate in having no casualties, but 1 pony killed and 2 horses wounded, not severe. My forces are in good shape, and I can maintain myself if I have supplies. The five days' half rations are up tonight. I urgently request that rations be sent at once. Respectively, Hayes, Lieutenant-Colonel, Commanding (ibid., 230; see also ibid., pt. 4, 313).

50. Hayes also reported that later in the day Dorrington's "Scouts discovered quantity gun cotton. Was carelessly exploded, wounding Corp. Gustave Raysck and Private William E. Brace, Company H, Thirty-fourth Infantry. Brace since died; Raysck will recover" (Lawton, ibid., pt. 2, 231).

Chapter 3: Northern Luzon

1. Several dates are cited as being the day on which Young's advance began. Brown says November 8 was the day, as do Young (*Annual Reports, 1900*, pt. 4, 274) and Sexton (*Soldiers in the Sun*, 182). Linn says it was the seventh (*Philippine War*, 147). Leach, recording the history of Company B, makes a direct reference to Brown when he says, "On November 10, 1899, one private left with General Young's Flying Brigade from Cabanatuan and made maps of all the roads traveled until Vigan was reached" ("Historical Sketch," 17). For an interesting ac-

count of what preparations were made for the march, which necessitated the abandoning of "all surplus weight," see Lieutenant Smedberg's orders in *Annual Reports, 1900*, pt. 4, 273.

2. One can assume he is stealing the pony and saddle. The skirmish Brown hears at Puncan was probably the one involving Lieutenant Colonel Hayes's 4th Cavalry. See *Annual Reports, 1900*, pt. 4, 313.

3. An entry dated November 13, 1899, states that "Hayes's Fourth Cavalry in vicinity of Carranglan has captured much insurgent property and nearly half battalion of 400 bolo-men transporting Aguinaldo's property north over mountains, together with his private secretary and seven officers" (Wilcox, ed., *Harper's History*, 291). The private secretary was Maj. Domingo Colmenar. See Hayes's reports in *Annual Reports, 1900*, pt. 4, 313–14.

4. The notion of "keep[ing] Aggie amused on the railroad" while a surprise attack was launched is clearly incorrect. He is accurate in guessing that Aguinaldo would disperse his army, but Brown probably did not envision the ensuing guerrilla war. For more on the capture of Aguinaldo's baggage, see the preceding note.

5. Brown may be referring to present-day Umingan. Lieutenant J. C. Castner's report mentions Lupao, Humingan [Umingan], and then Saint Quintin. See *Annual Reports, 1900*, pt. 5, 342.

6. At the time, Ballance was in the Villasis-Urdaneta area. Rather than move on Dagupan, the large town on the Lingayen Gulf as Brown assumed, Ballance was ordered to Binalonan after receiving information that Aguinaldo was headed in that direction. See *Annual Reports, 1900*, pt. 4, 277, 304–305.

7. See Hayes's complimentary comments on these men in ibid., 350.

8. They are attempting to ford the Agno River. See Castner, ibid., 342.

9. The town before San Filipe was probably San Manuel.

10. The language is Ilocano, which would be the local language for the rest of Brown's trip to Bangui. The language of the Macabebes was Kapampangan.

11. Aguinaldo was never wounded, but Young was chasing him.

12. Feuer reveals much about the 22d Infantry's march to Lingayen (*Combat Diary*, chap. 9). For more of Brown's time with the 22d Infantry in Pangasinan, see Ballance's report in *Annual Reports, 1900*, pt. 4, 304–305. This part of the journey is depicted on Brown's map "Sheet No. 4, Road Map from S. Manuel to Sto. Tomas."

13. Brown's observation is inaccurate, although there was some conflict between Ilocano and Tagalog groups. See Ochosa, *Tinio Brigade*, 54, 65; and Rosario Mendoza Cortes, *Pangasinan, 1801–1900: The Beginnings of Modernization*, 100–109.

14. The condition described by Brown is also found in a *New York Times* report that said U.S. forces in northern Luzon were "reduced one-third by sickness" and "shoeless" ("Young's Men in Distress," Dec. 12, 1899). Another primary account is found in William Oliver Trafton, *We Thought We Could Whip Them in Two Weeks*, 27–30. See also Sexton, *Soldiers in the Sun*, 203–204. Young told Lawton:

"Many of my people are sick from eating meat too soon after killing, and not sufficiently cooked" (Young to Lawton, Nov. 29, 1899, box 4, book 2, Samuel B. M. Young Papers, USAMHI, 496 [hereafter Young Papers]). Captain Ballance, describing the condition of his infantry at that time, wrote:

> November 25, arrived at San Fabian, where I had been informed I would find rations, shoes, and clothing. Rations were obtained, but not a single shoe. These men were in a very bad plight: most of them were sick with fever, dysentery, colds, dobie itch, bruised and bleeding feet, caused by half rations for over a month, no rations at all for days, living on what they could find of rice and caribao; rained on almost every day, wading through water and mud from 6 inches to 4 feet deep every day, swimming, wading, rafting, or bridging about fifty streams and rivers, going to bed every night with feet and ankles wet, and many nights with all their clothes wet, exposed to the cool nights of the winter season without a single blanket or covering of any kind; and yet these superb men were not only willing but anxious to push on to join their daring general whom they had been following for weeks. . . . Most of the men were suffering from fever and dysentery, but they kept to their physical work by sheer mental effort and American grit which was inspiring to observe. When the orders came for the battalion to remain at San Fabian the necessity for the men to continue their mental effort ceased, their physical natures were allowed to exert themselves, and 300 collapsed in one day as the result of fever and dysentery which they had contracted during the trip. Some of these men died from the effects of the strain through which they had passed; many will never recover from the hardships they underwent and the suffering and disease caused by them (*Annual Reports, 1900*, pt. 4, 305).

15. He is referring to Henry L. Ripley, who would later be made captain of the port of San Fernando. For more on Ripley, see Irving Hart, "Reminiscences of an Old Timer," *The American Oldtimer*, Mar., 1940, 45.
16. Judging by the mileage he reported, they probably camped a bit north of Agoo in La Union Province, at or near Aringay. This leg of the journey is recorded on "Sheet No. 5, Road Map from St. Tomas to S. Juan."
17. San Fernando was reported to have been captured on November 21 (*Annual Reports, 1900*, pt. 2, 289). See also Sexton, *Soldiers in the Sun*, 203.
18. This part of the journey is chronicled on "Sheet No. 6, Road Map from S. Juan to Sta. Cruz."
19. 1st Lt. William R. Smedberg Jr.
20. The battle at Tangadan Mountain or Pass is described and discussed by a number of writers. Participant Julius A. Penn offers this account:

Gen. Young had information about the strong position at Tangadan Pass, and on December 4 his command started up the coast form Narbacan. Col. Howze and Penn's Battalion leading. The carts with the sick and the wagon train of the Cavalry, were to be left on the coast road and later to proceed to Vigan. They were held where the trail left the coast and advanced about a mile when Lt. Decker commanding the scouts, four selected men from each company, reported the enemy on our front in a strongly entrenched position.

Leaving the companies in a sheltered and protected position on the trail, Gen. Young, Col. Howze and other officers reconnoitered the position. The scouts captured an insurgent Corporal, who was closely questioned. The position though reported to us was a strong one, was a surprise to all. Down the coast the Cavalry had found and assaulted and captured many trenches covering river crossings and steamer landings but here in front of us was a mountain with tier upon tier of trenches covering the crooked, narrow and steep trail and crowning all, or what appeared to us from below as covering all others, a great bald nob of a hill in the center. A natural redoubt, strengthened by a great circular trench at the summit and with steep, clean slopes that would have meant death to many in a direct assault. Below this redoubt was a very large trench in which at times during the day from three to four hundred men were seen. Then below this the many smaller trenches. Later in the action a second redoubt with two immense trenches were discovered at the summit of the Pass about eight hundred yards back of, and slightly higher that redoubt No. 1, and covering the trail perfectly between the redoubts.

The main ridge of the mountains was to our left as we faced the position, the grass covered crest, some two or three miles from us, and it apparently terminated in a high point about seven hundred yards north of redoubt No.1, and some five hundred feet above it. This was in fact, however, a spur from the main ridge, and a second spur parallel to the first and about three hundred yards to the eastward, extending further to the southward and cut off the summit redoubt from the trenches below No.1 as well as from any one on the spur overlooking redoubt No. 1. The main ridge at the summit redoubt was several hundred feet lower than the second spur. To the eastward of the summit redoubt was a broken, wooded country. To the southward of the redoubts were a few low hills and then beyond as a beautiful a coast valley as there exists on the Island. One great fertile plain, dotted with prosperous towns and villages some like Santa Maria, of exceptional beauty, and over the seaward a few small detached peaks broke the monotony of the sea line and gave glimpses of the sea that added greatly to the picture. The general direction of our advance was from the westward and almost parallel to the main ridge.

As a result of careful reconnaissance to the front of the enemy's position Gen. Young directed Lt. Col. Howze to detach Maj. Penn with eighty men to move to the left, climb the rugged mountains, gain the main ridge, and follow it to the point of the spur overlooking and commanding the great circular trench on the bold [bald?], redoubt No. 1. Lt. Decker with his twelve scouts were to hold the low hills to the left front. Penn's third company was to occupy the front, while Maj. Swigert's three small troops would occupy some low hills to the right of the trail and 1200 to 1800 yards from the trenches and make such a demonstration as would cover the turning movements of Maj. Penn. Lt. Col. Howze was placed in command of the whole, Gen. Young saying to him, "Col. Howze, it's your fight, a 34th Inf. fight."

About 10 A.M., Col. Howze started Maj. Penn's flanking column. . . . The flanking column followed the summit tail which crossing to the north slope of the ridge gave a view of the coast range running northwards and the extreme ruggedness of the range could only be equaled by the Teton Range of Wyoming and Idaho. The column passed rapidly along the trail, the deep worn path and tall grass almost hiding the column from view. . . . a few minutes of the day remained as it was nearly sundown. Down the slope in front was a canyon six hundred or seven hundred feet in depth and filled with tropical vegetation and upon the opposite summit four hundred feet below, lay the bald knob with its circular trench, Redoubt No. 1, well filled with insurgents. The big trench below it, glimpses of which we could see through the brush, was also filled. Lt. Col. Howze had already carried during the afternoon some of the lower trench with Capt. Rollis' company. Capts. Chase and Hunter were still carrying out their part of the program on the right, and Lt. Thayer's troop had been placed between Capt. Rollis' left and Lt. Decker's Scouts.

About the time Maj. Penn's column opened fire Lt. Col. Howze was joined by two companies of the 33rd and a third company was held in support. These companies of the 33rd under Col. Hare had been marching up the coast to overtake Gen. Young and arrived in time to take part in the charge which the followed the flank attack from the mountain top.

Considerable uneasiness had been felt by Gen. Young and Col. Howze as to the whereabouts of the flanking column which had experienced such difficulties in their all days climb of the mountain. Its volleys brought as much joy to them as it did sorrow for the insurgents. At the first volley the insurgents commenced retiring from the redoubt and at the 2nd volley at least two hundred insurgents were seen by Gen. Young leaving the big trench below it. Thirteen volleys were fired by Capt. Russell's Company and then Capt. French's Company was moved to the front and given the opportunity to clean their rifles, placing ten well directed volleys in the circular trench. Uncertainty as to the exact location of Col. Howze's position and possible changes in the Cavalry position prevented any firing from the mountain upon the lower trenches. The moral effect, however, was unquestionably good as the insurgents commenced to leave the trenches and several bold and vigorous charges by Col Howze and Capt. Rollis' company of the 34th and Capt. Hulen's and Lt. Lowe's companies of the 33rd carried one after another of the trenches including the big trench below Redoubt No. 1.

This last charge was made just after dark, up an almost perpendicular slope. Later Col. Howze with a few men entered Redoubt No. 1.

The flanking column on the mountain side ceased firing as darkness came over the scene and bivouaced for the night in their positions. The cheers below told of the trenches carried. By and by a large fire was built below near the big trench and we knew that that too had been won in the charges.

Perfect quiet was maintained in the mountain bivouac and no fire or lights allowed. Off in the wooded mountains to the eastward lights flickered now and then where some wounded insurgent was being borne away to some secure hiding place or was borne homeward to some of the towns or villages in the beautiful valley to the southward, everyone of which was showing that night a strong Beacon to guide their insurgent friends. . . . Our victory had not been one without its price in blood (*A Narrative of the Campaign in Northern Luzon, P.I. of the Second Battalion, 34th U.S. Inf. Volunteers in November and December, 1899 and January, 1900*, 9–13).

Other accounts of the battle can be found in Young, *Annual Reports, 1900*, pt. 4, 283–88; Hare, ibid., 322; Wilcox, ed., *Harper's History*, 321–22; Sexton, *Soldiers in the Sun*, 209–10); Ochosa, *Tinio Brigade*, 81–85); and Scott, *Ilocano Responses to American Aggression*, 51–52.

21. The name of the town actually is Santa. The editor of the 1901 edition probably thought Brown left out the personal name.

22. Brown is referring to the aftermath of the battle at Vigan during the early morning hours of December 4, 1899. This encounter, perhaps the most dramatic of the war, and ensuing skirmishes on the following days, can be found in the following sources: Lt. Col. James Parker, "Forty-Fifth U.S. Volunteer Infantry, Report of the Defense of Vigan, Luzon, P.I., December 4, 1899," in *Annual Reports, 1900*, pt. 5, 138–51; and Lt. Col. Webb C. Hayes, Thirty-First Infantry,

U.S.V., "Report of a March from Laoag, Province of Ilococ Norte, Luzon, P.I. to Mountain Passes East of Solsona, December 13 and 14, 1899," in ibid., 152–54b). For an extended description, see the relevant chapters in Parker, *Old Army*, and Trafton, *We Thought We Could*.

23. Although no attribution is made in *Annual Reports, 1900*, part 4, the map Brown was working on was surely "Sketch of the Engagement of the Prov. Cavalry Brigade 1st Div. 8th, Dec. 4, 1899." See also Brown's "Sheet No. 7, Road Map from Sta. Cruz to Santa."

24. This part of the march is found on "Sheet No. 8, From Santa to Badoc."

25. Young reported to Otis's command on December 10 that "Major Swigert, with 100 cavalry, should reach Batac, on coast road, tomorrow, with instructions to reconnoiter Bannajin [Banna?] to the east" (*Annual Reports, 1900*, pt. 2, 319).

26. The courier brought reports of insurgent forces under Tinio, who were holding American and Spanish prisoners. See Lawrence Benton, "Memories of the 33rd Vol. Infantry," *The American Oldtimer*, June, 1934, 21–24. For an account of other activities in the area at that time, see Hayes, "Report of a March from Laoag," 152–54b. Trafton, a member of Hare's party sent out to find the prisoners, details this experience in *We Thought We Could*, 50–57.

27. Brown's map titled "Sheet No. 9, Road Map from Badoc to Pasuquin" notes that about four miles east of Badoc "Maj. Swigert's Batt 3rd Cav. captured an Insurg. outpost Dec. 12, 1899" and approximately three miles east of the above it notes "Maj. Swigert Bat. 3rd Cav had two men killed Dec. 12, 1899." Maj. Samuel M. Swigert, 3d Cavalry, made this report to Otis concerning the operation:

> Dingras, December 13—11 A.M. [1899]—In accordance with orders received, I left my wagons at Batag on the 11th instant and started for Banna over the mountains at 3 P.M. There was no road at all. The command reached the foot of the mountains in the evening and captured 3 out of 5 insurgents that came down from the mountains. Three guns were captured and destroyed. The command left camp early the next morning, and about 10:30 A.M., in a small valley in the mountains, encountered a force of the enemy, stated by the natives to be two companies, amounting to about 120 insurgents. This force was engaged and scattered in all directions; 7 insurrectos were killed, 2 were captured, 1 of these wounded; 5 guns were captured and destroyed. Privates Harry Sweger and Charles W. Frazee were killed, and Private John Dillinger wounded, all of Troop A. After burying our 2 dead, the command proceeded on the 13th to Banna, where it arrived at 6 P.M., and received news there of Colonel Howze's command and Colonel Hare's command. These two commands left here for Salsona and thence northeast to Rancho Cabroogan, according to report of natives here. In order to cover as much country as possible, I shall move at once from here to Piddig, and probably

thence to Vintar. From Piddig, however, I shall be governed by information received on the road. The natives here report that Tinio, Natividad, and Aguinaldo, disguised, left here Saturday night with a force of three or four companies, some 500 men, going to Salsona and thence to Cabugaoan. I send this by courier who served us as interpreter from Batag over the mountains, and he is accompanied by a man who served as guide and informed us of the position of the insurrectos in the mountains. Both men merit being well paid. Without them we could have never gotten through the mountains (*Annual Reports, 1900*, pt. 4, 334).

Swigert was referring to Brig. Gen. Benito Natividad, a commander in the Vigan area. The *New York Times* reported: "Major Swigert, with a detachment of the Third Cavalry, had an engagement with insurgents near Dingras. Two Americans were killed and two wounded. Several Filipinos were killed" ("Aguinaldo Continues Fight," Dec. 18, 1899).

28. Capt. George K. Hunter, C Company, 3d Cavalry.
29. This last stage of the march is found on "Sheet No. 10, Road Map from Pasuquin to Bangui." The lighthouse he mentions is the Cape Bojeador lighthouse near Burgos, built by the Spanish in 1892.
30. Young landed in Bangui on December 13 and left on the sixteenth (*Annual Reports, 1900*, pt. 2, 321–22). See also "Filipinos Lose Negros Fight," *New York Times*, Dec. 16, 1899.
31. Brown here refers to the Boer War, a conflict with a complicated beginning and end. While there had been fighting between the British forces and the Orange Free Staters and Transvaalers (collectively known as the Boers) earlier in 1899, the first major confrontation occurred in December. The Boers defeated British forces on several occasions during the month, causing a hysterical patriotic reaction in Great Britain and much coverage in the world press. The British subdued the larger Boer forces in 1900, but the Boers continued to wage a guerrilla war that lasted until 1901. Peace eventually was achieved through negotiation. The United States remained officially neutral but sympathetic to the British cause.
32. According to Brown's map, "Sheet No. 10, Road Map from Pasuquin to Bangui," the nearest towns to Bangui were Claveria to the northeast and Nagpartian to the west. On today's map the next town would be Pagudpud to the northeast, Bucarog or Caramuagen to the southeast, or Lano to the west. It should be noted that the area around the bay, dotted by many small barrios, is still collectively known as Bangui. It should also be noted that a number of towns in the Ilocos region have changed their names over the last century.
33. The "natives" he is referring to could have been from one of several cultural minorities in northern Luzon. Captain B. H. McCalla of the USS *Newark* off Aparri reported to Young on December 28, 1899: "Igorrotes [Igorotes] were murdering natives south of Ilagan and burning buildings" (*Annual Reports, 1900*, pt. 4, 336) and later orders them punished. Scott, commenting in Trafton, says that

"resettled Isneg tribesmen" were near Solsona (*We Thought We Could,* 50). The Tinggians of the Abra region, usually supporters of the Filipino cause, were likewise nearby. Also possible would be the Kalingas, one-time headhunters of the Cordilleras.

34. The elusive Tinio was still in northern Luzon, and the rumored movement against the small U.S. force at Bangui was taken seriously, resulting in anxious communications between army and navy officers. Lieutenant Commander F. E. Beatty reported to William T. Burwell, captain of the USS *Wheeling,* on December 15: "Quite a number of . . . rumors which are being run down. Will act on anything of importance. The doctor (Spanish) [in Bangui] with his grandson are helping me all they know how. One of his grandsons has voluntarily gone up the mountain trail and says he will come back with positive knowledge of Tinio" (*Annual Reports, 1900,* pt. 4, 335). Brown's commanding officer, Captain Hunter, contacted Burwell on December 22 with the information that "Tinio is in this locality, but is moving daily, so that he cannot be positively located. My information leads me to believe that he has too many men for me to tackle" (ibid., 335). Burwell reported on December 23 that "as Captain Hunter needed rations, [I] came back to Bangui to supply him. Have landed 60 bluejackets and a company to reinforce Hunter. . . . I have extra rations and can keep my men and Hunter here indefinitely. Hunter states trails 'impassable for cavalry horses toward Palasi.' On some maps it is called Patapan; also, Pancan. Tinio's force reported 1,000 strong. Can not as yet locate him positively" (ibid., pt. 2, 324). Tinio was never located.

35. General Lawton was killed at San Mateo on December 18. His death had a deep impact on the U.S. forces.

36. He is referring to his cousin, Lt. William Henry Clifford Jr. According to MIT's 1896 yearbook, Clifford played the mandolin (*Technique,* 171).

37. After Brown left Company B in late October, the engineers under Lieutenant Oakes prepared the way for Young all the way to Binalonan. Company B was sent back to Cabanatuan at the beginning of December and arrived in Manila on the sixteenth, ending its relationship with Lawton's column. Early the following year it commenced building and repair work in the area south of Manila.

Chapter 4: Manila

1. For in-depth discussions of how the United States set up the colonial infrastructure, see Gates, *Schoolbooks and Krags;* Linn, *U.S. Army and Counterinsurgency;* Miller, *"Benevolent Assimilation";* and Wolff, *Little Brown Brother.*

2. The bell tower is that of Saint Williams.

3. The Philippines' climate is divided into a dry season (January–June) and a rainy season (July–December). January is usually the coolest month of the year on Luzon.

4. This is presumably the first time he showed any symptoms of typhoid.

5. Young records: "L[etter] R[eceived] 96 (Recd. Jan. 12, 1900) Dos Marines [Dasmarinas], Jan. 9, 1900. Oakes, Engineer—Orders Pvt. Brown to Manila to complete maps" (box 4, book 5, Young Papers). His subsequent orders to stay in Vigan were signed on January 13, 1900, by Lieutenant Smedberg (Special Order no. 9, box 3, Young Papers).

6. This would be Lieutenant Oakes.

7. The headquarters building in Vigan would have been the seminary in the public square, adjacent to Saint Paul's Cathedral. This plaza was where Colonel Parker and his men fought off Tinio's attack some weeks earlier. For a photo of the U.S. barracks, see *160 Photographs of J. D. Givens of SF: Period of Spanish-American War—1898*, 67.

8. See Trafton for another soldier's initial impression of Vigan (*We Thought We Could*, 34–35).

9. As noted, Cosmas says the army often misdiagnosed typhoid for malaria (*Army for Empire*, 272). If this was, in fact, a misdiagnosis, it could explain why Brown was not treated for typhoid immediately. The Spanish-American War Survey reveals that soldiers thought medical service was poor. Henry Augustus Stockman of the 22d Infantry said medical attention was "Rotton. When I had malaria typhoid the doctor was about to send me back to duty when the hospital seargant insisted that I be sent to the hospital. Four months later I was able to report for duty." It is interesting to note that Stockman combines both malaria and typhoid.

10. The *Romulus* was a small steamer. Owens's orders to be stationed at the Cape Bojeador lighthouse can be found in box 4, book 5, LR 456, Young Papers.

11. Brown is correct: American entrepreneurs of all shades and stripes were descending on the islands. For discussions of the American civilian invasion of the islands, see Lewis E. Gleeck's *Americans on the Philippine Frontiers* and *The Manila Americans, 1901–1964. The Bulletin of the American Historical Collection* carries numerous pieces concerning this migration.

12. This is Smedberg.

13. See Wilcox, ed., *Harper's History*, 300.

14. The order reads: "Private J. C. Brown, Company 'B' Engineer is relieved from duty at Vigan, and will proceed to Manila on the SS *Romulus*. The Subsistence Department will furnish travel rations for two days" (Special Order no. 36, Feb. 19, 1900, box 3, Young Papers).

15. It is unknown what Brown means by Oakes's "troubles." It could have been just a simple complaint; however, if one refers to the entry made on March 9, 1900, the Lieutenant, who is undoubtably Oakes, is distraught over the war.

16. Brown probably worked out of the Ayuntamiento Building, sometimes called the "Marble Palace," which, like the nearby Malacanang Palace, contained American administrative offices. The chief engineer was John Biddle (1859–1936). See chapter 5, note 4.

17. The Escolta was, up to the Second World War, Manila's premier street of commerce and entertainment. Brown's observation that the street was becoming

Americanized is correct: newspaper ads of the time reveal a large assortment of bars with names such as the "The Golden Eagle" and "The Olympia." For a good photograph of the Pasig River, the Escolta, and the surrounding environs in 1898 or 1899, see *Neely's Photographs: Fighting in the Philippines.*

18. There were several Spanish barracks. In Malate, two blocks north of the Malate Church, contemporary maps identify one area as the Malate Barracks. This area contains both the Cuartel de Malate and the Cuartel de España. The latter begs confusion with the Cuatel de España in Intramuros. For photos of that installation, see Jonathan Best, *A Philippine Album: American Era Photographs, 1900–1930*, 230; and Ramon Ma. Zaragoza, *Philippines: Images of the Past*, 205. Malate amd Ermita were, up until World War II, the American part of town. According to *A Pronouncing Gazetteer of the Philippine Islands*, Malate had "fine villas and residences. Ermita and Malate are the favorite headquarters for American families" (190). The *Gazetteer* also points out that the American civilian populatation of Manila in May of 1901 was 8,526 (183).

19. The 10-inch Krupp guns were fired at Dewey's fleet early throughout the May 1, 1898, battle of Manila Bay. The U.S. warships did not return fire for fear of civilian casualties. Neely's work includes a number of photographs of these guns.

20. From then until World War II, the primary U.S. Navy installation was at Cavite, the site where Dewey destroyed the Spanish fleet. After the war, the navy moved the facility to Subic Bay.

21. The USS *Brooklyn* was a cruiser. Brown is referring to Commodore Winfield Scott Schley's maneuver at the mouth of Santiago harbor as the Spanish fleet attempted to run the U.S. blockade on July 3, 1898. The *Brooklyn*, caught somewhat out of position as the Spanish fleet came out of the harbor, had to make a wide, sweeping turn away from the enemy ships in order to eventually engage them. Many observers thought the maneuver gave the appearance of "running away."

22. This was a ditty well known to U.S. troops. The voice in the song is supposedly that of Otis, and it is to a tune from *Pinafore*. See Wolff, *Little Brown Brother*, 294–95.

23. Unlike the 24th Infantry, the 48th and the 49th Volunteer Infantry Regiments had some African American officers.

24. Oakes's report says of Brown:

> During this time [August–December, 1899] one man had been detailed to make road maps of all routes traveled by the troops of the division. Accompanying the advance under General Young, maps were made showing the roads from San Fernando to Bangui, by way of San Isidro, Tayug, San Fabian, and Vigan.
>
> The maps enclosed are compiled from the road-map sketches made principally by Private J. C. Brown, Company B, Battalion of Engineers, whose industry, energy, and ability deserves the highest commendation (*Annual Reports, 1900*, pt. 4, 399).

25. Leila Herbert, "The First American: His Homes and his Households," pt. 4, "The Final Days at Mount Vernon," *Harper's Monthly*, Dec., 1899, 146–59. The piece is a romanticized view of George Washington after his presidency, including his death and burial.

26. According to Leach, "On February 14, Lieutenant Ferguson and 24 men of the company left with the expedition for the Camarines and returned May 18, 1900" ("Historical Sketch," 19).

27. This is William Brown Prescott (1888–1940), son of Linzee Prescott and Brown's sister Frances.

28. The piece reads, "Mr. John C. Brown, Co. B, Engineer Corps, who is in the Philippines, has been made a noncommissioned officer. His life is spent in a pleasant way in spite of hard work," *Portland (Maine) Sunday Times*, Feb. 11, 1900.

29. The island of Talin in Laguna de Bay was known for its stone quarry. A photograph of the quarry is in *Pronouncing Gazetteer*, 59.

30. Lawton was killed by a sharpshooter just outside the town of San Mateo.

31. Brown's "old Fort Malate" is Fort San Antonio Abad. Captain T. Bentley Mott also refers to the structure as "Fort Malate" before going on to describe how it was bombarded by the USS *Olympia* and then taken by the Colorado volunteers, an episode that occurred at Fort San Antonio Abad in February, 1899 (Feuer, *Combat Diary*, 69–70). Brown's direction, however, is a bit confusing. Fort San Antonio Abad was south of both the Cuartel de Espana and the Malate convent, not "above" the barracks as he claimed.

32. Rudyard Kipling's short story "In the Matter of a Private" describes how a British private in India—the butt of a comrade's jokes—runs amok in the heat and shoots several soldiers.

33. The VIII Corps's status was changed to the Division of the Philippines on April 1, 1900. The division was divided into four compartments, with Company B assigned to the Department of Southern Luzon. Lieutenant Oakes was in charge of this department.

34. There is the possibility that the lieutenant and the doctor saw symptoms of typhoid fever in the red swelling.

35. "Fenicule Fenicula" was a nineteenth-century song of Italian origin popular on both sides of the Atlantic.

36. The identity of the "Jim" mentioned here is unknown.

37. For a description of the return of the railroad to civilian hands in March, 1900, see *Annual Reports, 1900*, pt. 2, 514–19.

38. Company A, Battalion of Engineers, left Willets Point for the Philippines on May 24, 1898 (Leach, "Historical Sketch," 14).

39. On February 4, 1899, hostilities broke out near the San Juan bridge. This marked the beginning of the war.

40. The capture of the water pumping station at Marikina on February 6, 1899, by U.S. forces secured Manila's water supply from the Army of Liberation. See Faust, *Campaigning in the Philippines*, 132–33.

Chapter 5: Paranaque

1. The photo of the ferry is titled, "Native Carts and Horses Taken Across the Paranaque River in Bancas," in Wilcox, ed., *Harper's History*, 346.

2. Brown is moving from north to south. Paranaque was the scene of an intense firefight in early 1899. See Faust, *Campaigning in the Philippines*, 233–40. Camp Dewey was an early U.S. installation. Originally referred to as the "camp at Tambo," it was located on the Calle Real south of Malate and twenty-one miles north of Cavite, which would have put it just north of Paranaque. For a description of Camp Dewey and early activity in the Malate area, see James Rankin Young, *Reminiscences and Thrilling Stories of the War by Returned Heroes*, 320–38.

3. The large church is Saint Paul's, which was built in 1650. It is interesting to note that Paranaque was not quite the pastoral scene Brown initially perceived it to be. In fact, insurgents attacked the U.S. detachment at Paranaque on September 26, 1900, while Brown was probably hospitalized in Manila, (*Annual Reports, 1901*, pt. 2, 17).

4. The Paranaque bridge has existed in a number of different forms at or quite near the same location where Brown designed and began his pile structure. The completion of Brown's Paranaque bridge and its descendants constitutes a history in itself. In 1900, a report by Chief Engineer John Biddle speaks of the difficulties in getting material for the bridge and debates the merits of both U.S. and Filipino timber. See *Annual Reports of the War Department for the Fiscal Year Ended June 30, 1901*, vol. 1, pt. 2, 205–206. Two years later, the Bureau of Engineers reported: "data have been collected on the repair of the pile trestle bridge at Paranaque. This subject is practically complete" (*Annual Reports of the War Department for the Fiscal Year Ended June 30, 1903, Report of the Philippine Commission*, 215). This means that in less than three years Brown's bridge needed repairs. According to an engineering report the following year:

> Paranaque, Rizal Province.—Authorization on which to base designs and estimates for a bridge across estero at Paranaque, Rizal Province, is dated December 19, 1902. This bridge was built by the military authorities, probably in 1900, and consisted of a pile trestle 232 feet long, constructed of native timber. It was abandoned early in 1903, the piles having been destroyed by the action of sea worms. A ferry, consisting of three bancas to which a platform is attached, was substituted therefor. While the site is favorable for the erection of a steel bridge, a protected pile trestle was designed and recommended for construction on account of its suitability, convenience of maintenance, and because the first cost, P15,000, is about one-half that of a steel structure. The project is now before the Commission (*Annual Reports of the War Department for the Fiscal Year Ended June 30, 1904*, vol. 13, *Report of the Philippine Commission*, pt. 3, 204).

It was reported that act number 1342, enacted May 5, 1905, included "For the construction of a bridge at Paranaque, Province of Rizal, thirteen thousand pesos" (*Annual Reports of the War Department for the Fiscal Year Ended June 30, 1905*, vol. 14, *Report of the Philippine Commission*, 97).

It thus can be assumed that Brown's bridge was finished in 1900, although it is doubtful that he actually saw its completion. As noted above, Brown's bridge was subsequently eaten away by sea worms and was rebuilt several years later. A 1940 photo of the bridge shows a concrete structure (Isayas R. Salonga, ed., *Rizal Province Today: A Souvenir of the Province of Rizal Depicting Its History and Progress*, 47). A sharp confrontation between the defending Japanese and attacking Americans occurred at this bridge on February 4 and 5, 1945. During the engagement, in which the defenders were overrun, the bridge was partially destroyed. For an account of the battle and a photo of the damaged bridge, see Edward M. Flanagan Jr., *The Angels: A History of the 11th Airborne Division, 1943–1946*, 83. Today, the rebuilt structure looks virtually identical to its prewar ancestor.

5. Brown would have had a selection of American beers. Advertisements in American military and community newspapers in Manila like *The Manila Freedom* and *The Manila American* reveal a choice of Pabst's, Schlitz, Budweiser, and Lemps St. Louis Beer. Interestingly, many advertisements used health as a major theme. Anheuser Busch said its Black and Tan was "used in all the convalescent homes." An ad for a product called Walnutine went as follows:

THE TRUTH IN A NUTSHELL

Walnutine is a cordial especially compounded to tone the Stomach. A Great Relief in cases of dysentery cramps or any of the disordered conditions of the bowels. A bracer for the broken-down constitution!

For an idea of what a "native" saloon might have looked like, see the 1899 photograph of the Paranaque store titled, "Queer Inhabitants of Queer Houses," and the 1899 street scene, "A Novel Country and People—Village of Paranaque, Philippines" (Maria Serena I. Diokno, ed., *Voices and Scenes of the Past: The Philippine-American War*, 19, 131).

6. He is presumably referring to Lieutenant Colonel Ducat, but Brown does not reveal at any other point why he wants to remember the name.

7. Weber and Field's Music Hall was a popular turn-of-the-century Broadway theater. Koster and Bial's Music Hall, also in New York, gained fame as an early movie house: Edison demonstrated his vitascope there in 1896. The statement, "I suppose you have forgotten them by this time" is curious in that it does not appear to be directed at his mother, but rather at someone he knew or spent time with in New York. A list of songs that were popular with the troops at that time can be found in "Eighth Army War Songs," *The American Oldtimer*, July, 1938, 22–31. Many are recognizable standards: "The Sidewalks of New York," "Hail,

Hail," "Rally Round the Flag," "Good Old Summer Time," "Rosie O'Grady," and so forth.

8. Captain James Eads was a well-known army engineer who designed a number of bridges, including the Illinois and St. Louis bridge across the Mississippi.

9. The issue of Brown taking the preliminary examination for a commission engenders a bit of mystery. According to Brown, the failure of his application for the preliminary examination was due to his length of service. However, John Joseph Lenny records that no preliminary examinations were actually given during the years 1899, 1900, and 1901 (*Rankers: The Odyssey of the Enlisted Regular Soldier of America and Britain,* 112, 121–23). Were Brown or Lieutenant Oakes mistaken in the possibility of the examination? In any event, if his application had been approved, Brown would have qualified for the series of examinations given to all officer candidates. These included a physical examination, a number of written exams on English grammar and composition, the Constitution, international law, mathematics, geography, history, and army regulations. If the candidate failed any one of these tests he was finished and returned to his regular post. Once the written exams were passed, the candidate was tested on physical skills, drill regulations, and moral character. The board then reviewed the candidate's military record, his letters of recommendation, and other supporting evidence. At the time, obtaining a commission via the ranks was extremely difficult. First, few enlisted men had much political support, a necessary ingredient. Second, the officer corps had a tradition of rarely recommending noncommissioned officers for advancement, most likely because of social objections. Given his background, however, Brown probably stood a better chance than most. See Lenny, *Rankers,* 112; Edward M. Coffman, *The Old Army: A Portrait of the American Army in Peacetime, 1784–1898,* 224–25; and Marvin Fletcher, *America's First Black General: Benjamin O. Davis Sr., 1880–1970,* 25–26.

10. It can be assumed Brown's "low fevers" were some complication of typhoid. The doctor was probably Capt. William C. Warmsley. Warmsley settled in the Philippines, where he owned a drugstore and several tobacco plantations in northern Luzon. He continued to practice medicine and became the president of the Cagayan Province Board of Health. See Gatewood, *Black Americans,* 313–14. For an example of Warmsley's view of African Americans and opportunity outside the United States, see his letter from Cuba in Gatewood, *"Smoked Yankees,"* 231–32.

11. There is some uncertainty about this passage. Brown was both physically sick from the typhoid and certainly disappointed about being denied the opportunity to take the commissioning exam, but there is no real indication of what he meant by: "I was homesick I guess more than anything else. I was tempted to tear this up, but I send it to show that one has different moods, disagreeable as well as pleasant." If any passage within the manuscript was edited, this one seems the most likely candidate.

12. He means that the planks used to cross winter snow and spring mud were removed for the summer.

13. Brown's reference to the convent indicates that he was quartered near Saint Paul's, perhaps a hundred yards at most from the river.

14. The president's murder was indicative of the guerrilla war that was then beginning. Brown, like most U.S. soldiers and politicians, did not fully comprehend the depth of Filipino nationalism and thus had grown complacent after the previous year's victories. Guerrilla activity continued to plague U.S. forces for the next several years. See note 3 above.

15. Helen Holt Emerson went to Glen Cove, Maine, as a child and recalls the family residence and recreation circa 1910–20:

> It was a rambling, big summer place. It had been originally been two stories, wooden, sort of shingled, I think. My grandfather [Philip Henry Brown], whom I never saw, lifted the two stories up and put in a new first floor. They did this to several houses in the area around here. So it was then a three story summer cottage. But for the family it was rather a big house with three floors. The third floor was also for the maids, and they sweltered up there.
>
> The family moved up there from Portland every summer. They must have went by horse and carriage. It would not have been an easy little trip. My grandfather commuted every day to Portland. He came back at the end of the afternoon.
>
> They were there all summer. Their neighbors [were the Cliffords] and they had a wonderful time [together]. They had a sailboat. They had nice rocks to climb on. They had lovely meals and all kinds of family parties. Everyone loved going to Glen Cove. My generation went out there all the time.

16. Paranaque's population in 1899 was 9,863 (*Pronouncing Gazetteer*, 51).

17. He is referring to the insurgent trenches used in 1898 and part of 1899.

18. Company historian Leach notes the following: "On June 27, 1900, Lieutenant Ferguson with a detachment of 20 men left with the First China Relief Expedition and arrived at Taku July 6, 1900. The detachment were present with assault was made on the walled city at Tientsin July 13, 1900; with advance to relief of Pekin, August 4, and present at battle of Pietsang, August 5, Yangtsun, August 6, Chumen and other gates to sacred city of Pekin, August 15, 1900. Maps were made of the roads traveled from Tongku to Pekin and maps of the cities of Pekin and Tientsin were made by the detachment. This detachment returned to Manila June 5, 1901" ("Historical Sketch," 20).

19. The fascinating story of Capt. Oberlin M. Carter includes purported graft. Carter (West Point, 1880) was a brilliant Corps of Engineers officer married to a well-to-do socialite in Savannah, Georgia. After her death of typhoid fever, he was chosen to help study the possibility of building the Panama Canal. He inadvertently became involved in the dispute as to which route—the Nicaraguan or Panamanian—was preferred. His personal wealth invited suspicion by his professional rivals, and this eventually led to a sham trial, court-martial, and imprisonment in 1898 on charges of conspiracy, fraud, conduct unbecoming an officer, and embezzlement. Today he is considered innocent.

20. Presidential candidate William Jennings Bryan ran on an anti-imperialism platform in 1900. Many Filipino leaders tied their hopes for independence to Bryan's victory.

21. According to U.S. Marine Corps records, "Billy" Clifford was on duty in China from June 26 to October 9, 1900.

22. It is interesting to speculate whether Brown actually felt recovered or was cloaking his anxiety about his health.

23. Corporal Burke is surely the photographer whose works are included in the volumes of *Annual Reports*.

24. Senator Albert J. Beveridge was an annexationist and a major proponent of the war. He used the flag as a key rhetorical device in his address to the Senate on January 9, 1900, and in his famous "March of the Flag" speech in 1898. Brown was probably referring to a printing of the former. See Brands, *Bound to Empire*, 32–33.

25. Biddle's interrogation probably had some connection with the report mentioned in note 4 above.

26. The exact nature of the trip and speech are unknown, but given Mrs. Brown's social concerns it may have been about unwed mothers. Aunt Emily was Emily K. Brown.

27. Captain Charles King, who commanded a brigade of volunteers in Manila in 1899, was at that time a well-known novelist. His works centered on U.S. military life, especially in the American West. Brown's comment on *Ray's Recruit* (1898) is interesting in that there are remarkable similarities between fact and fiction. Not the least of which is that the protagonist in the novel is a young, fatherless "blonde" haired man named Gray, who, like Brown, becomes a "gentleman ranker." What might have hit a sensitive nerve for Brown is that the character attempts to jettison his former identity and replace it with a new one while in the army.

28. Leach records that on April 1, 1900, Company B under Lieutenant Oakes was assigned to repair roads and bridges in southern Luzon: "Headquarters of the company was established at the Convent de Malate, where a regular depot was equipped (quartermaster and engineer) to furnish transportation and supplies to the detachments left in charge of the work which was carried on at Paranaque, Bacoor, Imus, Dasmarinas" ("Historical Sketch," 20).

 The Malate Convent was situated next to the Malate Church, run presently by the Columban Order, on what is now M. H. Del Pilar Street. The church was originally built in 1588, remodeled in 1594, and rebuilt after the earthquake of 1863. The convent in 1900 is described as such in an unpublished draft document dated 1998 and titled "History of Malate Church": "The Augustinians remained in Malate until the early 1900s. In fact, one of the last parish priests there had made the convent such a notorious gambling house that the Archbishop agreed to government request that it be demolished. Actually, it was closed down when the Augustinians left, but never demolished. When the Spanish-American war was over, the Church came under the jurisdiction of the diocesan priests. . . . In 1910 an unfortunate fire destroyed the convento and damaged the church."

The convent was completely rebuilt after 1910, and then rebuilt again after the battle of Manila in 1945. Photographs of the church and convent, as well as the U.S. officer's headquarters in Malate, both dated 1899, can be found in Luning B. Ira, *Streets of Manila*, 184–85.

29. President McKinley established the Philippine Commission in 1899 to study and resolve Filipino and American disagreements.

30. Taku, China.

31. Brown's "disgraceful affair in St. Louis" is probably a reference to the strike by the Railway Employees' Union in May and June of 1900. The city's trolley-car system was initially shut down, and the resulting clashes between strikers, their supporters, passengers, and police led to several deaths. A sheriff's posse was formed in June to guard the rail lines, and more shootings occurred. The *St. Louis Post-Dispatch* carried daily stories on the strike during those months.

Chapter 6: California

1. Richard Harding Davis was an American journalist who covered the Spanish-American War.

2. This suggests that he did not fall sick until after his return to Manila, but that is highly unlikely.

3. Billy Clifford completed his service in China on October 9, 1900. He presumably arrived back in the Philippines a few days later.

4. She is referring to her brother, Nathan Clifford.

5. Molly Brown was a cousin to John and Helen.

6. Mrs. Brown died on December 20, 1900.

7. He had been transferred to the Van Nuys Hotel in Los Angeles.

Works Cited

Unpublished Manuscripts, Dissertations, and Papers

Clifford, George. Various records of William Clifford, Jr.

"History of Malate Church." Malate, Philippines, 1998.

Hoganson, Kristin Lee. "The 'Manly' Ideal of Politics and the Imperialist Impulse: Gender, U.S. Political Culture, and the Spanish-American and Philippine-American Wars." Ph.D. diss., Yale University, 1995.

Holt, Helen Clifford Brown. "Recollections of an Old Lady," dated 1951.

Paulet, Anne. "The Only Good Indian is a Dead Indian: The Use of United States Indian Policy as a Guide for the Conquest and Occupation of the Philippines, 1898–1905." Ph.D. diss., Rutgers University, 1995.

U.S. Army Military History Institute, Carlisle Barracks, Pa.
    Spanish-American War Survey
    Samuel B. M. Young Papers

Interviews

Emerson, Helen Holt, and Julia Holt Bradford. By author, Portland, Maine, February 5, 2000.

Newspapers

Manila American
Manila Freedom
New York Sun
New York Times
Portland (Maine) *Evening Express*
Portland (Maine) *Press Herald*
St. Louis Post-Dispatch
Sunday Telegram (Portland, Maine)
Washington Post

Articles

Abbot, Henry L. "Early Days of the Engineer School of Application." Occasional Paper no. 14. U.S. Army Engineer School, 1904.

Adams, Herbert. "John Brown's legacy." *Portland Press Herald,* November 10, 1989: 10–11.

Bass, Jason H. "Early Days in Manila." *The American Oldtimer,* August, 1939, 26.

Benton, Lawrence. "Memories of the 33rd Vol. Infantry." *The American Oldtimer,* June, 1934, 21–24.

Bunch, J. A. "Recollections of the Twenty-Fourth Infantry." *The American Oldtimer,* July, 1940, 34.

Coffman, Edward M. "Batson of the Philippine Scouts." *Parameters* 7, no. 3 (1977): 68–72.

Dunne, David M. "The Engineer School—Past and Present." *Military Engineer* 41, no. 284 (November–December, 1949): 411–16.

"Eighth Army War Songs." *The American Oldtimer,* July, 1938, 22–31.

Fischer, Leo. "The Macabebes." *The American Oldtimer,* April, 1936, 31–33.

Hart, Irving. "Reminiscences of an Old Timer." *The American Oldtimer,* March, 1940, 45.

Herbert, Leila "The First American: His Homes and his Households." Pt. 4, "The Final Days at Mount Vernon." *Harper's Monthly,* December, 1899, 146–59.

"History of the 36th Regiment United States Volunteers." *The American Oldtimer,* June, 1941, 12–18.

Lazar, Kay. "Medal's creator rose from humble roots." *Portland Press Herald,* September 1, 1995.

Leach, Smith S. "Historical Sketch of the First Battalion of Engineers During Its Tour Abroad." Occasional Paper no. 7. U.S. Army Engineer School, 1903.

Lobo, Matias M. "How the First Scouts Were Organized." *The American Oldtimer,* September, 1940, 27–33.

"Lowe's Scouts." *The American Oldtimer,* June, 1940, 20–24

May, Glenn. "Why the United States Won the Philippine-American War, 1899–1902." *The Bulletin of the American Historical Collection* 13 no. 1 (January–March 1985): 67–90.

Miller, Richard E. "Black Troops in the Philippines." *Bulletin of the American Historical Collection* 8 no. 4 (October-December, 1980): 75–88.

Munro, J. N. "The Philippine Native Scouts." *Journal of the United States Infantry Association* 2, no. 1 (July, 1905): 178–80.

U.S. Government Publications

Annual Reports of the War Department for the Fiscal Year Ended June 30, 1900. Vol. 1, *Report of Lt. General Commanding the Army,* pts. 2, 4, 5, and 6. Washington, D.C.: GPO, 1901.

Annual Reports of the War Department for the Fiscal Year Ended June 30, 1901. Vol. 1, pt. 2. Washington, D.C.: GPO, 1902.

Annual Reports of the War Department for the Fiscal Year Ended June 30, 1903. Vol. 7, *Report of the Philippine Commission.* Washington, D.C.: GPO, 1904.

Annual Reports of the War Department for the Fiscal Year Ended June 30, 1904. Vol. 13,
   Report of the Philippine Commission, pt. 3. Washington, D.C.: GPO, 1905.
Annual Reports of the War Department for the Fiscal Year Ended June 30, 1905. Vol. 14,
   Report of the Philippine Commission. Washington, D.C.: GPO, 1905.
A Pronouncing Gazetteer of the Philippine Islands. Washington, D.C.: Bureau of Insular
   Affairs, 1902.

Books

Agoncillo, Teodoro A. *History of the Philippine People.* 8th ed. Quezon City: Garotech, 1990.
Beale, Howard K. *Roosevelt and the Rise of America to World Power.* Baltimore: Johns
   Hopkins University Press, 1956.
Best, Jonathan. *A Philippine Album: American Era Photographs, 1900–1930.* Makati City:
   Bookmark, 1998.
Blount, James H. *The American Occupation of the Philippines, 1898–1912.* New York: G. P.
   Putnam's and Sons, 1912.
Brands, H. W. *Bound to Empire: the United States and the Philippines.* New York: Oxford
   University Press, 1992.
Bryan, William S., ed. *Our Islands and Their People.* New York: N. D. Thompson, 1899.
Coffman, Edward M. *The Old Army: A Portrait of the American Army in Peacetime, 1784–
   1898.* New York: Oxford University Press, 1986.
Cortes, Rosario Mendoza. *Pangasinan, 1801–1900: The Beginnings of Modernization.*
   Quezon City: New Day, 1990.
Cosmas, Graham A. *An Army for Empire: The United States Army in the Spanish-
   American War.* Shippensburg, Pa.: White Mane, 1994.
De Bevoise, Ken. *Agents of Apocalypse: Epidemic Disease in the Colonial Philippines.*
   Princeton, N.J.: Princeton University Press: 1995.
Different Views, Customs, and Traditions in the Philippines. N.p., n.d. Filipiniana
   Collection, Lopez Museum Library, Manila.
Diokno, Maria Serena I., ed. *Voices and Scenes of the Past: The Philippine-American War.*
   Manila: Jose W. Diokno Foundation, 1999.
Everett, Marshall. *Exciting Experiences in Our Wars with Spain and the Filipinos.* N.p.:
   n.p., 1899.
Faust, Karl Irving. *Campaigning in the Philippines.* San Francisco: Hicks-Judd, 1899.
Feuer, A. B. *Combat Diary: Episodes from the History of the Twenty-Second Regiment,
   1866–1905.* New York: Praeger, 1991.
Fiske, Bradley A. *War Time in Manila.* Boston: Gorham Press, 1913.
Flanagan, Edward M., Jr. *The Angels: A History of the 11th Airborne Division, 1943–1946.*
   Washington: Infantry Journal Press, 1948.
Fletcher, Marvin E. *America's First Black General: Benjamin O. Davis Sr., 1880–1970.*
   Lawrence: University Press of Kansas: 1989.
Foner, Jack D. *Blacks and the Military in American History: A New Perspective.* New
   York: Praeger, 1974.

Freidel, Frank. *The Splendid Little War.* Boston: Little, Brown, 1958.

Gates, John Morgan. *Schoolbooks and Krags: The United States Army in the Philippines, 1898–1902.* Westport, Conn.: Greenwood Press, 1973.

Gatewood, Willard B., Jr. *"Smoked Yankees" and the Struggle for Empire: Letters from Negro Soldiers, 1898–1902.* Urbana: University of Illinois Press, 1971.

———. *Black Americans and the White Man's Burden, 1898–1903.* Urbana: University of Illinois, 1975.

Gleeck, Lewis E. *Americans on the Philippine Frontiers.* Manila: Carmelo and Bauermann, 1964.

———. *The Manila Americans, 1901–1964.* Manila: Carmelo and Bauermann, 1977.

A History of the 22nd Infantry. Manila: E. C. McCullough, 1904.

Ira, Luning B. *Streets of Manila.* Manila: GCF Books, 1977.

King, Charles. *Ray's Recruit.* Philadelphia: Lippincott, 1898.

Kipling, Rudyard. "In the Matter of a Private." *Soldiers Three and Military Tales.* Pt. 2. New York: Charles Scribner Sons, 1898.

Lenny, John Joseph. *Rankers: The Odyssey of the Enlisted Regular Soldier of America and Britain.* New York: Greenberg, 1950.

Le Roy, James A. *The Americans in the Philippines.* 1914. Reprint, New York: AMS Press, n.d.

Lininger, Clarence. *The Best War at the Time.* New York: Robert Speller and Sons, 1964.

Linn, Brian McAllister. *The U.S. Army and Counterinsurgency in the Philippine War, 1899–1902.* Chapel Hill: University of North Carolina Press, 1989.

———. *The Philippine War: 1899–1902.* Lawrence: University Press of Kansas, 2000.

Manila Envelopes: Oregon Volunteer Lt. George F. Telfer's Spanish-American War Letters. Ed. Sara Bunnett The Oregon Historical Society Press, 1987.

March, Alden. *The History and Conquest of the Philippines and Our Other Island Possessions.* Philadelphia: Keeler-Kirkpatrick, 1899.

Massachusetts Institute of Technology. *Report of the Thirtieth Anniversary of the Class of Eighteen Ninety-Three.* Boston: MIT, 1923.

May, Glenn Anthony. *Battle for Batangas: A Philippine Province at War.* New Haven, Conn.: Yale University Press, 1991.

Miller, Stuart Creighton. *"Benevolent Assimilation": The Conquest of the Philippines, 1899–1903.* New Haven, Conn.: Yale University Press, 1982.

Neely's Photographs: Fighting in the Philippines. New York: F. Tennyson Neely, 1899.

Ochosa, Orlino. *The Tinio Brigade.* Quezon City: New Day, 1989.

160 Photographs of J. D. Givens of S[an] F[rancisco]: Period of Spanish-American War—1898. N.p., n.d. Filipiniana Collection, Lopez Museum Library, Manila.

Parker, James. *The Old Army: Memories, 1872–1918.* Philadelphia: Dorrance, 1929.

Penn, Julius A. *A Narrative of the Campaign in Northern Luzon, P.I. of the Second Battalion, 34th U.S. Inf. Volunteers in November and December, 1899 and January, 1900.* N.p, 1933.

Putney, Clifford. *Muscular Christianity: Manhood and Sports in Protestant America, 1880–1920.* Cambridge, Mass.: Harvard University Press, 2001.

Representative Men of Maine: A Collection of Portraits with Biographical Sketches of Residents of the State Who Have Achieved Success and Are Prominent in Commercial,

Industrial, Professional and Political Life, To Which Is Added the Portraits and Sketches of All the Governors Since the Formation of the State. Portland: Lakeside Press, 1893.

Roth, Russell. *Muddy Glory: America's 'Indian Wars' in the Philippines, 1899–1935.* Hanover: Christopher, 1981.

Salonga, Isayas R., ed. *Rizal Province Today: A Souvenir of the Province of Rizal Depicting Its History and Progress.* Manila: Salonga, 1940.

Sexton, William Thaddeus. *Soldiers in the Sun: An Adventure in Imperialism.* Harrisburg, Pa.: Military, 1939.

Scott, William Henry. *Ilocano Responses to American Aggression, 1900–1901.* Quezon City: New Day, 1986.

Sonnichsen, Albert. *Ten Months a Captive Among Filipinos.* New York: Charles Scribner's Sons, 1901.

Trafton, William Oliver. *We Thought We Could Whip Them in Two Weeks.* Ed. William Henry Scott. Quezon City: New Day, 1990.

U.S. Army Corps of Engineers. *The History of the U.S. Army Corps of Engineers.* Alexandria, Va.: Corps of Engineers, 1998.

U.S. Army Engineer School. *History and Traditions of the Corps of Engineers.* Fort Belvoir, Va.: Engineer School, 1953.

Welch, Richard E., Jr. *Response to Imperialism: The United States and the Philippine-American War, 1899–1902.* Chapel Hill: University of North Carolina Press, 1979.

Wilcox, Marion, ed. *Harper's History of the War in the Philippines.* New York: Harper Brothers, 1900.

Wolff, Leon. *Little Brown Brother: How the United States Purchased and Pacified the Philippine Islands at the Turn of the Century.* Garden City, N.Y.: Doubleday, 1960.

Woodruff, Charles E. *The Effects of Tropical Light on White Men.* New York: Rebman, 1905.

Worchester, Dean C. *The Philippines: Past and Present.* New York: Macmillan, 1914.

Young, James Rankin. *Reminiscences and Thrilling Stories of the War by Returned Heroes.* Kansas City: Topeka, 1898.

Zaragosa, Ramon Ma. *Philippines: Images of the Past.* Makati: Ramaza, 1993.

———. *Lost Era.* Makati: Ramaza, 1994.

Index

Brown, John Clifford, "Jack" (*cont.*)
170, 171, 202, 203, 204–205, 211, 213, 222, 223, 225, 227, 230–31, 232, 234, 236, 237, 239; Filipino troops, observations, 94, 113, 115–16, 117, 139, 150, 152, 158, 230–31; funeral, 15, 23, 247, 253; importance of observations, 3–5, 40–47, 256; influence of Indian Wars, 38–39; last days, 246–47, 249, 250–53; maps and mapmaking, 49, 57–58, 79, 80, 87, 88, 90, 94, 109, 132, 166, 172–74, 183, 186; marching, description, 156–57; nationalism, 36–38; Philippines, observations, 74, 98, 99, 137, 139, 140, 141, 142, 144, 145, 146, 150, 153, 157, 193, 201, 226; physical description, 15–16; public records, 15–17; prejudices, 39–40; promotion to corporal, 184–85, 239; records menu, 194–95; relationship to mother, 24–25, 28; rhetorical strategies, 24–25, 28–30; romantic interests, 54–55, 260n. 18; sailors, observations, 162, 163; sickness, 16–20, 23, 53–54, 166, 167, 172–73, 174, 199, 207, 208, 220–21, 249, 251; social class, 36–37, 101, 205; Spanish troops, observations, 158; volunteers, observations, 64, 127, 161, 164–65, 218–19, 220, 224, 232, 233–34; will, 3, 48. *See also* McMullen, Florence; Massachusetts Institute of Technology, alumni memoir; Warmsley, William C.
Brown, John Marshall (uncle), 6
Brown, Nathan Clifford, "Cliff" (brother), 7, 9, 13, 52, 247, 249, 250, 251, 252, 255
Brown, Philip Henry (father), 6, 7–8, 25, 27, 85, 288n. 15
Brown, Philip Greely, "Phip" (brother), 7, 9, 10–11, 13, 32, 47, 48, 51, 52, 54, 64, 101, 102, 182, 200, 235, 252, 253, 255
Bryan, William Jennings, 229, 243, 289n. 20
Bunch, J. A., 267n. 14
Burke, Corp. (also Bourke), 231, 233–34, 235, 237, 239, 271n. 31
Burwell, William T., 281n. 34

Cabiao, 117, 119
Cabanatuan, 79, 82, 124, 125, 134
Calumpit, 83, 87, 88, 268n. 6
Camp, Walter, 235
Camp Dewey, 209, 285n. 2
Carraglan, 135, 136
Carroll, Edward, 96, 109, 269n. 17
Carter, Oberlin M., 228, 288n. 19
Casey, Sergt., 83, 104, 114, 118, 270n. 25
Cavite, 181–82
Century (magazine), 223
Chickamauga, Georgia, 15, 22, 57, 205
China, 223, 226, 228, 229, 232, 242, 244, 245, 288n. 18
Chinese, 77, 84, 87, 93, 95, 120, 121, 173, 231, 268n. 13
City of Para (transport), 63, 67, 75, 213, 227, 264n. 3, 264n. 5, 267n. 14
Clark Field, 80–82
Clifford, Nathan (Supreme Court Justice), 7
Clifford, William Henry, 12
Clifford, William Henry, Jr., "Billy", 11, 164, 167, 180, 181–82, 183, 191, 192, 193, 202, 228, 229, 242, 249, 281n. 36
Collulit, 89, 102
Commission process, 287n. 9
Company A, Engineers, 192, 198, 204, 206, 212, 242
Company B, Engineers, 23, 62, 79, 80, 94, 105, 122, 185, 190, 207, 218, 220, 231, 232, 272n. 45, 281n. 37, 284n. 28, 284n. 33
Company C, Engineers, 63, 190
Constantino, Renato, 41
Cosmas, Graham A., 260n. 15

Dewey, George, Commodore, 41, 60
Diary of a Soldier in the Philippines, 3, 11, 24, 47–55, 249
Dagupan, 140
Dingras, 44
Dinwiddie, William, 271n. 32
Dorrington's Scouts, 127, 128, 273n. 50
Ducat, Arthur C., 213, 231, 237–39,